In memoriam Prof. Igor Kosír

This book has resulted from the projects supported by the Faculty of Social Sciences at the University of Wrocław, the Faculty of Political Science and International Relations at Matej Bel University and the International Visegrad Fund.

Joanna Dyduch, Sebastian Jakubowski,
Igor Kosír & Jaroslav Ušiak

POLAND AND SLOVAKIA: BILATERAL RELATIONS IN A MULTILATERAL CONTEXT (2004–2016)

Essays on Politics and Economics

ibidem-Verlag
Stuttgart

Bibliografische Information der Deutschen Nationalbibliothek
Die Deutsche Nationalbibliothek verzeichnet diese Publikation in der Deutschen Nationalbibliografie; detaillierte bibliografische Daten sind im Internet über http://dnb.d-nb.de abrufbar.

Bibliographic information published by the Deutsche Nationalbibliothek
Die Deutsche Nationalbibliothek lists this publication in the Deutsche Nationalbibliografie; detailed bibliographic data are available in the Internet at http://dnb.d-nb.de.

Peer reviews:
Doc. Ing. Saleh Mothana Obadi, PhD
Prof. Dr. habil. Robert Wiszniowski

English-language editing:
Paweł Burzała

∞

Gedruckt auf alterungsbeständigem, säurefreien Papier
Printed on acid-free paper

ISBN: 978-3-8382-0976-0

© *ibidem*-Verlag
Stuttgart 2017

Alle Rechte vorbehalten

Das Werk einschließlich aller seiner Teile ist urheberrechtlich geschützt. Jede Verwertung außerhalb der engen Grenzen des Urheberrechtsgesetzes ist ohne Zustimmung des Verlages unzulässig und strafbar. Dies gilt insbesondere für Vervielfältigungen, Übersetzungen, Mikroverfilmungen und elektronische Speicherformen sowie die Einspeicherung und Verarbeitung in elektronischen Systemen.

All rights reserved. No part of this publication may be reproduced, stored in or introduced into a retrieval system, or transmitted, in any form, or by any means (electronic, mechanical, photocopying, recording or otherwise) without the prior written permission of the publisher. Any person who does any unauthorized act in relation to this publication may be liable to criminal prosecution and civil claims for damages.

Printed in the EU

Contents

List of tables and figures IX

List of abbreviations XIII

Notes on contributors XV

Johanna Dyduch
Chapter one: Analyzing the bilateral relations between the European Union member states 1
   Introduction 1
   Historical determinants of Polish-Slovak relations 4
   Theoretical and methodological foundations and the origins of the book 9
   Organization of the book (overview of chapters) 23

Johanna Dyduch
Chapter two: Polish-Slovak political cooperation 27
   Introduction 27
   Dynamics of the relations in the bilateral context 32
      Brief assessment of the development of Poland and Slovakia's political environment (2004-2016) 32
      Analysis of strategic documents pertaining to foreign policy 36
         The Slovak Republic *36*
         The Republic of Poland *39*
         Summary of the analysis of strategic documents *43*
      Conditions and circumstances of Polish-Slovak bilateral political relations 44
         Legal basis *44*
         Social perception of Polish-Slovak bilateral relations *47*
      Most important achievements and developments in Polish-Slovak political relations 49

Dynamics of the relations in the multilateral context..................53
   Polish-Slovak relations in the context of European integration and both
   states EU membership..53
      Priorities of the Republic of Poland and the Slovak Republic in the
      context of European integration and EU membership..................55
      Polish-Slovak relations in the light of selected EU policies
      operationalization..57
   Visegrad Group as a sub-regional, multilateral platform for Polish-Slovak
   political relations..70
      Analysis of the cooperation and selected initiatives of Poland and
      Slovakia within the Visegrad Group......................................74
   Polish-Slovak relations in the light of global system dynamics (between
   US and Russia) Pan-Slavism vs. Euro-Atlanticism............................83
   Final summary of the political cooperation between the Slovak
   Republic and the Republic of Poland..92

Jaroslav Ušiak
Chapter three: Slovak-Polish cooperation in the field of defense and security 97
   Introduction..97
   Dynamics of the relations in the bilateral context........................100
      Brief assessment of the development of the security environment
      between 2004 and 2016..101
      Analysis of the strategic documents of the Slovak Republic and the
      Republic of Poland...108
         The Slovak Republic..109
         The Republic of Poland...111
         Summary of the analysis of strategic documents........................114
      The overview of bilateral cooperation between the Slovak Republic
      and the Republic of Poland..118
   Dynamics of Polish-Slovak relations in the multilateral context......127
      Cooperation within the Visegrad Group..................................127
      Polish-Slovak cooperation within international organizations
      (NATO, EU, OSCE, UN)..135
   Final summary of Polish-Slovak cooperation in the area of
   security and defense...149

Sebastian Jakubowski
Chapter four: Economic relations between Poland and Slovakia 153
    Introduction 153
    Poland and Slovakia—economic relations in bilateral context 154
        Mutual investments between Poland and Slovakia 156
        Mutual trade between Poland and Slovakia 164
    Poland and Slovakia—economic relations in the sub-regional context 176
    Poland and Slovakia—economic relations in the multilateral European context 182
        Slovak-Polish support for the development of the internal market 183
        Cooperation for the development of transport infrastructure 186
    Missed opportunities in Slovak-Polish cooperation 187
    Final remarks on economic relations between Slovakia and Poland 188

Igor Kosír
Chapter five: Polish-Slovak cooperation in other fields of neighborhood relations 191
    Introduction 191
    Dynamics of the relations in the bilateral context 192
        Brief assessment of the legal framework for bilateral relations in the sectors of education, science, culture and regional cooperation 193
        Overview of Polish-Slovak relations in the areas of education, science, culture and cross-border cooperation 194
            Education and science 194
            Cultural cooperation 199
            Cross-border cooperation 202
        Summary of development trends in the bilateral Polish-Slovak cooperation 205
    Dynamics of the relations in the multilateral context 206
        Importance of the European integration processes for the Slovak-Polish-Slovak neighborhood relations development 206
        Poland and Slovakia's role in multilateral regional cooperation within the framework of Euroregions 221
    Final summary of Polish-Slovak cooperation in the areas of education, science, culture and cross-border cooperation 223

Summary and conclusions **229**

Combined references **235**
    Documents, official statements and data 235
    Reports, Analyses 246
    Books, journal articles 250
    Other: newspaper articles, internet resources, miscellaneous
    sources. 259

Index of names **266**

List of tables and figures

Table 1. Planes of analysis with regard to the impact of international interdependence on Polish-Slovak relations. 3

Table 2. Core assumptions of the intergovernmental theory. 9

Table 3. Dimensions of Europeanization. 11

Table 4. Intergovernmentalism and Europeanization: an attempt at synthesis. 20

Table 5. Holders of power in Poland and Slovakia. 29

Table 6. The list of bilateral agreements concluded by Poland and Slovakia between 1993 and 2016. 44

Table 7. Rotating presidency of the Visegrad Group. 73

Table 8. Key similarities and differences in the perception of threats by Poland and Slovakia. 115

Table 9: Selected joint Visegrad group (V4) declarations related to defense and security. 129

Table 10: Overview of current and completed UN crisis management and other international operations in which Poland and Slovakia have been involved. 137

Table 11: Overview of current and completed NATO and EU international crisis management operations in which Poland and Slovakia have participated. 144

Table 12. Polish direct investments in Slovakia (end of year in million EUR). 159

Table 13. Slovak Direct Investments in Poland (end of year in million EUR). 160

Table 14. Total foreign investments and Slovak investments in Poland. 161

Table 15. Enterprises with Slovak capital—over 1 million USD. 162

Table 16. Enterprises with Slovak capital by number of people employed. 163

Table 17. Commodity imports and exports between Poland and Slovakia by CN/SITC/CPA/BEC section (in million EUR)...................164

Table 18. Export and Import of services between Poland and Slovakia (in million EUR). 165

Table 19. Polish import from and export to Slovakia of base metals and base metal-based articles (in million EUR)....................166

Table 20. Polish import and export to Slovakia of machinery and mechanical appliances, electrical and electronical equipment (in million EUR)....................167

Table 21. Polish import from and export to Slovakia of transport equipment (in million EUR). 168

Table 22. Polish import from and export to Slovakia of plastics and rubber articles (in million EUR)....................169

Table 23. Polish import from and export to Slovakia of chemicals (in million EUR)....................170

Table 24: Polish import from and export to Slovakia of mineral products (in million EUR). 171

Table 25: Polish import from and export to Slovakia of textiles and textile articles (in million EUR). 172

Table 26. Polish import of food products from Slovakia (in million EUR)....................173

Table 27. Polish export of food products to Slovakia (in million EUR)..174

Table 28. Polish import from and export to Slovakia of miscellaneous manufactured articles (in million EUR)....................175

Table 29. Annual growth rate of gross domestic product in selected economies. 178

Table 30. Gross domestic product at market prices (chain linked volumes—index 2004 = 100)....................179

Table 31. Gross Domestic Product per capita in purchasing power standards....................180

Table 32: An increase in the number of universities in Poland and Slovakia, 1990-2012....................195

Table 33. An increase in the numbers of university students in Poland and Slovakia, 1990-2012. 195

Table 34. Poland and Slovakia's integration with the EU and other international organizations. 207

Table 35. Key areas of future Visegrad cooperation identified in 2004. 209

Table 36. Selected joint Visegrad group (V4) declarations related to educational, scientific, cultural as well as cross-border cooperation. 213

Figure 1. Comparison of Poland and Slovakia's defense spending (as percentage of GDP). 117

List of abbreviations

Agency for the Cooperation of Energy Regulators (ACER)
Association of European Border Regions (AEBR)
Bologna Follow-up Group (BFUG)
Carpathian Euroregion (CER)
Central European Free Trade Agreement (CEFTA)
Central European Initiative (CEI)
Common Agricultural Policy (CAP)
Common Foreign and Security Policy (CFSP)
Common Security and Defence Policy (CSDP)
Council for Mutual Economic Assistance (CMEA)
Cross-Border Operation (CBO)
Deep and Comprehensive Free Trade Agreement (DCFTA)
Digital Single Market (DSM)
Eastern Partnership (EaP)
Economic and Monetary Union (EMU)
European Association of Development Agencies (EURADA)
European Commission (EC)
European Endowment for Democracy (EEfD)
European Free Trade Association (EFTA)
European Grouping of Territorial Cooperation (EGTC)
European Higher Education Area (EHEA)
European Neighborhood Policy (ENP)
European Security and Defence Policy (ESDP)
European Union (EU)
European Union Force in Bosnia and Herzegovina (EUFOR)
European University Association (EUA)
Foreign Direct Investment (FDI)
International Security Assistance Force (ISAF)
International Monetary Fund (IMF)
International Visegrad Fund (IVF)
Liquified Natural Gas (LNG)
NATO Response Force (NRF)
North Atlantic Treaty Organization (NATO)

Organization for Economic Cooperation and Development (OECD)
Organization for Security and Co-operation in Europe (OSCE)
Office for Democratic Institutions and Human Rights (ODHIR)
Purchasing Power Standards (PPS)
Polish Press Agency (pol. *Polska Agencja Prasowa*) (PAP)
Polish Central Statistical Office (pol. *Główny Urząd Statystyczny*) (GUS)
Trans-European Energy Network (TEN-E)
Trans-European Transport Network (TEN-T)
Treaty on the European Union (TEU)
Treaty on the Functioning of the European Union (TFEU)
World Economic Forum (WEF)
Visegrad Group (V4)
United Nations (UN)

Notes on contributors

Dr. Joanna Dyduch—Assistant Professor at the Department of European Studies at the University of Wrocław (Poland). Author of several scientific articles devoted to foreign policy analysis and energy policy. Author, editor and co-editor of books (e.g. *Selected Policies of the European Union. Evolution in the context of the Lisbon Treaty and the Europe 2020 Strategy*, Publishing House: ASPRA, Warszawa 2012; *European Union Development. Challenges and Strategies*, Publishing House: ASPRA, Warszawa 2013; *European Union as a Global Actor. Political integration: identity issues and foreign policy*, Publishing House: ASPRA, Warszawa 2014). Member of the Executive Committee of the European Association of Israel Studies at the School of Oriental and African Studies / University of London. Visiting scholar at various universities (e.g. SOAS University of London; Ben Gurion University of Negev Beer Sheva, Israel; Universidad CEU Cardenal Herrera in Valencia, Spain; Matej Bel University in Banská Bystrica, Slovak Republic).

Prof. Igor Kosír—Professor at the Department of International Relations and Diplomacy at the Matej Bel University in Banská Bystrica (Slovakia), responsible for the University's international cooperation as its Vice Rector (2010-2014). Author of several scientific articles devoted to world economy development, international economic integration and the European Union's external relations. Author, editor and co-editor of books (e.g. *Foreign Trade Policy of European Union*, Publishing House: Ekonóm, Bratislava 2007; *International Economic Integration: from Autarky to Global Economic Integration*, Publishing House: MBU, Banská Bystrica 2010; *European Perspectives of Western Balkans countries*, Publishing House: ABB, Prishtina 2015; *Alternatives of European Integration Development*, Publishing House: Ekonóm, Bratislava 2015). Visiting scholar at various universities (e.g. University of Reims Champagne-Ardenne in Reims, France; University of Sarajevo, Bosnia and Herzegovina; University of Batumi, Georgia).

Dr. Sebastian Jakubowski is a graduate of the University of Wrocław (Faculty of Law, Administration and Economics). Since 2005 he has been working at the University's Institute of Economic Sciences. Today he holds the position of an Assistant Professor. His research interests are focused on economic policy and structural changes that shaped Central and Eastern Europe after the collapse of communism. Dr Sebastian Jakubowski is also an organizer of a biannual International Wroclaw Symposiums of Economic Policy. His academic career is filled with numerous visits to foreign universities, such as the University of California (Santa Barbara, US), Leipzig University, the University of Latvia, the Vilnius Gediminas Technical University, the Šiauliai University, as well as the Fraunhofer MOEZ Institute in Leipzig.

Doc. Mgr. Jaroslav Ušiak, PhD—Associate Professor at the Faculty of Political Sciences and International Relations, Matej Bel University in Banská Bystrica (Slovak republic) and, since 2013, Editor-in-Chief of a scientific journal *Politické vedy* (*Political Sciences*) devoted to political sciences, international relations, modern history and security studies. He is an author and co-author of several books: *Bezpečnosť ako kategória* (*Security as a category*); *Security Policy of the Slovak Republic— Development, Cornerstone and Implications*. He has authored several articles devoted to international relations and security studies, focusing on regional security, mainly in Central Europe. He is a member of the Editorial Board of several scientific journals: *Současná Evropa* and *Defense and Strategy*. He has undertaken many research and lecture stays and participated in various conferences, both in his native Slovakia and a number of other countries, such as the Czech Republic, Poland, Hungary, Belgium, Slovenia, France, Ukraine and others.

Joanna Dyduch

Chapter one
Analyzing the bilateral relations between the European Union member states

Introduction

Despite their geographical closeness and similar socio-political experiences in the past, it seems that Poles and Slovaks know little about each other. Similarly, Polish-Slovak relations are, at best, only moderately dynamic given how many areas offer the two governments good opportunities for intensive cooperation. The existing, fairly narrow literature on Polish-Slovak bilateral relations characterizes them as good and friendly, but it is often noted that the potential for their further development is not being utilized. This is so for several reasons. First of all, priorities of national foreign policies basically put the relations between the two countries in the multilateral context (European Union, NATO, Visegrad Group). Secondly, the development of contacts is hindered by problems such as an unsatisfactory transport infrastructure (especially on the Polish side). Thirdly, compared to the importance attributed to ties with other neighbors, the topic of Polish-Slovak relations is almost absent from the socio-political discourse held in both countries. Moreover, unlike in the case of Polish-Russian or Slovak-Hungarian relations, the last two decades have not seen any controversial issues that would dictate the tone of conversation between Warsaw and Bratislava. Further still, not once has the narrative referring to common history been used for political purposes. All this results in a paradoxical situation where the ties between Poland and Slovakia are almost entirely overlooked not only by the media, but also by the academia. For Poles, Slovakia and its inhabitants remain relatively unknown neighbors.

Despite the above-mentioned considerations, a close look at Poland and Slovakia's bilateral relations and international activity reveals several interesting phenomena and a number of crosscutting interests relevant to the effectiveness of both countries' foreign and security policies. This warrants an attempt at describing and analyzing Polish-Slovak relations, and so filling the gap evident in the current academic discourse. Hopefully, research presented in this book will lead to pointing out key processes and phenomena that have affected the state of affairs between Warsaw and Bratislava.

The analysis will be focused on the period between 2004 and 2016. In 2004, both countries acceded to the European Union (EU)—a milestone that has had a huge impact on their strategies and approaches toward different policies (including foreign and neighborhood policies). The same year saw Slovakia join the North Atlantic Treaty Organization (NATO). Poland, along with Hungary and the Czech Republic, has been a full NATO member since 1999. The analysis reaches as far as 2016–12 years after the biggest enlargement in the EU's history. 2016 is also a time of serious challenges for both organizations, as several opportunities and threats have recently affected the European system as a whole and its individual actors.

The project that led to writing this book entailed research aimed at describing and diagnosing the evolution of Polish-Slovak relations from 2004 until 2016. It was focused on three dimensions: political, economic and social. It was also designed to reveal aspects and spheres in which Poland and Slovakia's interests coincide, as well as those that hold the highest potential for future development. Furthermore, the research was directed towards defining and analyzing issues that may hinder relations in specific areas—be it politically strategic problems of foreign and security policy or cooperation between regions. Finally, by using methodological principles of liberal intergovernmentalism and the theoretical framework of the discourse on Europeanization, the authors attempted to measure the extent to which Polish-Slovak relations are affected by the European integration process. As an additional aim, the research enabled verification of the Visegrad Group's effectiveness in pursuing its members' individual and collective interests.

The aims specified above provided the basis for the formulation of mutually complementary research questions that would guide the authors through the analysis of collected materials. The first of the questions concerned the state of Polish-Slovak relations throughout the relevant time period, taking into account their dynamic nature in both the bilateral and the multilateral dimension. The authors have tried to identify crucial areas in bilateral relations (i.e. where both countries have certain defined interests and whether these interests are shared or opposing) and main factors shaping them. It is worth noting that early in the research phase it became clear how much Polish-Slovak relations depend not only on both parties' motivations and interactions, but also on external influences. The importance of international interdependence has been considered at four complementary levels: local, sub-regional, regional (European) and global (see: Table 1).

Table 1. Planes of analysis with regard to the impact of international interdependence on Polish-Slovak relations.

Plane of analysis	Type of cooperation	Dominant issues
local	trans-border cooperation	• cultural cooperation • social issues (including e.g. environment protection)
sub-regional	cooperation among the V4	• social issues • political issues (including security) • economic issues
regional (European)	Cooperation within the EU	
Global	Cooperation within NATO Cooperation with other global players (e.g. Russia, US)	• security • political issues (including security) • economic issues

Source: own work.

The last question concerned how the international environment affects bilateral relations between Poland and Slovakia. One particularly important reference point was both countries' membership in various multilateral structures, from Euroregions and the Visegrad Group (V4) to the EU and NATO. The authors have assumed that such multilateral cooperation is legitimized on the premise that it allows governments to effectively (or, perhaps, even optimally) manage not only issues of common concern and those in which national interests coincide, but also those that could potentially lead to disagreements and conflicts. From this perspective, it can be said that Polish-Slovak cooperation and coordination of political activities on the international scene results primarily from increasing interdependencies inherent in the European system.

What follows from the above considerations is that the analysis of bilateral relations between any two EU member states (MS) requires researchers to account for the multilateral context. In this case, processes and phenomena that are particularly important stem from the European system which in its legal, institutional and socio-political form can be largely equated with the European Union. Such systemic perception of the EU should be coupled with the understanding of its internal complexity. One also needs to remember that the Union is increasingly intertwined with and affected by its international surroundings. The MS and EU institutions are, therefore, elements of the European system which, like every other entity of this kind, has its borders, outside which lies its external environment. The system has a two-ways communication with its environment—it influences and is influenced by it.

Historical determinants of Polish-Slovak relations

The set of historical circumstances shaping Polish-Slovak relations to this day has obviously been developing over the previous several decades. In general, the ties between Bratislava and Warsaw had for a long time been affected by the interests of nearby great powers more than by direct contacts between the two governments. The very beginning of contemporary Polish-Slovak relations came after World War I, when Poland and Czechoslovakia were reborn as independent states. Poland's restoration was famously included in Woodrow Wilson's Fourteen Points and was initially supported by the Soviet government which, in the Decree on Peace published in 1917, acknowledged the right of all nations to self-determination. The Brest-Litovsk Treaty and the Polish-Soviet peace treaty led to the final delimitation Poland's borders. Although Slovakia emerged as an independent state only in 1993, tracing the roots of its relations with Warsaw requires us to consider earlier historical developments between Poland and the Czechoslovak Republic formed in the aftermath of World War I. The emergence of Czechoslovakia was the first opportunity for the emancipation the Slovak nation. Slovaks' participation in the Austro-Hungarian army increased the awareness of the armed forces' role in national liberation and ultimately led to the formation of the Czechoslovak legion. National resistance constituted an important prerequisite for declaring ambitions to build a nation-state—a development that materialized as a result of the Versailles Treaty which stipulated the establishment of Czechoslovakia.

It was in the inter-war period when Poles and Slovaks began to interact, with both positive and negative consequences. The latter resulted from unresolved territorial disputes over Orava, Spiš and Tešínsko. The disagreement continued throughout the inter-war period (in 1938 Polish army attempted an occupation of the disputed lands, seizing the opportunity that presented itself when parts of Czechoslovakia were annexed by the Nazi Germany as a result of the Munich Treaty) and only ended in 1958, when the Czecho-Slovak-Polish treaty on the matter was signed by the communist governments. The brighter episodes included efforts to create anti-Nazi Czechoslovak divisions in several occupied countries, including Poland. The units participated in the defense of Tobruk and assisted Poles in their ultimately doomed resistance against the German invasion in September 1939. Polish soldiers participated in the Slovak national uprising during World War II, while Slovaks supported the Poles during the 1944 Warsaw uprising (Segeš 2015).

Geopolitical incorporation of both states into the Soviet sphere of influence after World War II represented a significant landmark. Interestingly, it quickly became apparent that the two societies differed in the extent to which they accepted or rejected the communist ideology. Consequently, they adopted different strategies of resistance. In Poland, the formation of the Solidarity movement and the involvement of the Catholic Church represented the rejection of communism in its political dimension. Meanwhile, Czechoslovakia chose the professional realm as one of its battlegrounds by keenly maintaining contacts with foreign (also Western) businesses. The society also employed a declaratory form of resistance, especially after the bloody events of 1968. While Western Europe pursued détente in the 1970s, Czechoslovak intellectuals released the Charter 77—a document that introduced a new concept of reforming the political and social reality by focusing on liberalization, democratization and gradual removal of the communist party's leading role in national politics.

Processes that were started by the dissolution of the Soviet Bloc and the democratic transition of Central and Eastern Europe were unquestionably crucial to Polish-Slovak relations as they are today. The division of Czechoslovakia was important for the shaping of the identity of the entire region, with societies and groups within them beginning to express their interests more freely. Pro-transformation sentiments and hopes for closer ties to Western Europe harbored by the citizens were translated into foreign policy priorities adopted by the governments. These circumstances can be seen as the reasons for forming the Visegrad Triangle in 1991. After Slovakia was established as an independent country in 1993, the organization was renamed the Visegrad Group. Shortly after Czechoslovakia, Hungary and Poland signed the Visegrad declaration, the European Communities invited the three states to negotiate Europe Agreements on Association (EAA)[1]—a move that constituted a very tangible token of support for the Euro-Atlantic strategic orientation adopted by Central European states (Kosír 2010). The name of the documents symbolized a historic return to Europe for the former members of the Soviet Bloc. The pro-European attitude all Visegrad states shared at that time changed the dimension and quality of bilateral ties in most areas. However, in the case of Poland and Slovakia, the perception of such relations was from the very first moments asymmetrical. While Bratislava considered Warsaw as its strategic partner and a natural regional leader, the Polish side attached considerably less importance to its southern neighbor.

As an active participant of the revolutionary changes that effectively eradicated the post-war bipolar order, Poland was able to quickly determine its strategic goals and oriented itself towards full participation in all important transatlantic structures. The country's position in European and global economy changed dramatically within a relatively short period of time. Apart from aspiring to Western political and eco-

---

[1] The new two Europe Agreements on Association (EAA) between the Communities and the Czech Republic and, parallelly, the Slovak Republic were negotiated and signed on 4th October 1993, after the Czechoslovak federation was dissolved at the end of 1992.

nomic bodies, Warsaw also supported the new quality of regional cooperation among Central European states.

In Slovakia, the domestic discourse was temporarily influenced by Slovenia's original effort to become a full EFTA member (the parallel wave of European integration)[2] and Russia's offer to negotiate bilateral free trade agreements with former CMEA states. Ultimately, Slovak political elites reached an informal agreement that would provide the basis for a pro-Western foreign policy. From then on, the government was committed to ensuring comprehensive security and development opportunities by joining NATO and the mainstream model of European integration.

At the December 1997 summit in Luxembourg, the EU decided to open the accession negotiations with six candidate countries: Cyprus, the Czech Republic, Estonia, Hungary, Poland and Slovenia. The process formally began in March 1998. Slovakia, alongside Bulgaria, Latvia, Lithuania, Malta and Romania, was included in the second group (so-called Helsinki group) of candidates to be admitted to the negotiation phase. The decision to start the procedure was made in December 1999.

For the purpose of determining accession terms, the EU adopted a "differentiation strategy"—i.e. it chose to approach each candidate on an individual basis. This meant that the prospective members had very limited possibilities to cooperate on the matter—a circumstance that was not conducive to building a regional solidarity and made it easier for the Union to exert pressure on each government. At the same time, however, some EU MS supported the Visegrad cooperation that occurred within the Central European Free Trade Agreement (CEFTA) concluded in 1992. In essence, CEFTA was not a political initiative. Moreover, its beneficiaries included states such as Germany which were keen to expand their export and investments in Central Europe. As it turned out, the desire to join the Union, visible particularly in the actions of all V4 members, spurred a surprising amount of competition that complicated the strengthening of genuine cooperation.

---

[2] EFTA was in that time a functional free trade area. Theoretically, it was easier to build this stage of integration. Slovenia's effort to reach EFTA membership was ultimately unsuccessful, but in 1996 the country signed its Europe Agreement on Association and later became one of the best-prepared new member states to join the EU in 2004.

The accession negotiations determined the condition on which each candidate would join the EU. Upon acceding to the Union, application were expected to adopt its acquis, i.e. detailed laws and rules based on the existing European treaties (Rome, Maastricht, Amsterdam and Nice Treaties). The negotiating process often focused on how exactly a given candidate would adopt, implement and enforce the acquis communautaire. This included the possibility of agreeing on certain transitional arrangements, necessarily limited in scope and duration. Such solutions had previously been employed with regard to other states joining the Communities. Ten candidates (namely Cyprus, the Czech Republic, Estonia, Hungary, Latvia, Lithuania, Malta, Poland, Slovakia and Slovenia) completed their negotiations in December 2002.

One factor that hindered the post-communist states in their pursuit of individual and collective interests during the pre-accession talks was the asymmetry in potentials and capabilities between the wealthy, integrated Western Europe and the underdeveloped, newly emancipated prospective members (Moravcsik & Vachudova 2003). Moreover, in their determination to join the European structures, countries such as Poland and Slovakia exposed themselves to Europeanization stimuli emanating from Brussels. At the same time, they had practically no instruments and possibilities to influence the political, legal and institutional developments within the Communities. Still, one needs to remember that the citizens and governments of the candidate countries consciously agreed to undertake far-reaching, often difficult and costly political, economic and social reforms so as to adjust to European standards. From their perspective, full EU membership was a reward worthy of such effort.

The results of the negotiations were incorporated in the accession treaties, submitted to the Council and the European Parliament for approval. Subsequently, the documents were returned to the candidate governments to undergo ratification procedures (including, in some cases, national referenda). In Slovakia, the turnout in the referendum proved relatively low at 52.1%, but an overwhelming majority (93.7%) of those who showed up at the polls said „yes" to EU membership. In Poland, the turnout was sligthly higher (58.9%), with 77.6% voting in favor of ratifying the accession treaty. Both referanda delivedered valid results and allowed the two countries, along with eight other candidates, to formally accede to the Union on 1st May 2004.

In one final remark, it should be noted that the patterns of relations between the new and old EU MS, based on "asymmetrical interdependence" (Moravcsik & Vachudova 2003: 46-52), remained in place after the 2004 enlargement.

Theoretical and methodological foundations and the origins of the book

The basic theory upon which the analytical process and its resulting conclusions are founded is liberal intergovernmentalism. This concept combines the liberal logic (used for explaining how preferences within states are shaped) with a realism-derived mechanism of intergovernmental negotiations, where a state's power is the decisive factor (see: Table 2). According to Moravcsik, 'the relationship between states and the surrounding domestic and transnational society in which they are embedded critically shapes state behavior by influencing the social purposes underlying state preferences — can be restated in terms of three core assumptions' (1997: 516). The assumptions mentioned here describe and explain the character of actors in international relations, their motivations and the nature of interactions between them. Moreover, they refer to the complexity of the international system, as well as its multidimensional structure.

Table 2. Core assumptions of the intergovernmental theory.

Assumption 1:	**The Primacy of Societal Actors.** The fundamental actors in international politics are individuals and private groups who, generally, are rational and risk-averse, and who organize exchange and collective action to promote differentiated interests under constraints imposed by material scarcity, conflicting values, and variations in societal influence.
Assumption 2:	**Representation and State Preferences.** States (or other political institutions) represent some subset of their domestic societies, on the basis of whose interests state officials define state preferences and act purposively in world politics.
Assumption 3:	**Interdependence and the International System.** The configuration of interdependent state preferences determines state behavior.

Source: Moravcsik (1997: 516-521).

Another concept that proved helpful in operationalizing the research was Europeanization. As a process-centered idea, it takes account of the dynamics of the phenomena to be examined. For the purpose of this analysis, Europeanization is understood as a multidimensional process / phenomenon. It involves 'construction, diffusion and institutionalization of formal and informal rules, procedures, policy paradigms, styles, "ways of doing things" and shared beliefs and norms which can be first defined and consolidated in the EU policy process and then incorporated in the logic of domestic (national and subnational) discourse, political structures and public policies' (Radaelli 2004: 3). At the same time, Europeanization is also about the bottom-up dimension: how the MS (acting either individually or in groups) influence the creation of common EU rules, norms, politics and policies. Both processes take place simultaneously and continuously. Literature on Europeanization recognizes two other phenomena: the so-called 'cross-loading' and 'ad extra' Europeanization (the latter is also known as 'Europeanization beyond Europe') (Schimmelfennig 2009). Each dimension influences all others and thus contributes to the overall structure of the European system (see: Table 3). Europeanization occurs in every aspect of European integration—economic, social and political. It also affects every realm of bilateral relations between EU MS.

Table 3. Dimensions of Europeanization.

bottom up (uploading)	top-down (downloading)	ad extra (beyond-Europe)	cross-loading
Influence of MS on the EU and its institutions.	Influence of the EU and its institutions on the MS.	EU's influence on its immediate and more distant environment, exerted by exporting its governance models and values.	Transfer of solutions between EU MS.
In case of foreign policy, the vital factor is the actual or desired impact of MS on EU institutions and the Union's overall agenda.	Goals, strategies and directions of MS' foreign policies are affected by the EU and its institutions.	This dimension of Europeanization may affect European states remaining outside the EU, non-European states maintaining relations with the EU, as well as international organizations.	The process may occur with or without the involvement of supranational institutions.
By Europeanizing their national interests, MS (consciously or not) affect each other's foreign policies, not only through bilateral contacts but also through their actions at the EU level.	Vertical process.	Vertical-horizontal process.	Horizontal process.
Vertical process.			

Source: (Dyduch 2016: 53).

Although each state tries to preserve its ability to shape the relations with other actors independently, bilateral relations between the EU MS are affected and influenced by their status as members of the Union. Therefore, while governments (including the ones in Warsaw and Bratislava) declare they are determined to preserve their prerogatives with regard to foreign policy, the ever-increasing interdependence within the European system calls for new methodologies and theories that would allow us to better explain how bilateral relations among EU MS are shaped in the context of dynamic integration processes.

One way to approach this challenge is to juxtapose the two previously mentioned theories. The task of finding common denominators for liberal intergovernmentalism and the concept of Europeanization forced the authors to focus on several key issues. First of all, both these approaches were developed to enable modelling and theorizing on the causes, course and consequences of European integration. The process is examined from several different perspectives, including that of the citizens, substantial social groups, states and supranational institutions. Hence, identifying crucial actors and describing relations among them is of vital importance. In liberal intergovernmentalism, the primary subjects of international relations are individuals and private groups that operate mostly within single states. Their preferences are the main driving force behind strategies developed by governments for operating at the supranational level. The theory assumes that in representing the interests of primary actors, states act rationally (at least to a certain minimal extent). The interests in question are considered to be mainly material, rather than abstract and ideological, in nature. Such rationalism means that actors calculate costs and benefits of undertaken actions—in other words, they wish to maximize their gains while avoiding risks. For Moravcsik, 'European integration is a series of rational choices made by national leaders in response to the international interdependence' (1998: 18). Hence, if at the national level there is belief that international cooperation will bring more benefits than unilateral actions or rivalry with other actors, governments are more willing to cooperate. By doing so, they reduce costs, maximize gains and avoid risks associated with being on the losing side of a political conflict. Additionally, as Moravcsik points out, 'most international interactions, (…) have a positive-sum component in which the interests, and thus the increasing influence, of more than one country or region are complementary, resulting in positive-sum or mixed-motive interactions' (2009: 407-408). The above considerations can be complemented by conceptual principles of the research agenda known as Europeanization. While theorists of Europeanization do not address the nature and goals of actors, they assume that the European integration, as a progressive process resulting from decisions made by political elites, needs to yield tangible benefits to the citizens of EU MS if it is to be continuously legitimized. The process is only functional if it guarantees the achievement of goals and interests endorsed by its participants while, at the same time, preserving a relative balance within the whole system. Such balance, in turn, results from a certain symmetry of various processes that Europeanization entails. In other words, it is maintained as long as the actors of integration are both recipients and creators of solutions to be adopted at the European level. It cannot be sustained if the role of some MS comes down to adopting solutions forced upon them, while others are free to shape the reality according to their own desires.

Secondly, the analysis presented in this book concerns phenomena and processes occurring within the European system. Both theories utilized here envision them as resulting from interactions between EU MS, as well as between MS and EU institutions. The latter form of contacts may take on a bilateral or multilateral (several governments negotiating with, for example, the European Commission) variant. By acting together, MS try to strengthen their positions vis-à-vis other actors in the European system. Governments can form coalitions not only among themselves, but also with European institutions: for instance, if they want to justify and legitimize their actions in the eyes of other countries or even their own societies (Czaputowicz 2008: 334). The varied (in terms of both form and content) dynamics of the European system affect foreign policies of MS and, consequently, bilateral relations among them. Both the intergovernmental approach and Europeanization perceive foreign policy as a purposeful activity aimed at increasing a given country's potential for socio-economic development and enhancing its security, both internal and external. However, as noted by Moravcsik, 'understanding of domestic policies is a precondition for (...) the analysis of the strategic interaction among states' (1993: 481).

After interests and preferences are generated at the national level, state institutions tasked with representing their societies carry those interests onto the supranational plane in the form of specific political strategies (Pollack 2005: 361). Given this model of how international preferences are shaped, the institutions at the national level (particularly governments) are not only actors of the system—they also constitute something of a transmission belt through which national-level actors (individuals and private groups) communicate with those at the supranational level (EU institutions).[3] The position held by national

---

[3] Under certain circumstances, one can (although only in a very limited scope) discern yet another phenomenon, described by J. Ruszkowski as a bypass Europeanization, whereby actors from two different, not 'adjacent' levels enter in contacts and relations 'by-passing' actors situated at the level that separates them (Ruszkowski 2013: 52-

governments in the European system can be used for the purpose of legitimizing political decisions, security measures or economic cooperation initiatives. This is so because decision-making elites communicate with their domestic public opinion to justify their political agendas, particularly those aspects that are unpopular. To do so, they present some solutions as adopted at the European level as a result of difficult negotiations and collective decisions (Moravcsik 1993: 494-95, 507). This mechanism of diffusing responsibility for certain actions relieves national political elites of the strong pressure originating from interest groups within their societies. Moreover, the EU's peculiar political and institutional structure allows governments to reduce costs and increase the effectiveness of international cooperation aimed at managing both economic and political interdependence.

The optimization of the way interdependence is governed and managed occurs through the institutionalization of cooperation. The process entails 'formal and informal rules, procedures, policy paradigms, styles, "ways of doing things" and shared beliefs and norms' created at the supranational level (Radaelli 2004: 3). It structures the European system and, therefore, limits the MS' leeway and independence. Paradoxically, though, European integration strengthens the state's position vis-à-vis internal interest groups by redistributing the sources of power and enabling governments to control internal matters more efficiently (Czaputowicz 2008: 337).

The distinction between the domestic and the international level of governments' activities is another common feature inherent in liberal intergovernmentalism and Europeanization. The concept of a 'two-level game', utilized by Moravcsik, links states' internal policies to their external relations. At the domestic level, governments strive to garner support for their actions by building coalitions based on existing social groups that then become their political base. When interacting with other actors at the international level, they aim to pursue interests and preferences expressed by their domestic supporters. However, as noted by Czaputowicz, many proponents of liberal intergovernmentalism (e.g.

---

53). One example of this dimension is a situation when supranational institutions (e.g. the European Commission) contact regional authorities directly, or when regional interest groups address supranational bodies (e.g. the European Parliament) without involving their national government.

William Coleman and Geoffrey Underhill) believe that contemporary states are actually engaged at three levels (domestic, regional—i.e. the EU—and global) rather than two, and that rules governing political behavior at each of these levels are somewhat different (Czaputowicz 2008: 334). The concept of an at-least-two-level game is also present in the theoretical discourse on Europeanization, which recognizes the multidimensional nature of interactions between the actors of the integration process. The dichotomy of *down-loading* and *up-loading*, focused on the impact of integration at the domestic and supranational level, is complemented by a more complex construct that includes the *ad extra* and *cross-loading* dimensions. The former corresponds to states' activity at the global level, while the latter—particularly interesting in the context of this book—refers to relations between countries within the EU. Balancing various dimensions of Europeanization, previously mentioned as a pre-condition for the continued functioning of the European system, is not a goal per se. It merely serves the purpose of optimizing the environment so as to allow all relevant actors (i.e. those perceived as legitimate subjects of international politics) to express and pursue their interests.

MS are both subjects and objects of the multidimensional Europeanization process. Similarly, supranational institutions constitute both objects and subjects of actions undertaken by governments. In liberal intergovernmentalism, the position and legitimacy of these institutions is the result of conscious decisions made by states that choose to delegate some of their prerogatives from the national to the supranational level. The scope and extent of European governments' readiness to transfer competences to EU institutions reflects calculations made at the national level (see: Moravcsik 1998: 486-487). Therefore, although EU bodies were established as stand-alone actors in the European system only through autonomous decisions of MS, their existence has led to a new order and distribution of power within the system. Furthermore, it has redefined patterns according to which bi- and multilateral relations between MS are shaped.

Theorists of Europeanization also claim that the process they examine has allowed actors other than states to generate and accumulate power (Saurugger & Radaelli 2008: 214). These newly empowered players are the EU's supranational institutions, collectively referred to by some authors as 'Brussels' (Pomorska 2011; Alecu de Flers & Müller 2012; Dyduch 2016). However, their emergence does not mean that all MS have relinquished their external sovereignty to the same extent. Instead, governance-related competences typically attributed to subjects of international politics are redistributed in a new, different way. At the same time, the process can affect the balance of power among domestic actors. It 'can (...) increase the power of (a) some actors such as the core executive in relations to other domestic actors and /or (b) the overall power of the state in relation to the civil society and the EU itself' (Saurugger & Radaelli 2008: 215). Ultimately, the phenomena described here can solidify a specific type of relations (which the proponents of liberal intergovernmentalism have termed 'asymmetric interdependence') between the actors of the European system. As Frank Schimmelfennig notes, according to the intergovernmental concept 'actors seek policy integration if they are convinced to reap higher net benefits than from unilateral, autonomous or only loosely coordinated national policies (...). Among the various forms of integration and substantive rules that produce such net benefits, actors strive to realize those that maximize their gains' (2015: 180). One example of this logic is the 2004 EU enlargement. For countries such Poland and Slovakia, it meant a substantial improvement of their position in the system. It also allowed dynamic socio-economic growth and enhanced political as well as strategic security. The so-called old EU MS were, in turn, 'promoting accession because they considered enlargement to be in their long-term economic and geopolitical interest' (Moravcsik & Vachudova 2003: 43).

The extent to which an EU member state can pursue its interests at the European level depends on the preferences, behaviors and willingness to cooperate on the part of other governments, as well as supranational institutions. This means that the dynamics of Polish-Slovak relations will be shaped not only by preferences and interactions between Warsaw and Bratislava, but also by the actions of other actors within the European system (e.g. other members of the V4) and subjects from outside the system (e.g. Russia or the USA).

Supranationalization of the decision-making process and the establishment of increasingly advanced governance mechanisms for the European system have some further consequences for the way bilateral relations between MS are shaped. Certain political actions, including bi-

and multilateral relations between governments, are no longer a purely international affair. Foreign policy (particularly its European dimension) is somewhat internalized—a fact that has changed the nature of relations between the EU MS. While governments of other European countries are still considered foreign entities, their status is different from that of governments of non-EU states. This is so because certain areas of bilateral relations within the Union are now regulated at the supranational level. In matters not regulated by the European law, bi- and multilateral agreements still hold their traditional function, but their stipulations cannot go against any provisions of the *acquis communautaire*.

Moreover, it has to be kept in mind that EU membership is generally conducive to the intensification and systematization of contacts between MS, both logistically / organizationally and in terms of the socialization process. Regular meetings of national representatives, particularly in the EU Council and the European Council, create a specific organizational culture characterized by consensual, pluralistic and collective approach to decision-making.

The model described above allows the authors to analyze Polish-Slovak relations in the context adequate to their dynamics. It is clear that these relations are dictated by social preferences stemming from geographical, social, cultural and political closeness, as well as by international interdependence, both economic and geopolitical. The sole fact that Poland and Slovakia are neighbors (with all the complexity of social, cultural and political factors this entails) generates certain problems and needs, many of which can be met only through international coordination. The aforementioned interdependence is both the cause and consequence of Polish-Slovak cooperation, be it in a bilateral formula or within multilateral structures.

The third element common to liberal intergovernmentalism and Europeanization is the category of international interdependence. In the discourse on the latter theory, it is seen as both the determinant and the outcome of the Europeanization process. Meanwhile, the proponents of the intergovernmental theory define it as the link between phenomena, processes and subjects of the international system, and consider the impact all these elements have on one another. The process whereby states influence each other within the European system is driven by their domestically created preferences. Intergovernmentalists maintain that interdependence is a constant feature in relations between various participants of the European system, and that it can be managed effectively through 'negotiated policy coordination' (Moravcsik 1993: 474). Moreover, 'costs and benefits of international economic interdependence are the primary determinants of national preferences' (Moravcsik 1993: 480). This means that all behaviors exhibited by states at the international level, including their readiness to form coalitions or, more broadly, their approach to shaping bi- and multilateral relations, result from preferences formulated domestically. The perception of European integration and preferences based on that perception are also 'national and issue specific'—'they result from a domestic process of preference formation and are oriented towards increasing (and possibly maximizing) national welfare in the issue-area at hand' (Schimmelfennig 2015: 179). In liberal intergovernmentalism, domestic groups articulate preferences, while governments aggregate them through a process that entails internal convergence of identities, perceptions and calculations on the part of various relevant social groups and public bodies. Next, such aggregated interest, often referred to as 'national interest', is brought to the agenda of issues that actors of the European (or international) system need to face. The outcomes of interactions between these actors influence the process of national preference formation through a feedback mechanism.

As noted by several researchers, Europeanization can also encompass domestic interest groups and social movements. Although European integration has affected the way these subjects act and organize themselves, their nature as actors linked primarily to the domestic policy network remains unchanged. Nonetheless, as Reiner Eising notes, 'European integration has promoted extensions and modification of established practices and, for the most part, reaffirmed the power of the organization that had built up capacities to articulate, aggregate and represent the interest of their constituencies' (Eising 2007: 180). In other words, Eising indicates that domestic groups have strengthened their position in the public sphere as a result of the integration process. This, in turn, has given them the possibility to develop 'persuasive policy concepts' (Eising 2007: 181) that can be discussed and included at the supranational level (e.g. in EU legal regulations). Mindful of this phenomenon, decision-makers in EU MS are now more likely to cooperate with their counterparts in other countries, while effective social movements and interest groups are encouraged to internationalize their activities. This is visible in how MS include the European legal, political, economic and social context in their operational strategies.

When analyzing relations between two neighboring EU MS (such as Poland and Slovakia) that share some historic and political experiences, one would be well advised to use Moravcsik's category of 'international policy externalities' which arise where 'the policies of one government create costs and benefits for politically significant social groups outside its national jurisdiction' (Moravcsik 1993: 485). In a sense, this concept corresponds to the *cross-loading* category of Europeanization, whereby one member state uses the EU's legal and institutional structures to influence other MS. This happens because governments, being rational actors, believe that their ability to pursue their interests is affected by policies adopted by their foreign counterparts. In other words, interdependence can be considered as a vital feature of bi- and multilateral relations between states operating in the international system. This is particularly significant given the advanced stage of European integration. In some policy areas, the lack of unanimity can completely paralyze the decision-making process and thus prevent the achievement of goals which some actors consider beneficial, but others see as undesirable. This is true for political issues (such as foreign and security policy), as well as tax and social policies. In those areas where the process of integration is most advanced—namely, the European Single Market—the existence of EU regulations not only affects, but practically determines bilateral relations between MS. The greatest extent of communitization occurs in agricultural, trade, competition, regional and cohesion policies. It is worth noting that strong incentives for cooperation are present also in some areas that are currently less communitized, but exhibit a clear trend of progressing integration: e.g. consumer protection and energy policies. The latter is linked to MS' internal security and will serve here as an important case study confirming the assumptions of liberal intergovernmentalism.

Conclusions from the above considerations point to the fact that economic interdependence implies the need for strictly political cooperation. Underpinned by issues of security, political integration is justified on the grounds that it contributes to the stability of the European system and reduces threats generated by the external environment. This, in turn, calls for enhancing institutional mechanisms of governance at the supranational level, which is not possible without transferring competences previously held by states to Brussels.

To summarize, it can be said that this volume utilizes a model version of 'common grounds' on which Poles and Slovaks meet. The 'meetings' occur in the conditions of European integration. They result (and are often caused by) in an increasing interdependence that can be examined through the lens of a multidimensional Europeanization process. The model distinguishes four interaction levels: local, sub-regional, regional (European) and global (international).

Table 4. Intergovernmentalism and Europeanization: an attempt at synthesis.

	Intergovernmentalism	Europeanization	Level of cohesion H-high, M-medium, L-low, I –inconsistent C- complementary
Character of the analysis	Systems analysis	Systems analysis	H
Subjects of the analysis	Primary actors: individuals and private groups Secondary actors: State institutions (governments and other public bodies) EU institutions (supranational and intergovernmental institutions)	EU MS EU Institutions	C
Scope of the analysis	Actors' preferences	The impact of integration on a state's behavior	C
Nature of interactions	Voluntary / rational	Voluntary / rational	H
Key analytical concepts	Two-level game (domestic and international)	Two-level system transforming into → multi-level system	H/C

Dimensions of processes and interactions	Multidimensional—unspecified	Bottom-up: EU MS seek to influence (co-create) EU policies; Top-down: MS are subjected to influence and stimuli from the EU; Cross-loading: EU MS seek to influence policies and political behavior of other MS; Ad-extra: the EU exports the European model of governance and management outside and tries to spread European values	C
Source of interdependence	Globalization European integration	European integration Globalization	H
Form of interactions between participants	Bilateral as well as multilateral relations	Bilateral as well as multilateral relations	H
Mechanism and instruments of crucial processes	Intergovernmentalism is not focused on mechanisms and instruments utilized in the international relations	Socialization, learning, adaptation	C

Source: own work.

Finally, when juxtaposing liberal intergovernmentalism and Europeanization, one needs to address key processes and their mechanisms (depending how exactly they refer to a given research agenda). While the intergovernmental theory does not really cover this aspect, the discourse on Europeanization gives it substantial attention. Moravcsik and some of his fellow theorists (e.g. M. Vachudova and F. Schimmelfennig) merely mention mechanisms such as cooperation (as the antithesis of rivalry) which in an international system, particularly one as structured as the EU, usually take the form of negotiations or bargaining—activities that intergovernmentalism sees as the expression of actors' rationality. Meanwhile, scholars dealing with Europeanization[4] consider the analysis of mechanisms as one of the key elements in their research template (Moumoutzis & Zartaloudis 2016). Typically, the literature provides the following categories of mechanisms within Europeanization: socialization, learning and adaptation (Smith 2000; Ladrech 2010; Moumoutzis 2011; Alecu de Flers & Müller 2012). Socialization is defined as a process in the course of which actors in a given community are introduced to common rules, norms and political paradigms. This results in the development of supranational attitudes toward common European goals (Alecu de Flers & Müller 2012: 25). The phenomenon is a consequence of continuous interactions between actors of the integration process. These interactions, in turn, increase interdependence and lead to further socialization.

The mechanism of learning is closely linked to the existence and functioning of the European institutional system. The organization and work of EU institutions is characterized by a tendency to seek consensus and the practice of sharing information. According to Ladrech, the intensity and regularity of cooperation in certain (sometimes interconnected) policy areas 'provides structured patterns of interaction, based on principles and norms' (2010: 201). Such situation is conducive to promoting specific values. The EU and its administrative-bureaucratic apparatus can be compared to a platform that presents MS with a chance to express and act on their preferences at the European level. This enables mutual learning and pooling of resources required to achieve common goals.

The third mechanism mentioned by researchers of Europeanization is adaptation—it occurs particularly in the period directly preceding a country's accession to the Union. In the case of those MS that wield less power and possess fewer resources, the trend of adjustment may continue even after they join the EU. The process entails adaptation to norms, standards and expectations stemming from the membership status or regular contacts with the Union. The pressure to adapt has

---

[4] The issue of mechanisms and instruments of Europeanization is discussed in more detail in Dyduch, Joanna (2016). 'Europeizacja polskiej polityki zagranicznej w perspektywie realizmu strukturalnego' [Eng. 'Europeanization of Polish foreign policy from the perspective of structural realism'], Wrocław: Wydawnictwo Uniwersytetu Wrocławskiego.

various underpinnings and determinants—it is usually based on the strategy of conditionality. In essence, 'international organization promises rewards (such as financial assistance or membership) to target a state on the condition that the state fulfils one or more conditions (such as policy adjustment or institutional change) set by the international organization' (Schimmelfennig & Sedelmeier 2007: 88-89).

If one accepts the notion that Europeanization results in a specific pattern of political power distribution (and, hence, the distribution of costs and gains from integration), one has to determine which actors control the Europeanization process. In the case of foreign policy, it can be a state or a group of states. Such assertion, together with conclusions regarding mechanisms of Europeanization, naturally opens the door to a dialogue between theorists of Europeanization and proponents of liberal intergovernmentalism. Both Moravcsik and other authors who employ the intergovernmental theory (Moravcsik & Vachudova 2003; Schimmelfennig 2015) emphasize the importance of adaptation, socialization and learning for cooperation between rational actors that understand the positive and negative aspects of international interdependence.

It seems, therefore, that complementing liberal intergovernmentalism with assumptions from the concept of Europeanization is an effort that will serve to optimize further analysis. The tenets of both these approaches, although frequently convergent, are not identical. They can, however, be treated as complementary.

Organization of the book (overview of chapters)

The book consists of five main chapters, of which this one, focused on theoretical and methodological issues, is the first. Subsequent chapters encompass the most important realms of Polish-Slovak bilateral relations in the multilateral context. The main purpose of the second chapter is to present the development of Polish-Slovak political relations under the conditions of deep international interdependence, shaped by (among other factors) the process of European integration. The author assesses how both countries' participation in multilateral cooperation (which clearly dominated their political relations) affected their effectiveness in pursuing both shared and individual interests and goals. In order to identify crucial factors that determined the overall shape of cooperation between Warsaw and Bratislava, the author has reviewed a substantial volume of both primary and secondary sources. This has led to distinguishing spheres (or, sometimes, single issues) that were the focus of bilateral relations.

Chapter three, entitled 'Slovak-Polish cooperation in the field of defense and security', is centered around observations on the extent to which national interests of both states shaped their joint attitudes and positions at the bi- and multilateral level during the analyzed period. Its first part presents the development of bilateral relations based on evolutionary tendencies observed in both states' security environment and the analysis of their strategic documents and contractual agreements establishing mutual bilateral cooperation, along with meetings at various levels between the representatives of the two governments. The second part outlines Polish-Slovak cooperation within the framework of international organizations—the Visegrad Group (V4), North Atlantic Treaty Organization (NATO), European Union (EU) and Organization for Security and Cooperation in Europe (OSCE), as well as the United Nations (UN).

The main goal of the fourth chapter is to analyze economic relations between the Slovak Republic and Poland. In the opening pages, the author examines direct bilateral economic cooperation. The second part is focused on strong economic ties between Germany, Slovakia and Poland. Berlin's dominance in Central Europe is the most important factor that shaped Polish-Slovak cooperation at the sub-regional level. The analysis also encompasses the European context of bilateral cooperation. The last pages are devoted to how Poland and Slovakia worked together to improve the absorption of European funds, develop the energy sector and transport infrastructure, as well as support the EU's internal market. The analysis is concluded by pointing out missed opportunities in Polish-Slovak cooperation.

Finally, the fifth chapter analyzes significant progress in various areas of neighborhood cooperation made within the larger framework of European integration. It scrutinizes to what extent national interests, resulting from social preferences formulated in the two states, have shaped the governments' attitudes and positions with regard to both bi- and multilateral cooperation in areas such as science, culture, as well as preservation of heritage and folklore. The chapter also includes the analysis of bilateral regional cross-border cooperation, as well as multilateral cooperation within the broader formula of Euroregions.

The book makes use of a very rich, diverse research material, including primary and secondary sources. Research and knowledge contained in already existing, fairly broad literature has also been employed. Materials used for this monograph include sources written in native languages of the authors, as well as in English.

The authors hope this volume becomes of interest to the academia and students of European studies, economics and related sciences, as well as any person interested in issues related to Polish-Slovak cooperation.

Publishing this book would not have been possible without the support of the Faculty of Social Sciences of the University of Wrocław and the Faculty of Political Science and International Relations of the Matej Bel University in Banská Bystrica. The authors would also like to gratefully acknowledge the support granted them by the International Visegrad Fund. Our personal thanks go to dr Rafał Juchnowski, deputy head of the Chair of European Studies at the University of Wrocław, who effectively supported the project from the very beginning. Finally, many thanks to Jana Miková and Joanna Wojas whose work facilitated the cooperation and joint work on the book.

Joanna Dyduch

Chapter two
Polish-Slovak political cooperation

Introduction

Polish-Slovak political relations constitute simultaneously an independent sphere (both in bi- and multilateral context) and a complex set of determinants for relations in other areas, discussed in subsequent parts of this book. The following chapter covers the particular section of relations that is the exclusive responsibility of public bodies authorized to take on, on behalf of the state, legal and international-political commitments (e.g. by creating temporary and long-term coalitions and alliances). Issues to be examined here refer to political processes such as allocation and redistribution of power (e.g. political elites' attitudes toward integration or vital global developments). Moreover, the analysis encompasses questions concerning the way public bodies exercise their decision-making authority—including their competences in the field of foreign policy. Importantly, following Moravcsik, the author has assumed that the bodies in question represent interests articulated by domestic groups, rather than their own agenda.

The political dimension of Polish-Slovak relations constitutes a complex matter. It is shaped by various processes and phenomena occurring at both domestic and international level, some of which result directly from bilateral contacts, while others are driven by the multilateral sphere. In the case of the former, we shall look primarily at issues and events specific to relations between these two particular states. As for the latter, the analysis is focused on situations generated by both governments' broader international activity—most of all, their participation in institutionalized forms of multilateral cooperation. Additionally, the author attempts to assess how the dynamics of Polish-Slovak bilateral relations affect the directions and effectiveness of activities undertaken by the aforementioned multilateral bodies. The most significant example of such cooperation is, of course, the European system which, for the purpose of this chapter, is considered synonymous with the European Union. Another important case is the Visegrad Group—a multilateral forum for the governments of the Czech Republic, Hungary, Poland and Slovakia. Over the last quarter of a century, this sub-regional formation has established a rich history and developed its own unique identity, shaped by pressures emanating from the European system, the dynamics of relations among the four governments and social preferences formulated independently in each country (corresponding to at least two dimensions of Europeanization: downloading and cross-loading). Usually, the latter factor has no direct link with international politics—it typically refers to domestic social and economic issues at the local, regional or national level. However, when national decision-makers conceptualize policies (including foreign policy) and strategies (also those regarding alliances and cooperation with other countries), they are bound to treat such preferences as crucial directives. Hence, strategies related to foreign policy reflect interests expressed by domestic groups. The actions undertaken by national decision-making elites within the European system should, according to the theory of liberal intergovernmentalism, be legitimized and endorsed domestically (with elections being the most clear-cut example of such legitimization). Having the above considerations in mind, the author examines—by referring to the results of public opinion polls—the impact of preferences articulated by Polish and Slovak citizens on the views and actions of their political representatives.

It is the author's opinion that a detailed analysis should be preceded by a brief presentation of Poland and Slovakia's political elites. In the timeframe considered here (i.e. 2004-2016), both countries experienced alternations of power. This meant not only a change of individuals holding key posts, but also (particularly in Poland) a shift in political orientation and ideological focus. Of course, the reshuffling of political scenes did not occur simultaneously in both states. These domestic political developments must be taken into account when one tries to divide Polish-Slovak relations into clearly defined periods. The table below should be helpful in understanding and interpreting events and processes to be discussed throughout this chapter.

Table 5. Holders of power in Poland and Slovakia.

Republic of Poland					Slovak Republic			
Time in power	Government: Prime Minister and parties involved in the governing coalition	Time in power	President (determined by a general election, appointed for a 5-year long term of office)	Time in power	Government: Prime Minister and parties involved in the governing coalition	Time in power	President (determined by a general election, appointed for a 5-year long term of office)
19.10.2001-02.05.2004	**Leszek Miller**—Prime Minister Governing coalition: - Democratic Left Alliance - Labor Union - Polish People's Party (until 2003)	23.12.1995-23.12.2005	**Aleksander Kwaśniewski**	30.10.1998-15.10.2002	**Mikuláš Dzurinda**—Prime Minister Governing coalition: - the Slovak Democratic Coalition: the Party of Hungarian Coalition, the Party of Democratic Left, the Party of Civic Understanding	15.06.2004-15.06.2014	**Ivan Gašparovič**
02.05.2004-31.10.2005	**Marek Belka**—Prime Minister Governing coalition: - Democratic Left Alliance - Labor Union			16.10.2002-04.07.2006	**Mikuláš Dzurinda**—Prime Minister Governing coalition: - Slovak Christian-Democratic Union		
31.10.2005-14.07.2006	**Kazimierz Marcinkiewicz**—Prime Minister Governing coalition: - Law and Justice - The Center - League of Polish Families (from May 2006) - Self-Defense (from May 2006)	23.12.2005-10.04.2010	**Lech Kaczyński**	04.07.2006-08.07.2010	**Robert Fico**—Prime Minister Governing coalition: - SMER Direction—Social Democracy - The Slovak National Party; - People's Party - Movement for Democratic Slovakia		

14.07.2006-16.11.2007	**Jarosław Kaczyński**—Prime Minister Governing coalition: - Law and Justice - League of Polish Families - Self-Defense	06.08.2010-06.08.2015	**Bronisław Komorowski**[5]	08.07.2010-04.04.2012	**Iveta Radičová**—Prime Minister Governing coalition: - Slovak Democratic and Christian Union–Democratic Party SDKU-DS - Freedom and Solidarity (SaS), - Christian Democratic Movement (KDH), - Most-Hid the ethnic Hungarian party		
16.11.2007-22.09.2014	**Donald Tusk**—Prime Minister Governing coalition: - Civic Platform - Polish People's Party			04.04.2012-23.03.2016	**Robert Fico**—Prime Minister Single-party government: - SMER Direction—Social Democracy ()		
22.09.2014-16.11.2015	**Ewa Kopacz**—Prime Minister Governing coalition: - Civic Platform - Polish People's Party	06.08.2015-......	**Andrzej Duda**	23.03.2016-......	**Robert Fico**—Prime Minister Governing coalition: - SMER Direction—Social Democracy - Slovak National Party - Most-Hid - Network (former member of Christian Democratic Movement)	15.06.2014-......	**Andrej Kiska**
16.11.2015-......	**Beata Szydło**—Prime Minister Single-party government: - Law and Justice						

Source: own work, based on: (Úrad vlády Slovenskej republiky 2016; Premier RP 2016).

---

[5] Based on art. 131 of Polish Constitution, Bronisław Komorowski, as the Speaker of the Sejm, became the acting President after Lech Kaczyński died in the airplane crash on 10th of April 2010. He performed this role for three months, until 8th of July, when he resigned from the position of the Speaker (with Grzegorz Schetyna being his successor).

When analyzing the impact of international interdependence on Polish-Slovak relations, we shall focus on the sub-regional level, with particular attention being devoted to the cooperation among the countries of the Visegrad Group (V4). Regional cooperation (i.e. within the EU) and its impact on bilateral relations is also examined. Finally, the chapter moves on to the global dimension, presenting both states' individual and joint engagement with key players such as Russia and the United States.

Naturally, concepts and activities developed as parts of foreign policy are determined not only by domestic processes and phenomena, but also by those generated at the international level. As indicated in the introduction, authors acknowledge interdependence between the actors as an important feature of the international system (and its subsystems, including the EU). Therefore, foreign policy strategies formulated by governments in Warsaw and Bratislava reflect, in their essence, a mixture of influences—they have frequently changed in response to either domestic or international developments. Such interdependence meant that national decision-makers were constantly under pressure to find ways of ensuring security and economic growth for their fellow citizens. On many occasions, it spurred them to seek and work out compromises in order to accommodate divergent interests, as well as reduce costs and risks associated with international political rivalry (Moravcsik 1997).

The main purpose of this chapter is to present the historical development of Polish-Slovak political relations under the conditions of deep international interdependence driven by, among other factors, the process of European integration. Secondly, the author assesses how both countries' participation in multilateral cooperation (which clearly dominated their political relations) affected their effectiveness in pursuing both shared and individual interests and goals. In order to identify crucial factors that determined the overall shape of cooperation between Warsaw and Bratislava, the author has reviewed a substantial volume of both primary and secondary sources. This has led to distinguishing spheres (or, sometimes, single issues) that were the focus of bilateral relations. The chapter progresses from identifying those spheres to describing connections between them and, subsequently, presenting them in a systematized manner. The analysis and synthesis of research material has been conducted according to the theoretical model that juxtaposes liberal intergovernmentalism with the concept of Europeanization (as elaborated in chapter 1).

Dynamics of the relations in the bilateral context

The aim of this section is to describe and analyze bilateral relations between Poland and Slovakia. It begins with a closer look at how both governments formulated their foreign policies. The author attempts to explain how changes in the political environment that occurred over the period encompassed by this book affected Poland and Slovakia's strategic goals and interests. To that end, attitudes and views expressed in official documents are confronted with actions and achievements recorded in the area of bilateral relations.

Brief assessment of the development of Poland and Slovakia's political environment (2004-2016)

When analyzing conceptual bases of Polish and Slovak foreign policies, one needs to start by periodizing them. In this case, the crucial factor around which such periodization can be attempted is the alteration of power that followed national elections—in both Bratislava and Warsaw, changes of governments prompted reorganizations (sometimes even a redefinition) of foreign policy priorities. Within the time scope encompassed by this book (2004-2016), one can identify four clearly distinguishable periods, each with its own specific set of characteristics. Importantly, the aforementioned changes in policy directions and goals did not occur simultaneously in both states. Furthermore, socio-political divisions that shaped domestic political scenes in Poland and Slovakia differed substantially. The following paragraphs contain a brief presentation of stages in the development of Polish and Slovak foreign policies throughout the analyzed period.

In the case of Slovakia, the first period coincided with the coalition government led by Mikuláš Dzurinda (1998-2006). The coalition itself was based on the anti-Mečiar sentiment, as the cabinet declared its unambiguous support for integrating the country with European structures. Dzurinda's main goal was to overcome international isolation by introducing a series of political and economic reforms bringing Slovakia closer to standards espoused by Western Europe. At the same time, his concept of foreign policy featured the notion of normalizing relations with the Russian Federation—a prospect that Bratislava found tempting mainly due to the potential seen in economic cooperation (Vlček & Kaščáková 2012: 77-93).

The second period began in June 2006, when the social-democratic party won the parliamentary election and its leader, Robert Fico, was tasked with creating a coalition cabinet. The composition of the coalition, together with Fico's personal views regarding international politics, meant an ideological volte-face akin to a return to policies pursued earlier by Vladimir Mečiar. Slovak diplomacy turned a keen eye to Moscow, cooling its interest in any initiatives that would strengthen Euro-Atlantic structures. Fico's first term of office as the Prime Minister also saw a crisis in relations between Bratislava and Budapest—a circumstance that hindered cooperation within the entire Visegrad Group and, generally, resulted in Slovakia being branded by its European partners as something of an enfant terrible.

The next election, held in 2010, ended the rule of Fico's first cabinet. The new coalition, led by Christian Democrats, formed a government with Iveta Radičová as the Prime Minister. For a brief two years (the third period in our classification), Radičová directed her country back towards Europe, replicating earlier efforts made by Mikuláš Dzurinda. As a result, between 2010 and 2012 European matters „became more a part of the Slovak political life" (Gabrizová 2014: 63). Slovakia's first female Prime Minister declared willingness to restore and enhance good relations with Euro-Atlantic structures. However, her plans in that respect came to an abrupt end when her cabinet was given a vote of no confidence after the parliament failed to ratify the European Financial Stability Facility (The Economist 2011; Kałan 2012: 96).

The fall of Radičová's cabinet meant an earlier parliamentary election that ended with a landslide victory for Robert Fico, who was able to form a single-party government. He kept his post after the 2016 election, but was forced to seek partners for a coalition cabinet, as Social Democrats lost their absolute majority in the parliament. Fico's second tenure in power was a somewhat different affair than the first one—this time, Bratislava made an effort to skillfully find the balance between managing pressure exerted by other actors within the international system on the one hand, and meeting the expectations of the domestic electorate on the other hand. As a result, Slovakia was able to maintain decent relations with Russia without straying too far from the mainstream of Europe's attitude towards Moscow. Although Fico's view on dealing with the migration crisis was heavily criticized in Brussels, his cabinet managed to cooperate closely on this matter with partners from the Visegrad Group. Since 2012, Bratislava's relations with NATO have also been less tumultuous, allowing Fico to consolidate this element of foreign policy.

In a final word of comment to this section, it is worth noting that throughout the time examined here, Slovak governments declared their determination to preserve the conceptual continuity in foreign policy. Most of all, however, direction and priorities were driven by the country's membership in the EU—an aspect to be discussed later in this chapter.

When it comes to analyzing Polish foreign policy since 2004, the first period to be mentioned lasted from 2001 to 2005, when the predominant force in the parliament was the post-communist social-democratic party. The coalition government led by Leszek Miller and, subsequently, a minority cabinet of Marek Belka pursued integration with Western political structures by prioritizing the completion of Poland's accession to the EU and close cooperation with the USA. The first priority was embodied by the willingness to embrace the socializing, adaptive mechanisms of Europeanization that Warsaw was exposed to in the process of accession negotiations. The second one was reflected in advancing political and military alliance with Washington.

Poland's European policy changed noticeably after the parliamentary and presidential elections of 2005. The Law and Justice party that governed from 2005 to 2007 (since 2006 in a coalition with two other partners) represented a somewhat Euro-sceptic outlook, contesting changes proposed at the supranational level that would lead to the EU's federalization. Warsaw maintained and wished to further strengthen its ties with the USA, particularly with regard to security matters. Throughout this second period in the development of Polish foreign policy, both the cabinet and the president declared interest in building a coalition of Central European states—an initiative that, in some sense, was meant to challenge the Franco-German dominance in the Union and the primacy of Paris's and Berlin's national interests. Such stance sparked a skeptical reaction not only from the two aforementioned governments, but also from Brussels.

Jarosław Kaczyński's decision to dissolve the government brought about an early election that began an eight-year long (2007-2015) rule of a coalition formed by the center-right-leaning Civic Platform and the agrarian Polish People's Party. During that third period, Warsaw systematically built the pro-European direction of its foreign policy, sometimes at the expense of other areas (transatlantic cooperation, Central and Eastern European regional cooperation).

The final, fourth stage began in 2015. First, Law and Justice's candidate, Andrzej Duda, won the presidential election in May. In October, Kaczyński's formation emerged victorious from the parliamentary election, forming a single-party government. The new cabinet reverted, both conceptually and symbolically, to policies pursued between 2005 and 2007. At the same time, it has been highly critical of the achievements of its predecessors. Notably, although concepts included in Kaczyński's narrative are not, strictly speaking, new, some of them are redefined in a rather innovative way. One such example is the idea to build a coalition of countries stretching between the Baltic, Adriatic and Black Seas (including, of course, Poland and Slovakia).

In summary, it is important to realize that Polish decision-makers (primarily those from the two biggest parties: the Civic Platform and Law and Justice), unlike their Slovak counterparts, did not attempt to build a lasting consensus as to mid- and long-term priorities of foreign policy. Hence, Warsaw's approach was characterized by a lack of continuity, with international-political issues being the subject of internal disputes and disagreements—a predicament that Slovakia managed to avoid.

When one takes the periodization described above as a background that determined the development of Polish-Slovak relations, an important conclusion is that a genuine ideological convergence occurred only briefly (from 2010 to 2012) between cabinets led by Donald Tusk and Iveta Radičová respectively. It was the only period during which the two governments shared foreign policy goals and the way they positioned themselves on the European political scene—in the European

Parliament, both were members of the European People's Party. Some ideological and political similarities have also emerged between the cabinets of Robert Fico and Beata Szydło: both are proponents of an extensive social benefits system and strive to appease large social groups. However, with regard to several important issues of international politics, the two governing parties differ substantially. Their rapprochement in reaction to the refugee crisis has been devoid of deeper conceptual foundations—unlike in the case of Hungarian-Polish relations, built on the basis of ideological similarities represented by the cabinets of Victor Orban and Beata Szydło. Domestic socio-political developments marginalized Polish-Slovak relations to a mere function of their status as neighbors, with a sprinkling of minor, temporary issues of little importance to the strategic dimension. That being said, if such hypothesis is to be credibly verified, a more in-depth analysis is required. This is why the next section is focused on a precise examination of foreign policy priorities adopted by Bratislava and Warsaw, as expressed in strategic documents prepared by the highest national authorities. We shall devote particular attention to how both countries defined their role and importance for each other.

Analysis of strategic documents pertaining to foreign policy

Analytical conclusions for key priorities and directions of Polish and Slovak foreign policies were drawn based on official government documents such as: political agendas, reports on the achievement of policy goals and, particularly for Poland, the annual addresses delivered by the minister of foreign affairs in the Sejm.

The Slovak Republic

Being aware of their country's objective limitations (such as demographic potential and geopolitical position), Slovak decision-makers were fairly—to the degree the aforementioned limitations allowed—active in international politics. In areas deemed crucial to Slovakia's interests, they made efforts to be not just present, but actually influential. However, given Slovakia's stature in international politics, they could not hope to exert such influence through traditionally understood power. Instead, they adroitly positioned their country as a relatively neutral mediator or moderator / coordinator of political processes. This approach characterized their foreign policy even before Slovakia joined NATO and the EU in 2004. The essence of Slovakia's attempt to define its role was rooted "in the spirit of the principles of effective multilateralism" (Ministry of Foreign and European Affairs of the Slovak Republic 2010a: 2). In other words, Slovak diplomacy was strongly convinced that the international relations should be organized through strong, negotiated and enforceable multilateral regimes. According to both previous and current agendas published by the government, its activities in the international arena should be based on the needs of Slovak citizens and the economic interests of the state (Government Office of the Slovak Republic 2016a). Such statement clearly indicates the liberal intergovernmental perspective on justifying foreign policy directions adopted by the officials in Bratislava.

Integration with Western structures (primarily the EU) was consistently considered the main priority of Slovak foreign policy (Ministry of Foreign and European Affairs of the Slovak Republic 2009: 2). Slovakia supported the deepening of European integration and consolidation of EU institutions. Its participation in this process was backed by its efforts to implement the Union's policies and specialized programs. As beneficiaries of the EU's structural funds and direct payments, Slovaks perceived their membership as a source of stability, as well as socio-economic development. The government's view, according to which its position in international bargaining was largely dependent on the strength and effectiveness of the entire organization, was reflected in its declared determination to be a "predictable and reliable partner within the EU". Thus, Slovakia wanted to strengthen the "position and impact of the European Union in the global economy and global processes", while at the same time preserving the "ability of the EU to respect the specificities of its individual MS in the process of integration" (Government Office of the Slovak Republic 2016a).

Bratislava's most important partners throughout the analyzed time period were its neighbors. Examination of strategic documents reveals that relations with the neighboring states were always at the forefront of its foreign policy. In nearly all publications, the first (and, hence, the most important) partner to be mentioned was the Czech Republic. Other prioritized countries included Poland, relations with which were usually described as "traditionally friendly, intensive and forthcoming" (Minister of Foreign and European Affairs of the Slovak Republic 2009: 3). Thus, as stated in one of the analyzed documents, "the development of privileged relations with the Czech Republic and traditionally good relations with Poland remain among Slovakia's priority interests" (Ministry of Foreign and European Affairs of the Slovak Republic 2010a). As for Polish-Slovak bilateral relations, the continued emphasis was placed on "developing cross-border infrastructure (...), including progress in interconnecting road and highway networks", as well as "solidarity and cooperation in terms of energy security" (Minister of Foreign and European Affairs of the Slovak Republic 2011: 3, 2013).

Slovakia implemented its policy toward its neighbors in a traditional bilateral formula. However, the multilateral dimension, operationalized at the sub-regional level through the Visegrad platform, was also very prominent. Most of the examined documents indicated that "the Visegrad Group maintained its special status in Slovakia's foreign policy activities in the region" (Ministry of Foreign and European Affairs of the Slovak Republic 2009). Bratislava's active participation in the Group's work was considered as crucial to the regional and cross-border cooperation among Central European countries. Detailed goals of the Slovak foreign policy with regard to V4 included "strengthening of the consultation mechanism; concerted action and formulation of common position of Visegrad Group countries concerning important issues of the EU agenda, such as budget, regional development, external energy security and allocation of posts in EU bodies to candidates and representatives from V4 countries; concerted action aimed at reducing the impact of the global economic and financial crisis" (Ministry of Foreign and European Affairs of the Slovak Republic 2010a; Ministry of Foreign and European Affairs of the Slovak Republic 2011b).

When it comes to a broader European perspective, Slovakia's preferred direction of developing strategic relations encompassed the Western Balkans and, to a lesser extent, Eastern European countries (Ukraine, Belarus), along with the southern Caucasus (particularly Georgia). Finally, Bratislava considered Russia as its very important partner. This meant that even after its accession to Western integration structures, Slovak diplomacy was keen to maintain pragmatic, profitable relations with the Russian Federation (Ministry of Foreign and European Affairs of the Slovak Republic 2010a). The focus of these relations was the economic dimension. With that in mind, Slovaks intended to position themselves as advocates of "stronger ties between Russia and the European political, economic and security projects" (Ministry of Foreign and European Affairs of the Slovak Republic 2009: 6). One issue that proved particularly important for Russian-Slovak relations in both bi- and multilateral context was the "supply of strategic raw materials from the Russian Federation and their transit to European customers" via Slovakia (Ministry of Foreign and European Affairs of the Slovak Republic 2011a: 7).

Slovakia's approach to defining the role of the United States of America in its foreign policy was somewhat interesting. On the one hand, the USA was described as a "key partner and ally of the Slovak Republic" (Ministry of Foreign and European Affairs of the Slovak Republic 2010a). On the other hand, relations with Washington were clearly inserted into the Euro-Atlantic context, which suggested that the multilateral formula was seen as more important than the purely bilateral political and strategic dialogue. Such a position may be explained by Slovakia's pragmatic attitude toward its development and security. Bratislava wished to concentrate its bilateral relations with the USA around "scientific and technical cooperation between Slovak entities and their American partners" (Minister of Foreign and European Affairs of the Slovak Republic 2011a: 6).

The Republic of Poland

In the early 1990s, major political formations in Poland established a consensus regarding strategic aims of foreign policy by agreeing that the government should make utmost efforts to integrate the country with NATO and the EU. When that goal was completed with Poland's accession to the Union in 2004, the consensus naturally lost its validity. Subsequently, political elites (and the society at large as well) developed differing opinions as to how to use their newly reached status as a fully-fledged member of the European family. Questions arose also with regard to the future of transatlantic relations and reconciling the need to strengthen Europe as an independent actor of global politics with the notion of maintaining a strategic relationship with the USA. Another thorny issue was the attitude towards Russia. As the two biggest political parties grew more and more apart in their visions of a desirable foreign policy, the consensus that once preserved its continuity ceased to exist altogether.

In the time scope analyzed here, the only comprehensive publication that defined mid- and long-term goals and interests to be pursued through foreign policy was a strategy entitled "Priorities of Polish foreign policy, 2012-2016" published by the Ministry of Foreign Affairs in 2012 (Ministerstwo Spraw Zagranicznych Rzeczypospolitej Polskiej 2012a). The document was prepared to "present the vision, priorities and general tasks to be performed as parts of foreign policy through 2016". The government recognized that "society's support is indispensable for its effective implementation" (Ibidem: 2) and, in doing so, confirmed Moravcsik's notion of a link between political actions and their social legitimization, acknowledging that such actions are shaped by the most effective and influential social groups.

The first of foreign policy priorities mentioned in the document was related to Poland's membership in the EU. The government declared it would work toward "building a competitive, open and safe Union, based on the principle of solidarity", and that it aspired to "participate constructively in the EU's decision-making process" (Ibidem: 6). The second one regarded the strengthening of Poland's position "as a reliable ally in a stable transatlantic order" (Ibidem). The strategy signaled a conviction that the USA held a privileged position as a major partner in the Euro-Atlantic structure. The third place was granted to the task of "solidifying cooperation among the Visegrad Group states", as the government stressed that "Poland is open to different dimensions of regional cooperation". Further priorities included "increasing the role of development cooperation in Polish foreign policy" and "supporting activities aimed at spreading human rights, the rule of law and democracy" (Ibidem). The authors considered the promotion of Poland abroad as an instrument to strengthen its international position. The next task was to devise a new strategy for Polish diasporas in various countries. Government officials believed the previous mentality—whereby the onus was on the state to support its citizens living abroad—should be reversed so as to make diasporas responsible for promoting and supporting their motherland. Finally, the last priority concerned the continuing professionalization of Polish diplomatic service (Ibidem: 7).

The strategy also referred to the importance of other states for Polish foreign policy. Germany was named as Poland's key partner in bilateral relations (Ibidem: 17). Substantial role was also accorded to France and Great Britain as the other major EU MS. Among countries from outside the EU mentioned in the document, Ukraine seemed to be considered particularly vital, as it was named as a strategic partner (Ibidem: 18). With regard to Moscow, the authors declared that "Poland intends to maintain good, pragmatic relations with Russia, on the basis of the principle of reciprocity" (Ibidem).

The strategy labelled Poland's southern neighbors (i.e. Czech Republic and Slovakia) as its "European allies". The only direct reference to relations with Slovakia comes in the context of regional cooperation (the strategy's third priority), where Bratislava is categorized as a regional partner at the southern flank. Otherwise, Polish-Slovak relations were considered as a part of the multilateral dimension, embodied by the work of the Visegrad Group. The most important area of connections between the Czech Republic, Hungary, Poland and Slovakia was economic cooperation, including trade and investments. It was emphasized that "Poland, the Czech Republic, Slovakia and Hungary need common solutions that would not only satisfy their particular interests, but also allow them to pursue an effective European policy" (Ibidem: 19).

One would expect to find more information on the vision, concept and tasks of Polish diplomacy with regard to Slovakia in the Minister of Foreign Affairs' annual communique on the priorities of Polish foreign policy, presented each year to the Parliament. However, the analysis of these documents published between 2004 and 2016 revealed that Slovakia was mentioned only sporadically—always in the context of the Visegrad cooperation, when the ministers emphasized the need to coordinate the V4's efforts at the EU level and develop regional cooperation, particularly in the areas of infrastructure, movement of people and culture (Ministerstwo Spraw Zagranicznych RP 2004, 2007, 2008, 2011, 2012). One speech notable from the perspective of Polish-Slovak relations was an expose delivered by the Minister of Foreign Affairs in 2013. In it, Radosław Sikorski referred to Slovakia as a positive example of the benefits of adopting the common European currency. Moreover, Sikorski mentioned Bratislava not only when speaking about the Visegrad Group as a whole—he outlined specific bilateral projects to be implemented, including the construction of a gas pipeline connecting the two countries, as well as a common initiative to host the 2022 winter Olympic Games. The subject of Polish-Slovak cooperation on energy security re-emerged in the 2014 expose. This time, however, it was written into the broader international-political context, as Polish government acknowledged the consequences of international interdependence. In this particular case, the Minister was referring to long-term plans for transferring gas from Hungary, Poland and Slovakia to Ukraine (Ministerstwo Spraw Zagranicznych RP 2014). Polish diplomacy developed such plans as an expression of solidarity with Ukraine—a neighboring country that was embroiled in a political and military conflict with Russia. The concept of connecting national gas networks was also a case of a pragmatic approach, whereby cooperation was seen as a tool to prevent socio-economic destabilization and political turmoil in Poland's immediate vicinity. The same line of thinking was later employed by the new government formed after the 2015 parliamentary election, as evidenced in Minister Waszczykowski's 2016 address. W. Waszczykowski broadened the scope of the energy security issue in Polish Slovak relations by including a critical appraisal of the Nord Stream 2 project developed jointly by Germany and Russia. He noted that "the pipeline reduces Slovakia's importance as a transit country, and so damages the economic interests of our southern ally", while at the same time "weakening the position of our eastern partner [i.e. Ukraine—J.D.]" (Ministerstwo Spraw Zagranicznych RP 2014). Furthermore, the shift in the priorities of Polish foreign policy resulted in a proposal for intergovernmental consultations between Bratislava, Prague and Warsaw, as Waszczykowski vowed to "seek synergy with the efforts made by the Slovak presidency in the EU Council with regard to, among other matters, the review of the EU budget, the development of the digital market, the Energy Union, the migration crisis and the situation in Ukraine" (Ibidem).

Interestingly, some of the annual addresses delivered by Polish Ministers of Foreign Affairs did not contain any direct references to Slovakia—that was the case in 2005, 2006, 2009, 2010 and 2015. Bratislava was mentioned only indirectly, through descriptions of the Visegrad cooperation as one of the pillars of Warsaw's regional activity.

After Poland acceded to the EU, its successive governments attempted (at least declaratively) to construct foreign policy goals in a manner that would make them clearer and link them to specific benefits it would bring to citizens. The concepts around which they were formed, particularly between 2007 and 2015, marginalized the aspect of competition (or, even more, an open rivalry) within the European system. Instead, Warsaw chose to stress the cooperative tendencies and rationality of Europe's major actors. Consequently, the policy was built primarily as a way of managing relations with foreign partners to the benefit of domestic interest groups, with the task of preserving the country's good image often at its core. This approach changed in the aftermath of the 2014 crisis in Ukraine and the annexation of Crimea.

Summary of the analysis of strategic documents

Several observations can be made to summarize the conclusions stemming from the lecture of strategic documents mentioned above. First of all, the goals of Polish and Slovak foreign policies were, in general, not divergent—in a great majority of situations, they were either identical or complementary. This enabled both parties to preserve an atmosphere conducive to the development of bilateral political dialogue. The two governments were similar in identifying areas of common interest: energy security, cross-border cooperation, coordination of policies at the European level. Discrepancies that emerged throughout the period analyzed here were related to a narrow set of issues: specifically, to the perception of the role and importance of Russia and the United States.

Secondly, both Bratislava and Warsaw have increasingly tried to take account of the interests expressed by their domestic social groups when formulating their foreign policies. This trend was spurred by, among other factors, the progressing process of Europeanization and the gradual fading of distinction between European and internal policies of each member state. As many policies (including those crucial to Polish-Slovak relations, e.g. regional, energy and trade policies) have been communitized, interests expressed directly by citizens have become a more influential force in the European political process.

Finally, the fact that Polish-Slovak bilateral relations were mentioned only briefly in strategic documents is a reflection of their fairly uninterrupted, trouble-free character, rather than a suggestion of their insignificance. This preliminary conclusion will be verified in subsequent parts of this book.

Conditions and circumstances of Polish-Slovak bilateral political relations

Legal basis

The body of legal documents that regulate Polish-Slovak relations is relatively large—since 1994, 197 normative acts of various types have been signed by representatives of both states (Sejm RP 2016). The most important ones are, of course, bilateral intergovernmental agreements. It should be noted that after Poland and Slovakia acceded to the EU in 2004, some (or, in case of certain documents, all) stipulations contained in agreements concluded between 1996 and 2004 became invalid. This was true particularly for regulations regarding trade—an area that since 2004 has been governed by the rules of the European Single Market. When both countries joined the Schengen zone in 2007, the same happened to regulations on border controls and cross-border movement of people.

Table 6. The list of bilateral agreements concluded by Poland and Slovakia between 1993 and 2016.

Signing date	Title	In force
18th August 1994 1st August 2013	Agreement between the Republic of Poland and the Slovak Republic regarding the removal of double taxation on personal income and property Protocol	Yes—with changes resulting from the stipulations of the Protocol
6th July 1995	Agreement between the Republic of Poland and the Slovak Republic regarding legal relations and cooperation on the common border	Yes
18th August 1994	Agreement between the Government of the Republic of Poland and the Government of the Slovak Republic regarding cross-border rail traffic	Yes
23rd August 1996	Agreement between the Republic of Poland and the Slovak Republic regarding complementing and facilitating the implementation of the European Convention on Extradition dated 13th December 1957	Yes

6th December 1996	Agreement between the Republic of Poland and the Slovak Republic regarding local border traffic	No
25th March 1997	Agreement between the Republic of Poland and the Slovak Republic regarding complementing and facilitating the implementation of the European Convention on Mutual Assistance in Criminal Matters dated 20th April 1959	Yes
14th May 1997	Agreement between the Government of the Republic of Poland and the Government of the Slovak Republic regarding water resource management in interstate waters	Yes
16th April 1998	Agreement between the Government of the Republic of Poland and the Government of the Slovak Republic regarding international road transport	Yes
1st July 1999	Agreement between the Government of the Republic of Poland and the Government of the Slovak Republic regarding border crossing points, crossing the border on interstate tourist trails and the rules for crossing the border outside crossing points	No
23rd March 2000	Agreement between the Government of the Republic of Poland and the Government of the Slovak Republic regarding cultural, educational and scientific cooperation	Yes
24th January 2000	Agreement between the Republic of Poland and the Slovak Republic amending the Agreement between the Republic of Poland and the Slovak Republic regarding local border traffic dated 6th December 1996	No
4th January 2002	Agreement between the Government of the Republic of Poland and the Government of the Slovak Republic regarding the change of opening hours of the Szczawnica-Lesnica border crossing point	No
2nd April 2002	Agreement between the Government of the Republic of Poland and the Government of the Slovak Republic amending the Annex no. 3 to the Agreement between the Government of the Republic of Poland and the Government of the Slovak Republic regarding border crossing points, crossing the border on interstate tourist trails and the rules for crossing the border outside crossing points dated 1st July 1999	No
28th April 2001	Agreement between the Government of the Republic of Poland and the Government of the Slovak Republic regarding international combined transport	Yes
4th January 2000	Agreement between the Government of the Republic of Poland and the Government of the Slovak Republic regarding cooperation and mutual assistance in the eventuality of catastrophes, natural disasters and other major accidents	Yes

Date	Agreement	Ratified
29th July 2002	Agreement between the Government of the Republic of Poland and the Government of the Slovak Republic regarding mutual protection of classified information	
18th November 2004	Agreement between the Government of the Republic of Poland and the Government of the Slovak Republic regarding scientific and technical cooperation	Yes
23rd November 2004	Agreement between the Government of the Republic of Poland and the Government of the Slovak Republic regarding the construction of a new road connection and a border bridge across the river Poprad in the vicinity of the towns of Piwniczna and Mniszek nad Popradem	Yes
18th July 2005	Agreement between the Government of the Republic of Poland and the Government of the Slovak Republic regarding mutual recognition of periods of studying, as well as the equivalence of documents confirming the level of education and academic degrees obtained in the Republic of Poland and the Slovak Republic	No
23rd March 2004	Agreement between the Republic of Poland and the Slovak Republic regarding cooperation in combating crime and common activities in border areas	Yes
10th February 2012	Agreement between the Government of the Republic of Poland and the Government of the Slovak Republic regarding mutual visa representation	Yes
22nd November 2013	Agreement between the Government of the Republic of Poland and the Government of the Slovak Republic regarding cooperation for the purpose of implementing the project of constructing a gas pipeline connecting Polish and Slovak gas transmission networks	Yes
13th November 2013	Agreement between the Government of the Republic of Poland and the Government of the Slovak Republic regarding mutual protection of classified information	Yes
16th March 2016	Agreement between the Government of the Republic of Poland and the Government of the Slovak Republic amending the Agreement between the Government of the Republic of Poland and the Government of the Slovak Republic regarding mutual recognition of periods of studying, as well as the equivalence of documents confirming the level of education and academic degrees obtained in the Republic of Poland and the Slovak Republic	Yes

Source: own work, based on Internetowy System Aktów Prawnych (Sejm RP 2016).

The scope of subjects covered in bilateral agreements listed above includes primarily issues related to cross-border cooperation and socio-cultural-scientific cooperation. The dynamics of bilateral relations, as assessed based on the quantitative (the number of documents) and qualitative (matters covered in those documents) criteria, points to a low level of politicization. Instead of being focused around political agendas, Polish-Slovak cooperation was shaped by the influence of domestic interest groups that were concerned, first and foremost, with pragmatic aspects and expected results that would be tangible and useful to the citizens.

Social perception of Polish-Slovak bilateral relations
Following the theoretical approach that complements the liberal intergovernmentalism with Europeanization, we shall now take a brief look at Poles and Slovaks' mutual perception. The subject of Polish-Slovak relations only sporadically emerged in public debates ongoing in both countries and, even when it did, it did not spark particularly heated discussions, be it within the societies or among political leaders. Unlike some other, more troubled bilateral ties (e.g. Slovak-Hungarian or Polish-German), Poland and Slovakia's relations as neighbors have been generally considered as "the most trouble-free" ones (Lubicz-Miszewski 2008: 151). This is so because their shared history—particularly those episodes that might generate animosity (such as the conflict over the territories of Spisz and Orawa, or Slovaks' collaboration with the Nazis during WWII)—was not politicized by either side. Moreover, the subject of Slovakia's internal and foreign policy was practically absent from socio-political discourse in Poland. As noted by R. Zenderowski, "individual public broadcasters, but especially commercial ones, are generally not interested in Slovakia as such, recognizing it as a country of little interest and having little importance in international politics" (Zenderowski 2013: 142).

At the same time, Poles seem to have a positive image of their country's political relations with Slovakia and are sympathetic towards their southern neighbors. This has been confirmed by public opinion polls conducted throughout the entire period analyzed in this book. In 2004, Polish society considered the Czech Republic and Slovakia as examples of good neighbors, while Russia as a negative counter-example. 38% of respondents explicitly described Slovakia as a good neighbor, while only 2% were of the opposite opinion (OBOP 2004). In one of the most recent polls, conducted in 2015, 42% of respondents deemed Polish-Slovak relations to be good. Merely 14% believed they were negative, but as much as 30% described them as "neither good nor bad". Another 14% did not have any opinion on this matter (CBOS 2015a). Compared to the social perception of Poland's relations with its other neighbors, such as Russia, Lithuania, Belarus or even Ukraine, Polish-Slovak ties are clearly considered as positive. Furthermore, the same poll revealed that Czechs and Slovaks are Poles' favorite neighbors. 50% of respondents declared sympathy for the Czechs, while 48% stated they liked the Slovaks (CBOS 2015b). A negative sentiment towards these nations was voiced by only 14% and 12% of respondents respectively (Ibidem). Importantly, the results of the 2015 poll simply confirmed a consistent tendency exhibited by the Polish society over a long period of time: Poles have been increasingly positive towards other Central European nations, particularly Czechs and Slovaks (Dębicki 2013: 17). Finally, Polish people's opinion on their southern neighbors seems to be correlated with the near absence of the subject of Polish-Slovak relations from the public debate. One might argue that the less attention the media devote to problems between Bratislava and Warsaw, the more positive the nation's view of these relations is.

Assessing Slovaks' attitude towards Poland and the Poles is somewhat more difficult, since within the time scope examined here there were no public opinion polls on this subject. One must therefore consider statements from Slovak opinion-forming circles. In general, it seems that Slovaks are not as optimistic in their assessment of Poland as Poles are when talking about Slovakia. Poles are often perceived through the lens of stereotypes. Moreover, Slovaks believe Poland does not treat their country as an equal partner in bilateral relations and uses its superiority (in terms of potential, population etc.) to take a dominant position in certain areas. For instance, Polish trade practices are sometimes judged as unfair and Polish goods are considered to be low-quality (Aktuality.sk 2014). Slovaks see Poles as clients who like to bargain in order to 'get more for less'. Slovak General Consul in Kraków, Ivan Škorupa, observed in a press interview: "When Slovaks see that something costs three euros, they either pay the amount and buy it, or just walk away. You [the Poles—J.D.] often bargain. I think it is rooted deeply in your culture. In times of socialism, you had private shops, some people engaged in trade, they exchanged goods and looked for ways to earn. It seems you are still able to make better use of money than us" (Gazeta Krakowska 2014). Such view was confirmed by a Pole living in Bratislava, Joanna Matloňová, who is the editor-in-chief of the Polish-Slovak Forum. As noted by Matloňová, "when Slovaks talk about Polish people, they often use the word 'entrepreneurship'—some mean it as a complement, but others associate it with scheming and being cunning in the negative sense of the term" (Bankier 2014). Only a narrow group of Slovak intellectuals possesses a well-grounded knowledge of Poland, its cultural heritage, the nation, the depth of changes that occurred after 1989 and contemporary socio-political problems (Gazeta Krakowska 2014).

The limited interest both nations have in each other is frequently limited to singular issues discussed at a given moment by the media. Magdaléna Vášáryová, who between 2000 and 2005 acted as Slovakia's Ambassador in Warsaw, summarized the problem as follows: "Polish-Slovak relations are like a sinusoid: sometimes you forget us, and sometimes you think well of us (...) I know that a lot of people in your country have no opinion at all about Slovakia simply because they don't know anything about us" (Vášáryová 2006). The same is true if one reverses the perspective—Slovaks do not know much about Poland and Poles. The state of relations between the two societies—and, as a result, their perception of bilateral political relations—is shaped largely during Slovaks' shopping sprees to Poland and Poles' holiday stays in Slovak resorts. In both cases, the impression is not always unequivocally positive (Dziennik Zachodni 2013).

Most important achievements and developments in Polish-Slovak political relations

As an introduction to this part, let us begin with two quotes presenting opinions that, while seemingly divergent, can be neatly synthesized to serve as a starting point for further analysis. The first one comes from Piotr Bajda, who observed the following: „the actions of Robert Fico's government presented Polish diplomacy with quite a challenge. Instead of continuing a smooth development of bilateral and regional relations,

Slovak decision-makers put clear emphasis on promoting direct relations with major European actors. This forced our government to reconsider the role of the Visegrad Group and cooperation with Eastern European partners. We could no longer hope that Bratislava would understand or support Poland's initiatives in international politics if they threatened, even slightly, Slovakia's relations with the EU's biggest MS or Russia. Slovakia was not interested in having Warsaw as its strategic partner to the same extent as Prague or the Baltic states were" (Bajda 2010: 273). The second quote comes from Jakub Łoginow, who assessed that "after Slovakia joined NATO and the EU, our southern neighbor ceased to be of any interest to Polish foreign policy (...). We assumed that all goals pertaining to that country had been achieved, our relations were exemplary and, hence, did not require any attention" (Łoginow 2013).

Indeed, after the 2004 EU enlargement Polish-Slovak relations generally developed in the right direction, although the two governments were primarily absorbed by matters other than their mutual contacts. Poland and Slovakia did not follow their accession to the EU with any bilateral approaches. Neither Bratislava nor Warsaw were particularly interested in obtaining mutual support for their initiatives and interests or in tightening their relations in general. The sole exception was Slovakia's decision to put forward its candidacy for a non-permanent seat in the UN Security Council. Its diplomatic efforts in Warsaw were headed by Ambassador Magda Vášáryová and resulted in Slovakia being the only country from Central and Eastern Europe running for the post. Poland, along with all other Central European states, fully supported Bratislava's candidacy (Ukielski 2008: 241). Otherwise, when Poland and Slovakia did act in unison on the international scene, it was through the V4 formula. Certain differences that emerged in their European policies did not cause any significant tensions in bilateral contacts.

Bilateral relations between Bratislava and Warsaw experienced a slight setback after the 2006 parliamentary election in Slovakia. Although the new, left-wing government did not fundamentally reorient the country's foreign policy, it shifted the emphasis when formulating its strategy for international relations (Ukielski 2009: 263). The changes had a negative impact on the atmosphere of Polish-Slovak bilateral contacts (albeit to a much lesser extent than in the case of Slovak-Hungarian relations). In October 2006, Prime Minister Fico visited Warsaw—an event during which bilateral relations were described as "above standard". However, reality did not reflect this rather optimistic assessment. Throughout that year there were no meetings at the ministerial level—consultations of vice-ministers were also postponed. Such state of affairs was a consequence of more than a mere lack of mutual interest or vagueness as to supposedly shared goals. It resulted from an increasing divergence in the perceptions of the desirable future of European integration and cooperation with Russia and the USA. Of some importance was also the difference in attitudes towards western aspirations expressed by countries such as Ukraine and Georgia.

Certain rapprochement began in 2007, after a new government, headed by Donald Tusk, took office in November. Bratislava had already made some friendly gestures earlier during the year: for instance, it enthusiastically supported Wrocław's bid to host EXPO 2012. However, a genuine, full-scale restoration of closer relations required the alternation of power in Slovakia and occurred when Iveta Radičová commenced her tenure as the Prime Minister in July 2010. Her Christian-democratic government, underpinned by liberal tendencies, was ideologically close to Tusk's cabinet and constituted a much more natural partner than Fico's left-leaning nationalists. Newly defined priorities of Slovak foreign policy opened up the possibility of recreating positive foundations for bilateral political cooperation on European matters and other issues of international politics alike.

Over the following two years, that positive atmosphere fostered pragmatic cooperation to the point where Slovakia went as far as branding it a "strategic partnership". The early parliamentary election in 2012 and Robert Fico's return to the post of Prime Minister threatened to disrupt that dynamic. However, social-democrats seemed to have learned their lesson from their previous stint in power. This time, they embarked on a much more conciliatory policy, presenting themselves as predictable partners open to constructive cooperation. Both Bratislava and Warsaw continued to pay closer attention to their relations. Consequently, March 2013 saw the first joint government meeting, held in Poprad (Ministry of Foreign and European Affairs of the Slovak Republic 2014b). Apart from making very friendly declarations, the two cabinets decided to make a joint bid for the 2022 Winter Olympic games. They also discussed issues related to energy security and the development of transport infrastructure. Another vital topic was the need to coordinate their European agenda (Government Office of the Republic of Poland 2013). Despite readiness expressed by Donald Tusk and, later Beata Szydło, the second such meeting did not take place before the end of 2016. Bilateral dialogue was continued through mutual visits of Polish and Slovak politicians. The Presidents of both countries met regularly on the occasion of opening an annual cross-country skiing competition, the course of which starts in the Slovak town of Oravice and finishes in Witów, Poland. Their common presence at the event has since become something akin to a tradition: Bronisław Komorowski visited Oravice three times, meeting Ivan Gašparovič in 2013 and 2014, and Andrej Kiska in 2015 (Ambasada RP w Bratysławie 2015). The tradition was upheld also in 2016, when Andrzej Duda met Andrej Kiska in the resort of Tatrzańska Łomnica. The two Presidents stated that "Poland and Slovakia share many needs and visions of the future", and that matters crucial to their relations (including the improvement of road and rail connections, as well as support for tourism and business) stemmed primarily from the expectations of their citizens (PAP 2016a).

The drive to infuse Polish-Slovak relations with more dynamism and solid content came primarily from trans-border initiatives aimed at developing infrastructure, fostering socio-economic growth and protecting the environment. Many of these projects were implemented with the support of EU funds (for instance Interreg), while others were devised within the framework of Euroregions. More details on this topic can be found in chapter five. Here, it might be useful to note that central governments of both countries (particularly Slovakia) often pointed out the need to improve the quality of road and rail infrastructure, especially by connecting road and highway networks (Ministry of Foreign and European Affairs of the Slovak Republic 2010a; Ministry of Foreign and European Affairs of the Slovak Republic 2009). Tasks seen as crucial in this context included the completion of cross-border road transport infrastructure along the expressway section between Prešov and Rzeszów, as well as modernization of railway infrastructure (Ministry of Foreign and European Affairs of the Slovak Republic 2010b).

Dynamics of the relations in the multilateral context

This part of the chapter is aimed at explaining how Polish-Slovak bilateral relations were implemented in the multilateral formula. The key reference objects here are the European Union and the Visegrad Group. Importantly, there is a significant link between both countries' membership in the EU and the dynamics of the V4 as a platform for bilateral cooperation. The analysis is aided by employing the concept of Europeanization and its dimensions, particularly *downloading*, *uploading* and *cross-loading*. It is apparent that the Group often intensified its activity in reaction to processes initiated at the supranational (European) level. At the same time, the European Commission's decisions acted as a catalyst for regional cooperation—this corresponds to the downloading dimension. Conversely, by effectively coordinating their positions, the V4 members were sometimes able to influence decisions made in Brussels, thus showcasing the uploading dimension. Finally, the combined impact of Visegrad cooperation and European integration processes allowed the cross-loading effect, whereby EU MS influenced and Europeanized each other. Similarly to the analysis of the bilateral context, we shall consider sources of political decisions and actions undertaken at the international forum, including the role of national interest groups.

Polish-Slovak relations in the context of European integration and both states EU membership

After Poland and Slovakia acceded to the European Union, their relations were naturally remodeled. First of all, some bilateral agreements (particularly those on economic matters—see the table) simply lost validity and were replaced by the Union's legal order that has now applied to both countries. Secondly, once the goal of joining the EU had been achieved, the main ideological driving force behind Polish-Slovak cooperation was gone. This produced a certain conceptual void and uncertainty as to mutual preferences. Of course, in the aftermath of their accession both Bratislava and Warsaw acknowledged the need for further cooperation within the EU. This, however, required the two states to redefine their regional identities and perception of partners.

EU membership changed not only the backdrop of bilateral relations, but also the very character of foreign policies implemented by Poland and Slovakia: their scope and goals. Prior to the accession, European policy constituted an element of those foreign policies. Since 2004, it has become a part of internal policy logic. In other words, in relations with other EU MS, the distinction between internal and foreign policies has become blurred (Dyduch 2016: 36).

aturally, in order to find their footing in this new reality, decision-makers in Bratislava and Warsaw had to expose themselves to the mechanisms of Europeanization. In 2010, when characterizing Slovakia's foreign policy, president Ivan Gašparovič stated: "we gradually get used to the fact that we should approach European matters as domestic policy issues rather than foreign policy agenda" (Gašparovič 2010: 12). The same shift applied to Polish foreign policy. After the accession, the European agenda often included topics typical of the domestic domain, such as agricultural and social policies. Some areas that had previously been treated as strictly domestic (e.g. regional development) were now closely linked to the EU's cohesion policy and, as such, came into the orbit of diplomatic activities. Moreover, when pursuing goals related to cross-border regional cooperation, Poland and Slovakia had to account for the influence of Brussels. From a different perspective, EU membership became an impulse not only for cooperation, but also for certain rivalry, as all MS competed for funding and position in the European system. Throughout the time period analyzed here, European policy strategies formulated by Polish and Slovak politicians frequently differed to a significant extent. Presented below are selected issues around which Poland and Slovakia focused their activity in the Union—with particular focus on those that affected their bilateral relations. Firstly, we shall examine Bratislava and Warsaw's vision of their place in the Union immediately after their accession. / Then, we will move on to preferences with regard to specific EU policies that caused the two countries to interact. We will omit economic and security aspects, as those are discussed elsewhere in the book. Instead, we will look into their involvement in the conceptualization and implementation of the Common Foreign and Security Policy, the Eastern Partnership and the energy policy.

Priorities of the Republic of Poland and the Slovak Republic in the context of European integration and EU membership

The starting point for our considerations is a brief examination of Poland's and Slovakia's strategies for their EU membership. The example to be used here is their attitude towards the introduction of new European treaties that would remodel the community and affect each state's position in it. Newcomers to the Union were from the very beginning subjected to strong adaptational pressure, emanating from both Brussels and particular "old" MS. They were pressed not only to adjust their legal and institutional systems to EU standards, but also to accept common principles and patterns of cooperation. In addition, at the time of its enlargement, the Union itself was undergoing dynamic changes. It is a commonly accepted notion that the scale of the enlargement produced the need for deep institutional reforms. The community had already attempted to address the problem before it accepted ten new members: in 2001 it adopted the Nice Treaty. However, numerous politicians across Western Europe contested the stipulations of the Treaty even before it entered into force in 2003, pointing out that further changes were inevitable and calling for the commencement of negotiations on another treaty. Driven by a sense of urgency, the decision-makers agreed on the continuation of reforms and embarked on an ambitious effort to design a constitutional treaty for the EU. Signed in 2004 in Rome, the document was meant to strengthen supranational institutions and change the voting system in the EU Council. The so-called Nice system (weighted voting) was to be replaced with a double majority system. Warsaw defended the weighted voting method in the belief it would allow a more effective pursuit of Polish interests. Slovakia, on the other hand, did not object to the new reform proposals and accepted the outcome of the intergovernmental conference. The ratification process began fairly well, with Lithuania, Hungary, Slovenia, Italy, Greece, Austria, Germany, Slovakia and Spain completing the procedure within months of the Rome summit. Then, however, citizens of France and the Netherlands rejected the treaty in national referenda, held on 29th of May and 1st of June 2005 respectively (Banat & Pałłasz 2006: 43).

Despite the failure of the ratification process, most decision-makers in EU MS remained convinced the community needed the reform—not only due to the enlargement, but also to handle emerging global challenges. The first voices advocating the return to the negotiating table—from France and Germany, among others—came late in 2005 and in the first months of 2006. It was decided that the new project should be based on those stipulations of the Constitutional Treaty that did not raise any controversies. When Germany assumed the presidency in the EU Council in the first half of 2007, Berlin campaigned to include in the new treaty as much of the original proposal as possible, with only cosmetic changes (Missiroli 2010: 428). At that time, Slovakia was seen by Brussels as something of an enfant terrible due to its tense relations with Hungary and Prime Minister Robert Fico's uncompromising rhetoric, which even led to the suspension of his party's (SMER) membership in the socialist political group in the European Parliament. Some observers believed that by endorsing the new proposal practically without any reservations, Fico tried to manage his negative image and prove Bratislava's "Europeanness" (Ukielski 2009: 264). Others pointed to the fact that the majority of Slovak society and political elites had considered EU membership as a key foreign policy goal since at least 1998. Being aware of their country's limited territorial and demographic potential, decision-makers in Bratislava did not aspire to have a substantial impact on the direction of European integration. Instead, they valued the membership for all pragmatic advantages it offered and, hence, looked to position themselves in the mainstream of European politics.

Poland, meanwhile, remained skeptical and from the Autumn 2005 onwards, consistently objected to the planned reform. Having gained the status of a full member of the European community, the government in Warsaw believed it was now entitled to have its say on the Union's future and was no longer obliged to blindly follow whatever was proposed by the major actors. It saw the stipulations of the accession treaty (based explicitly on the Nice system) as fairly permanent conditions of its membership. This attitude made EU decision-makers convinced that Warsaw did not understand the rules of European politics. They believed that by rejecting further political integration, Poland acted to the detriment of the Union. Finally, after several rounds of tumultuous negotiations, a compromise on the new treaty was reached in June 2007. Warsaw agreed to the proposed new EU Council decision-making procedure in exchange for being excluded from the obligations of the Charter of Fundamental Rights and including in the Lisbon Treaty a chapter on energy policy.

In summary, the initial period of EU membership saw Poland and Slovakia differ in the way they defined their place in the Union. This divergence affected their bilateral relations and interactions within the European system. Poland wished to be an equal partner to Europe's major players and a co-creator of processes that the community would undergo. Warsaw's right to a seat at the decision-making table was implied in the internal discourse on European politics held in Poland. The concept was particularly relevant in the discussion of political issues, including the redistribution of powers within the community. Slovakia took on an entirely different stance: it opted to refrain from pursuing political ambitions and instead focused on optimizing the outcome of its membership by maximizing gains and reducing costs.

Polish-Slovak relations in the light of selected EU policies operationalization

Issues related to the European Union and stemming from Poland and Slovakia's membership in it were consistently one of the most important areas handled by the two governments. When one considers Polish and Slovak European policies against the backdrop of a complex, interactive European system, it becomes apparent that the system became a space for bilateral relations. It enabled various dimensions of the Europeanization process. This was particularly true when Bratislava and Warsaw consulted their positions on the operationalization of certain policies or cooperated towards the achievement of commonly determined goals. Moreover, the activities undertaken by the two governments at the European level, coupled with the downloading process, drove the system's internal feedback loop by shaping bilateral relations.

Common Foreign and Security Policy (CFSP) constituted one of the important areas where Polish and Slovak interests, as defined in their foreign policy priorities, crossed and affected bilateral relations. Since the issues to be examined here are chosen according to their impact on the bilateral aspect, the sphere most relevant to the analysis presented in this chapter is the European Neighborhood Policy (ENP) and one of its specific initiatives—the Eastern Partnership (EaP). These particular areas absorbed both Polish and Slovak diplomats, frequently becoming a subject of common decision-making and coordinated actions. This was due to several reasons, key among which were historical and geopolitical considerations, as well as the fact that since 2004 Poland and Slovakia have shared the responsibility of protecting the EU's external borders.

Warsaw articulated its preferences as to the EU's new neighborhood policy as soon as the subject was first raised: in late 2002 and early 2003. The fact it did so even before completing its accession procedure serves to highlight the importance Polish government attached to the task of adding a well-defined, consistent Eastern dimension to the Union's foreign policy. From the very beginning, the key points in Poland's proposals referred to Ukraine and Belarus—Warsaw called for creating very specific relations between Brussels, Kiev and Minsk. It supported Ukraine's European aspirations and suggested that the extent of cooperation with Belarus should be 'conditional' (i.e. dependent on the implementation of democratic reforms that the EU called for). Polish government also supported the notion of further EU enlargement, so as to include Ukraine and the Western Balkans. It proposed creating a long-term perspective for Belarus' accession. The first proposals for neighborhood policy developed at the supranational level were not entirely satisfactory from Warsaw's point of view. Therefore, Polish government remained an active participant of the discussion throughout the subsequent months, presenting other EU MS with a document prepared by the Ministry of Foreign Affairs, entitled „The Polish View on the EU New Neighbors Initiative" (The Warsaw Voice 2003).

Slovakia was far less involved in the discourse, particularly at the common European forum. Lucia Najšlová described its stance as that of "learners and followers" (2011: 109). However, it should be noted that the problem of post-accession foreign policy directions was not ignored by Slovak politicians and experts. As soon as 2002, an influential think-tank, Slovak Foreign Policy Association, started a debate that would quickly attract attention from the country's top politicians. The discussions produced an agreement as to the need to further develop relations with Eastern-European partners—primarily Ukraine and Belarus—as well as the countries of Western Balkans. The need was seen as equally relevant at both domestic and common European level (Najšlová 2012: 123-124). Similarly to Poland, Slovakia attached particular importance to the situation of Ukraine. However, while Warsaw voiced its position independently from any other proposals that came from within the Union, Bratislava considered its eastern policy almost exclusively within the common European context. This was so because the Slovak government believed it would be able to exert more influence in this area if acting through the EU channels.

The concept for the Union's approach to the problem was outlined in a document entitled "The European Neighbourhood Policy—Strategy Paper" (European Commission 2003a), published in May 2004. The Paper defined goals, geographical scope and instruments of the European Neighbourhood Policy (ENP). The Policy was to be aimed at stabilizing and ensuring security in the EU's immediate vicinity. In its essence, the ENP was a regional incarnation of foreign policy: it was designed to grant the Union's neighbors the benefit of privileged relations with the community, but stop short of promising them the prospect of full membership. This basic assumption went clearly against Bratislava and Warsaw's desire to maintain the attitude of open door.

The geographical scope of ENP encompassed North Africa (Morocco, Algeria, Tunisia, Libya), the Middle East (Egypt, Palestine, Israel, Syria and Lebanon), southern Caucasus (Georgia, Armenia and Azerbaijan), as well as Southern and Eastern Europe (Moldova, Ukraine and Belarus). One notable absence from the above list is, of course, Russia. Moscow's reaction to the concept whereby the Union would build bilateral relations with its neighbors through the framework of ENP was highly critical. Refusing to participate in the program, Russia accused the EU of using the proposal to disguise an expansionist policy.

As the conceptual debate over the shape of ENP continued, two directions of foreign policy emerged as being of primary interest. The first one, championed by France, Spain and Italy, encompassed the Mediterranean area. The second one, supported by Germany and the new MS, targeted Eastern Europe. The initial period of implementing the ENP showed that with regard to its eastern neighbors, the EU was only ready for "soft" engagement, rather than for a consistent, detailed strategy that would lead to, for instance, full integration of this region. This vagueness of intentions and lack of clear perspective or criteria for further integration brought about some criticism and caused dissatisfaction on the part of the Union's most pro-European-oriented neighbors. This meant that certain actors within the EU (among them Poland and Slovakia) would try to introduce more purpose and details in the eastern aspect of the ENP.

The result of these attempts materialized in the shape of a joint Polish-Swedish proposal announced in May 2008. Suggested as an initiative within the ENP, the EaP was discussed by the European Council as soon as the following month. The concept envisioned creating a regional forum for cooperation with Ukraine, Moldova, Georgia, Azerbaijan, Armenia and (though only through expert groups) Belarus. EaP was designed as an integral part of the ENP. Accepting the idea presented by governments of Poland and Sweden as a valid starting point, The European Council tasked the Commission with preparing a more detailed proposal for the principles that would govern the EaP. The Commission based its work on an implementation document adopted in December the same year. The success of the initiative owed much to a substantial effort that Stockholm and Warsaw put into consulting it with their partners (including numerous MS and the EC). As early as March 2008, both countries' diplomatic services made initial enquiries to probe the attitudes of other European actors. Poland made particular effort to gain the support of the remaining Visegrad Group members, including Slovakia. Although Bratislava did not directly participate in the elaboration of conceptual framework for the EaP, it was very open towards the prospect of adding a regional dimension to the ENP. Slovak diplomats described the EaP as "one of the most important initiatives under EU foreign policy" and emphasized that "Slovakia is fully committed to its successful implementation" (Minister of Foreign and European Affairs of the Slovak Republic 2009).

The EaP was inaugurated on 7th of May 2009, during a summit attended by representatives of all EU MS and the partner countries. However, right from the outset even the strongest proponents of the new initiative had different perceptions of how it might be used. The Slovak government believed it should be focused on functional aspects: primarily social and economic issues. Political cooperation—including the prospect of future EU membership—was not to be emphasized. Meanwhile, Poland was interested in using the Partnership as a geopolitical instrument that would allow the Union to shape its political surroundings and extend Europe's sphere of influence at the expense of Russia. This was to be achieved through the *ad extra* dimension of Europeanization. Warsaw considered Ukraine, Belarus and Georgia as key partner countries. Slovakia was equally precise in its preferences as to the geographical focus of the EaP: "as part of the Eastern Partnership policy, Slovakia focused mainly on supporting the European direction of Moldova, Ukraine and Georgia" (Ministry of Foreign and European Affairs of the Slovak Republic 2011b). Bratislava and Warsaw shared a particularly keen interest in the developments regarding Ukraine, and it was this common foreign policy focus that prompted their closer cooperation. Of similar importance was the fact that both governments called for the revision of the ENP so as to more consistently apply the principle of more aid for more democracy and reforms. Still, Poland was far more vocal and unequivocal in stating the need to continue the process of enlargement.

Soon after its introduction, the EaP started losing most of its impetus. The atmosphere around it reflected the fact that the expectations harbored by the EU's neighbors at the outset (particularly Ukraine and Georgia) were now quickly dwindling. As Kiev and several other governments tried to manoeuver their way around some of the requirements put forth by Brussels, signals of their equivocal attitude were increasingly difficult to ignore. Consequently, Western Europe's patience and empathy for their predicaments was gradually wearing thin. These developments meant that once relations between the Union and non-EU EaP countries ceased to be treated as a priority, the effectiveness of the ad extra and cross-loading dimensions of Europeanization largely diminished. The second summit of the Partnership that took place in Warsaw in September 2011 (at that time Poland held the Presidency in the EU Council) confirmed the decreasing importance of the initiative, particularly in its political aspect. Slovak diplomats stated they would support the Polish Presidency but emphasized they would do so only with the prospect of promoting their country's interests (Ministry of Foreign and European Affairs of the Slovak Republic

2011a). Rather than striving to develop the eastern direction of the ENP, Bratislava was already focused on the negotiations of the new multi-annual 2014-2020 financial framework. Its position was dictated by the desire to keep the Cohesion Policy among the priorities on the expenditure side of the EU budget (Ministry of Foreign and European Affairs of the Slovak Republic 2011a). For that matter, questions relating to the future of the Union's budget were also of prime concern to Polish politicians and temporarily gained far more importance than any ambitions to shape Europe's foreign policy.

Tensions rising in relations between the EU and Kiev found their symbolic expression when Ukraine's former Prime Minister, Julia Tymoshenko, was arrested and subjected to a show trial. Poland's ex-President, Aleksander Kwaśniewski, and former President of the European Parliament, Pat Cox, intervened on the EU's behalf to protest the highly dubious legal procedure. Nonetheless, even as the Union was increasingly dissatisfied with violations of democratic principles in Ukraine, Slovakia and Poland insisted on continuing the "critical dialogue" with Kiev (Marušiak 2015: 35).

The third EaP summit, held during Lithuania's Presidency, in November 2013, brought a new opening in the development of the ENP's eastern direction. Unexpectedly, the meeting led to a flurry of events and processes that would ultimately rebuild the EU's eastern policy and affect international-political situation in Eastern Europe. The stone that would start the avalanche came with Ukraine's announcement that it would not to sign the agreement on its association with the EU, painstakingly negotiated and prepared over the previous months. The decision meant the process of granting Ukraine the status of an associated member (and thus bringing it closer to Western political structures) would be suspended. This caused outrage among the pro-European part of the Ukrainian society and resulted in mass protests that, ultimately, led to the ousting of President Viktor Yanukovych. At that time, many experts believed the EU should have responded to these developments by intensifying its cooperation with Kiev (Duleba 2014). On their part, Ukraine's new Prime Minister, Arseniy Yatsenyuk, and President Petro Poroshenko, elected in March 2014, renewed efforts to sign the association agreement, along with an annex on free trade (Deep and Comprehensive Free Trade Agreement, or DCFTA). Taking advantage of the renewed impetus, Brussels responded by swiftly returning to the negotiating table. The political part of the agreement was signed in March, almost immediately after Poroshenko's presidential victory. Stipulations referring to trade were agreed on and signed soon afterwards, in June. From then on, the fate of the agreement lied with the ratification process. Ukrainian Supreme Council accepted a project of the ratification bill in September and the document was quickly signed by President Poroshenko. However, before the agreement would come into force, it needed to be ratified also by all EU MS, as well as the European Parliament. Only a couple of countries (including Slovakia) completed the procedure before the end of 2014. Interestingly, Poland, having long been one of the strongest advocates of Ukraine's pro-European aspirations, was one of the MS that took their time to ratify the document—Warsaw finalized the ratification process in March 2015.

Notably, one of the issues that inserted some dynamism into the cooperation under the EaP (and, more broadly, the entire ENP) was the challenge of liberalizing the visa system for the EU's eastern neighbors. Eastern European governments have repeatedly asked Brussels to scrap the visa requirement for their citizens. While the cause was generally supported by both Poland and Slovakia, the two governments differed somewhat in the way they operationalized their visa policies towards Ukraine in the period before their accession to the Union. Slovakia introduced a visa system for its eastern neighbor as soon as 2001. Meanwhile, Poland was one of the last new (i.e. those joining in 2004) EU MS to do so. Kiev's bilateral negotiations with Bratislava and Warsaw on small border traffic proceeded almost simultaneously. Both agreements were signed in 2008 and entered into force the following year, allowing local residents (those living within a 30 km radius from the border) to cross the border for periods not exceeding three months based on a special permit, without the need to apply for a visa (Marušiak 2014: 107; Dyduch 2016: 353). The problem of liberalizing traffic between the EU and its neighbors was tackled not only on a bilateral basis, but also through multilateral and regional cooperation (particularly between Poland, Slovakia and Ukraine). Solutions agreed on during various talks were important for both political and socio-economic reasons, as they advanced the dynamics of mutual relations in all the aforementioned configurations (i.e. bilateral, regional-multilateral and European).

When one leaves the confines of the EaP and considers other areas of the EU's foreign policy, it is possible to note several other international-political initiatives that created space for interaction and, sometimes, deliberate cooperation between Bratislava and Warsaw. Obviously, pursuing national interests at the European level requires that a government garners support of other MS and relevant actors of the system. One interesting case of such effort was an initiative undertaken by Polish Minister of Foreign Affairs, Radosław Sikorski, who in 2011 proposed establishing the European Endowment for Democracy (EEfD)—a fund designed to support democratic transition in the EU's neighboring countries (Brudzińska 2012). Initial reactions from some EU officials (among them Catherine Ashton and Commissioner Štefan Füle) suggested that the EEfD could become an important instrument of the ENP (Cicha 2012: 28). However, when Polish diplomacy tried to capitalize on these declarations and develop a specific proposal (using its Presidency), all it managed to achieve was a decision that the fund would serve to support the European foreign policy goals, but would not be institutionally linked to any EU structures. It was determined that the initiative would be financed by the European Commission (EC) and voluntary donations from the member states. Its budget for the first three years was to approximate €25m. Poland would provide the largest individual donation in the amount of €5m, with the Netherlands and Sweden adding €1m each. Switzerland would provide €830 000. The EC allocated €6m. Slovakia's contribution, while purely symbolic (€60 000), was a very telling and potent sign of support, especially given how few actors actually joined the initiative. After Warsaw failed to turn EEfD into an EU-wide project that might help it pursue important, prestigious foreign policy goal, it was ultimately decided that the fund would be launched as a private foundation under Belgian law. In recognition of their gesture, Slovaks were invited to build the structures and operationalize EEfD's activities (Minister of Foreign Affairs of the Slovak Republic 2012a, 2013). For Slovakia, supporting the concept made sense for several different reasons. First of all, sharing the EU's external border, the country was highly interested in enhancing instruments that Brussels could use to shape its relations with its partners. Secondly, the Slovak ministry responsible for foreign policy, led at that time by Miroslav Lajĉak, saw Europeanizing its activities as a way to multiply its own potential. Thirdly, the government believed the EEfD provided very cost-effective means to gain a seat and role in European discussion on foreign policy issues (or at least one narrow aspect of it).

Another opportunity for political cooperation between Poland and Slovakia at the European level came with Croatia's quest to join the EU. At the time Poland held the Presidency in the EU Council, Zagreb's accession negotiations were nearing their successful conclusion. As was mentioned previously, Slovakia considered the Western Balkans as one of the key directions of its foreign policy. Therefore, Bratislava became increasingly involved in the finalization of negotiations. In May 2011, Slovak diplomats joined their Austrian counterparts on a visit to Zagreb—a gesture that was seen as an important attempt at preserving the dynamics of the procedure (Ministry of Foreign and European Affairs of the Slovak Republic 2011b). Slovakia took the opportunity to emphasize the need to continue the enlargement process, referring particularly to Montenegro and Serbia. Such rhetoric was, of course, in perfect concert with Poland's ambitions as a promoter of the EU's eastern expansion. In and of itself, Croatia was not on Warsaw's list of key partners—be it politically, strategically or economically. However, since Zagreb's accession was strongly supported by Germany, Polish authorities made efforts to complete the procedure in order to preserve their close and, at that time, cordial relations with Berlin. Moreover, Warsaw saw the enlargement as a fitting contribution to the success of its Presidency. The fact of holding the lead in the EU Council motivated the government to expand its involvement in various European undertakings. This, in turn, spurred the cross-loading phenomenon, as Warsaw became more receptive and responsive to the interests and needs expressed by other member states with regard to external relations.

The above considerations can be summarized through several conclusions. Both Poland and Slovakia advocated an active neighborhood policy—particularly in its eastern dimension. They did, however, differ somewhat in their perceptions of geographical and functional priorities. While Warsaw was focused primarily on the EU's cooperation with Ukraine and Georgia, Slovakia paid close attention to the developments in the Western Balkans. Bratislava emphasized economic and social cooperation, leaving purely political dialogue on the fringes of its agenda (with the notion it should be very pragmatic if it was to occur at all). Polish government was far more vocal in its support for the normative aspect of the EU's neighborhood policy and identified the ad extra Europeanization with the process of democratization. Still, all the above differences did not prevent the two countries from deepening their cooperation with regard to the ENP. Finally, both Poland and Slovakia were in favor of continuing the open door policy and preserving the dynamics of the enlargement process based on the Copenhagen criteria. They maintained that a clear prospect of EU membership—something without which the policy of conditionality, so effective in the 1990s, would no longer be rational—remained the Union's most effective instrument for shaping and stabilizing its immediate neighboring areas (Ministry of Foreign and European Affairs of the Slovak Republic 2011b).

The second area where Polish and Slovak interests and needs coincided was the EU's energy policy—a topic that was also strongly linked to national foreign policies. After 2000, the energy policy was subjected to the process of Europeanization due to several factors. Firstly, the Union was increasingly dependent on the import of strategic resources. Secondly, a number of its member states voiced growing concerns over the environmental impact of energy production, particularly the global warming phenomenon. Therefore, they advocated the inclusion of environmental considerations in the process of formulating European policy directions. These developments provided an impulse that would infuse Polish-Slovak relations with a certain new quality, as the two countries found a new, strategically important area in which they could coordinate their activities in the pursuit of security at the European level.

A breakthrough in Europe's approach to energy security resulted primarily from disagreements over gas supply contracts that occurred between Russia and Ukraine in 2006 and 2009. In the latter case, the supply cuts affected not only Ukraine, but also many EU countries. Slovakia was among the countries most-troubled by these events: Moscow's move nearly paralyzed its entire industrial sector and even threatened the security of supply to individual consumers. It is estimated that the cuts cost Slovakia €100m a day, or a total of €1 billion over the duration of the crisis, leading to a decrease in GDP by as much as 1,5 per cent (Nosko & Ševce 2010). In a way, the January 2009 gas crisis motivated EU member states to redefine their cooperation on energy security. From then on, such cooperation was placed at the supranational level, meaning that the development of energy policy would depend primarily on the initiative of the EC and other supranational bodies. At the same time, the fact that numerous MS (Poland and Slovakia among them) had to rely on importing energy sources became one of the key determinants in the development of energy policy, providing it with a strong external dimension. In other words, the policy would from then on be designed to secure the supply of resources not only by regulating the internal market, but also by integrated planning and reacting to contingencies occurring outside the Union. Consequently, for Poland and Slovakia the energy policy became an area inherently linked to their foreign policies.

Increasing demand for energy sources and the politicization of global trade in these commodities pushed European states to initiate communitization of the energy policy. It seems that, so far, the biggest success in this area has been the inclusion of a separate chapter dedicated to the energy sector in the Lisbon Treaty. New stipulations were thus added to the Treaty on the Functioning of the European Union (TFEU). As stated in the Treaty, the EU energy policy is aimed at ensuring the correct functioning of the energy market and the security of supply for the entire Union, as well as supporting the pursuit of energy efficiency and energy saving, the development of new (also renewable) forms of energy and the process of interconnecting various transit networks. The above goals are to be pursued "in a spirit of solidarity between MS" (TFEU, art. 194). It is worth noting that the principle of solidarity was explicitly stated in the Treaty thanks to the initiative of the Polish government, which was on that occasion supported by other V4 countries. Although the so-called old MS (most of all France, Germany and Great Britain) were not enthusiastic about the proposal, Warsaw's resolve on this matter, coupled with its readiness to reach a compromise on other issues, ultimately prevailed.

The reforms written into the Lisbon Treaty led to several changes aimed at developing and consolidating the EU energy policy. The policy was gradually institutionalized and equipped with a number of instruments, one of which came in the shape of a new body: the Agency for the Cooperation of Energy Regulators (ACER). Slovakia's effort to promote Bratislava as a possible host city for the Agency ultimately failed (Slovenian capital, Ljubljana, was chosen instead), resulting in a symbolic blow to the prestige of Slovak diplomacy. Nonetheless, the Ministry of Foreign and European Affairs was quick to state that "Slovakia highly appreciated Poland's approach, which considerably contributed to ensuring uniform support by the V4 countries to Slovakia's candidacy for the seat of the ACER despite the failure of one of the V4 members" (Minister of Foreign and European Affairs of the Slovak Republic (2009). As one may notice, the statement, while praising Warsaw, at the same time pointed the finger of accusation at Hungary which, according to the Slovak Minister, dropped its support for Bratislava's bid in retaliation to Slovakia's passing of a law restricting the use of minority languages (EurActive 2009).

Polish-Slovak cooperation on the energy policy in the context of the EU's supranational decision-making spawned both diplomatic initiatives and specific infrastructural undertakings. The purpose of the latter was to enhance energy security by constructing an integrated (also in the physical sense) market. Put simply, Bratislava and Warsaw planned to link elements of the transit infrastructure located in various MS with the use of so-called interconnectors (installations that would provide a physical connection between electricity and gas transit and distribution networks) and reverses (facilities that made it possible to use a pipeline to send gas in both directions). In Eastern and Central Europe, one of such undertakings was the gas interconnection between Poland and Slovakia that would become a key element of the North-South European Energy Corridor (Salamonová 2014: 47). The Corridor was designed to secure gas supply in the event of another crisis and prepare this part of Europe for a gradual decrease of supply from Ukraine. In October 2013, the EC determined that a trans-border gas pipeline connecting distribution networks in Poland and Slovakia was a project of common interest. Bilateral intergovernmental agreement on the construction of interconnectors was signed by the two countries in November the same year. Its implementation was entrusted to two companies: Gaz-System and Eustream. Investments such as interconnectors should be considered as particularly crucial, since without this infrastructure the principle of solidarity written into the Lisbon Treaty simply cannot be employed in practice. Recognizing the importance of the project, Polish and Slovak diplomats expended much effort to create regulations regarding guidelines for Trans-European Networks in transport, energy and telecommunications (TEN-E, TEN-T and TEN-Tele). These laws created a framework for what the EU describes as projects of common interest[6]. It should be mentioned that the V4 worked closely together both on the regulations and a number of energy projects, inter alia the connections between electricity and gas transit and distribution networks (Minister of Foreign Affairs of the Slovak Republic 2014a).

Bratislava's and Warsaw's positions converged even more when in 2014 Prime Minister Donald Tusk presented the proposal for creating the so-called European Energy Union. The presentation was preceded by consultations with a number of EU MS and representatives of the EC, including Slovakia's European Commissioner, Maroš Šefčovič, appointed to Jean-Claude Juncker's Commission specifically to lead the efforts on forming the Energy Union (Government Office of the Republic of Poland 2014a). Since many European leaders and official in Brussels were at that time highly interested in further consolidating and communitizing the energy policy, Tusk's proposal found substantial support and was adopted as a basis for a common concept. As soon as February 2015, the Commission announced its "Energy Union" package. When recollecting the events that led to the introduction of the package, Šefčovič emphasized that "Energy Union is the result of vast collaborative work, following the political agenda of President Juncker. But the core principle of integrating Europe's energy markets is to a large extent 'made in Poland', conceptualized by Council President Donald Tusk and President Jerzy Buzek who revived the legacy of President Delors. The Energy Union now encompasses much more than the original concept but it still resonates well among Poles as I recently discovered when visiting the country" (Šefčovič 2015). Importantly, for both Polish

---

[6] Projects of common interest are the key energy infrastructure projects, which aim to create an integrated EU energy market. These are essential for completing the European internal energy market and for reaching the EU's energy policy objectives of affordable, secure and sustainable energy (European Commission 2016).

and Slovak officials the Energy Union project has become a key reference point in the debate on the Europeanization of the energy policy. One can also notice an interesting systemic synergy effect, whereby the area of energy security constitutes a plane for the crossing of various interests, perspective and ideas, many of which are developed by politicians whose careers see them migrate from the domestic to the supranational level.

In summary to the impact of certain EU policies on Polish-Slovak relations, it can be said that it was predominantly indirect. Operationalization of these policies generated a certain legal and institutional context for the two countries' European and broader foreign policies. Acting in the peculiarly organized European system, governments accommodated their interests to its nature. This enabled mechanisms of Europeanization such as adaptation and, later, also socialization and learning. The examples cited above serve to illustrate how European integration made Bratislava and Warsaw more receptive towards the interest of their EU partners. It may be argued that such receptiveness was often deliberately used to generate sympathy for their own interests. In line with the concept of liberal intergovernmentalism, the process of seeking areas of shared interest was implemented through bargaining and negotiations.

As Poland and Slovakia found their footing as EU members, they became not only geopolitical neighbors, but also potential partners in initiatives spawned within the Union's multi-level governance system. Neglecting the influence of Europeanization for the development of bilateral relations would constitute a serious error of judgement.

Visegrad Group as a sub-regional, multilateral platform for Polish-Slovak political relations

Shortly after the 2004 EU enlargement, the Visegrad Group seemed destined to lose its importance as a tool for pursuing strategic goals of foreign policies adopted by its members. It was argued that the Group's role had previously been based around the four states' desire to join the Union and, consequently, it would now become irrelevant. Opinions that called for using the Group as a quasi-political body and a tool to influence European politics and various EU policies were questioned and criticized (Ukielski 2010a).

Such criticism, however, proved to be largely misguided. First of all, the Czech Republic, Hungary, Poland and Slovakia invariably shared an interest in stabilizing the Union's external environment by extending the Euro-Atlantic sphere of influence. Secondly, the V4 was capable of not only maintaining, but also strengthening its brand, already recognized throughout Europe. By continuing their cooperation, the four states enhanced their ability to influence processes occurring in the European system. When it came to intergovernmental negotiations that provided European integration with specific content, V4 members began routinely coordinating their positions and acting in unison whenever their domestically determined interests proved convergent. It can therefore be assumed that, in a way, EU membership "revitalised the cooperation agenda of the Visegrad Group" and that the Group's "*modus operandi* (...) should be regarded as a specific vehicle for cooperation and coordination around EU affairs (...)" (Dangerfield 2014: 73).

The symbolic new political opening in the functioning of the Visegrad cooperation came in the immediate aftermath of the 2004 enlargement. On 12th of May, less than two weeks after its members joined the Union, the Group held a summit in a Czech town of Kroměříže. In a declaration signed during the meeting, the four prime ministers emphasized their willingness to continue cooperation for the building of democratic Europe (Visegrad Group 2012a). They declared involvement in the developing of the CFSP (including the "Wider Europe—New Neighborhood" policy and the strategy towards Western Balkans); consultations, co-operation and exchange of experience in the area of Justice and Home Affairs, Schengen co-operation, including protection and management of the EU external borders; visa policy; creating new possibilities and forms of economic cooperation within the European Economic Area; consultations on national preparations for joining the EMU; active participation in the development of the Common Security and Defence Policy (CSDP), as a contribution to the strengthening of relations between the EU and NATO and deepening of substantive dialogue between both organizations (Visegrad Group 2012b). Of particular importance was the fact that the four leaders stressed their readiness to use the Group as a forum for consultations, policy coordination and seeking common grounds in determining their attitude toward matters considered important by Bratislava, Budapest,

Prague and Warsaw (Czyż 2014: 21). This emphasis on utilizing synergy between the Visegrad cooperation and EU membership was coupled with a broad, expansive definition of possible areas of cooperation that encompassed most key aspects of European integration. Such approach re-established the Group as an instrument to be used in European politics. Since the way various actors position themselves within the European system is fairly complex and depends on factors emanating from different levels (local, sub-regional, regional), the political game conducted within the EU—which the V4 was now a part of—is imbued with a very peculiar character.

Although the Visegrad Group was never granted the status of an international organization and its institutionalization has remained relatively low, mechanisms developed throughout the course of its existence allowed its members to act systemically. Operationally, the Group's functioning has been based on regular meetings of heads of states and governmental representatives (ministries or experts). This determined its strictly intergovernmental character. The only fully institutionalized form of Visegrad cooperation remains the International Visegrad Fund (IVF) which supports cultural, academic, educational and scientific projects, including youth exchanges, cross-border cooperation initiatives and tourism promotion. To organize and systematize its work, the Group uses the mechanism of annually rotating presidency. The state holding the presidency is responsible for arranging and coordinating the Group's operations. It is also granted the privilege and duty of preparing the presidency agenda, along with a specific list of priorities to be pursued (Wiszniowski & Glinka 2015).

Table 7. Rotating presidency of the Visegrad Group.

Country	Presidency period
Poland	2004/2005
Hungary	2005/2006
Slovakia	2006/2007
Czech Republic	2007/2008
Poland	2008/2009
Hungary	2009/2010
Slovakia	2010/2011
Czech Republic	2011/2012
Poland	2012/2013
Hungary	2013/2014
Slovakia	2014/2015
Poland	2016/2017

Source: own work.

The events of 2011 provided an interesting example of how the presidency shaped Polish-Slovak bilateral relations. As it happened, Slovakia's presidency in the Group, which lasted from 1st of July 2010 until 30th of June 2011, was followed immediately by Poland's six month-long presidency in the EU Council, which began on 1st of July 2011. Polish government understood that its success at the helm of the Council depended largely on its ability to build a multilateral consensus at the supranational level and on how effectively individual EU MS would implement decision made in Brussels. As it turned out, Warsaw found the Visegrad formula particularly conducive to the use of the downloading dimension of Europeanization. By intensifying political and diplomatic cooperation with Bratislava, Polish authorities contributed to effective communication and cooperation within the Group, thus optimizing their preparations to lead the EU's work. For Slovakia, the annual leadership in the Group, coupled with Poland's stint of the EU Council presidency, constituted an opportunity to articulate and pursue its particular interests more effectively, be it through the V4 or at the forum of the entire Union. This complex process occurring at various levels of the European system was linked to different dimensions of Europeanization: downloading (for which Poland was partly responsible during its Council presidency), uploading (which Slovakia led with regard to the V4's common interests during its presidency in the

Group) and cross-loading (which occurred in relations between various EU MS).

In the context of European political processes, characterized by a consultative manner of developing solutions, it is worth to mention the V4+ formula, which at that time was keenly utilized by the leaders of the Visegrad countries. One illustration of how V4 PLUS contributed to the EU's work was a meeting of foreign affairs ministers of the Visegrad Group and the EaP partner countries, organized in Bratislava and attended by Germany's foreign affairs minister, Guido Westerwelle, Slovakia's European Commissioner, Štefan Füle, and the EU's High Representative for Foreign Affairs and Security Policy, Catherine Ashton. Another example was the participation of German and Austrian Chancellors, along with the Ukrainian Prime Minister, in a summit held on the occasion of the 20th anniversary of establishing the Visegrad Group (Ministry of Foreign and European Affairs of the Slovak Republic 2011b). It can be said that for both Bratislava and Warsaw, functional cooperation with the use of the Visegrad platform provided a method of aggregating the potential needed to act effectively at the EU forum. It was also a useful instrument of managing these states' image, as in the late 2000s the Group became an attractive political brand that symbolized a flexible space for dialogue and negotiations.

Finally, mechanisms employed in the implementation of the Visegrad cooperation were conducive to learning and socialization—those key aspects characteristic also for the process of Europeanization. As the V4 members became increasingly adept at developing common positions (however difficult this might have been at times), the key remaining challenge was the ability to act effectively on the decisions made jointly at the negotiating table.

Analysis of the cooperation and selected initiatives of Poland and Slovakia within the Visegrad Group

For Slovaks, participation in V4 essentially multiplied their power in Central and Eastern Europe, and consequently the EU. The same could be said about Poland, although Warsaw had somewhat larger aspirations to leading a bloc within the EU that could balance the influence of strong Western European players. One of constant priorities of Poland's participation in the activities of the Visegrad Group was the coordination of efforts concerning goals related to or resulting from their membership in the EU. Other objectives related to V4 cooperation on matters of domestic sectoral policies and regional politics should also be interpreted through this lens, even though they were also very strongly influenced by solutions worked out by the EU. Accordingly, after the V4 members acceded to the EU, the number of meetings between their politicians and representatives visibly increased, while cooperation between corresponding ministries tightened.

Additionally, the agenda of the V4 after the accession was permanently broadened by the addition of international political issues and the members' stance on the CFSP and foreign affairs of the EU. Particular attention was given to the EU's burgeoning eastern policy. Poland's main interest was in relationships with the EaP members (particularly Ukraine), while other member countries, especially Slovakia, were keen on building good relationships with the countries of Western Balkans. It should be noted in this context that over the years the V4 formula was repeatedly used to intensify cooperation between its members and other countries of Eastern and Southern Europe—Baltic and Western Balkan countries. Such cooperation materialized as the Visegrad Plus (V4+) formula.

One of the first, and decidedly the most important project initiated after the V4 members had acceded to the EU was the cooperation on expanding the Schengen Area to encompass the Visegrad countries. Consultations between the V4 governments began as early as September 2003 and resulted in a tightened cooperation among Foreign Ministries and the establishment of the V4 Working Group for Schengen Cooperation. In 2004, the report concluding the activities of the Working Group stated that "the individual legislation and practices concerning Schengen *acquis* are compatible or / and harmonized enough to submit the application of all four Visegrad countries together" (Zelenická 2009: 57). However, the optimism expressed in the report had been premature, as, despite declarations, the degree to which each V4 member was prepared to be included in the Schengen system differed noticeably. This resulted in a very real possibility that not all the members would be able to join the Schengen Area. The EC expressed its most serious doubt about Slovakia's state of preparations—a development which resulted in tensions between Bratislava and Prague. The Czechs accused Slovakia of causing a delay and wanted to restore border control on the Czech-Slovak border. In addition, Poland experienced some difficulties in securing its northern border on the Baltic Sea. (Zelenická 2009: 57). Warsaw made consistent efforts to maintain the unity within the Visegrad Group, which would increase the pressure on Brussels, and consequently, its chances for successful application. It is because of this unified, joint stance on keeping the expansion of the Schengen Area on schedule that all Visegrad countries became full members of the Schengen system on 21st December 2007. This, in turn, improved bilateral relations between Poland and Slovakia, especially in the social dimension, and greatly expedited economic cooperation. Slovakia was perhaps the greatest beneficiary of the liberalization of border traffic, as in a matter of few years it became one of Central and Eastern Europe's major logistical centers for both transport and international trade—these issues are discussed in the following chapters.

The relations among the Group were animated not only by the desire to pursue common interests, but also by the idea of maintaining a reasonably continuous political dialogue which would result in better management of contentious issues and make it easier to work out common stances and policies in less controversial subjects. However, it took a relatively long time for the member countries to agree on the mechanisms of systemic cooperation. In December 2007, on the initiative of Anna Fotyga, Polish Minister of Foreign Affairs, the V4 countries met before the European Council summit to consult with Lithuania, Latvia and Estonia. This practice, while occasionally repeated, has never become a routine. It should be mentioned, however, that it met with a rather cold reception from other European leaders. In particular, French president Nicolas Sarkozy warned the V4 governments "not to make a habit of a pre-summit meetings" (Dangerfield 2012: 963). By and large, the heads of the V4 countries ignored such voices and attempted to jointly articulate their common interest on the EU arena. An example of such conduct was the EU's attempt on tackling the climate and energy package in 2008, 2009, and 2014. In that case, the V4 leaders, along with their counterparts from the Balkan republics, Bulgaria, and Romania, managed to reach a common view and so significantly improve their negotiating position. Both in 2009 and in 2014, the V4 leaders (with Bulgaria and Romania supporting them) demanded that ambitious pro-environmental objectives for curbing CO_2 emissions be toned down. Statements published before the summit underscored that the EU's climate policy should reflect the specificity and capabilities of its members' economies (Ministerstwo Ochrony Środowiska 2014).

The Visegrad Group formula achieved a particular relevance on the occasion of the aforementioned natural gas crisis of 2009. While prior to the events of 2009 the issues of energy policy and energy security had already been the subject of meetings and discussions among V4 representatives (on various levels: from experts to the highest representatives), cooperation never went beyond joint proclamations. Even though the earlier crisis caused by the Ukraine-Russia gas dispute of 2006 sparked some interest in the risk stemming from dependence on imported resources, the debate was then limited to European institutions and did not result in any specific actions.

The main difference between the crises of 2009 and 2006 was their scale (in 2009, the interruption in gas transfer lasted 11 days and affected 17 European countries, including 12 EU MS) (Mišík 2012: 58). While the crisis (as far as foreign policy was concerned) had distinctly different economic and political consequences for each V4 country, individual intra-system convergence of needs and perceptions pushed the four partners to close ranks and led to actual, content-filled cooperation. Major V4 initiatives pertaining to energy security that originated throughout that period included: creating the V4 High Level Energy Working Group (in 2009), organizing the Energy Security Summit in 2010 in Bratislava in the V4+ format (V4 countries plus Austria, Bosnia and Hercegovina, Bulgaria, Romania, Serbia, and Slovenia), publishing a joint V4 letter to Günther Oettinger, the European Commissioner for Energy, and lobbying for the North-South energy corridor to become an EU priority. The Visegrad Cooperation led the establishment of a High Level Working Group on the North-South Interconnection, chaired by the EC and including, apart from the V4, Bulgaria, Romania and Croatia (Mišík 2012: 65-68). The idea of creating north-south interconnections in Central and South Eastern Europe became a core concept of further cooperation. Thus, since 2009 energy security issues have been a permanent feature, both in relations between V4 countries and in bilateral Polish-Slovak relations. In fact, it could even be concluded that cooperation on energy security launched Polish-Slovak cooperation into a new era.

The countries of the Visegrad Group have also made an effort to coordinate the stance towards the escalation of the next Russian-Ukrainian conflict and, later, the annexation of Crimea in 2014. The joint response of the V4 countries to the events in Ukraine was issued far more rapidly than during the previous crisis. Even though the governments in question differed visibly in the assessment of these events and their political consequences, they were able to agree on a position condemning 'the illegal annexation of Crimea and Sevastopol, [...] aggressive actions of Russia towards Ukraine and provocations taking place along the eastern border of NATO' (Government Office of the Republic of Poland 2014b). As usual, Poland was quick to show an unequivocal support for Ukraine's European aspirations. Meanwhile, Slovakia remains "cautiously silent" and later tried to take a "moderate position" (Gerasymchuk 2014: 49). Predictably, such difference marred the otherwise joint attitude of the V4. The Czech Republic seconded Poland in advocating a harsh stance towards Moscow, while Hungary and Slovakia presented a much more moderate opinion by opting to continue their dialogue and cooperation with Russia, especially on matters of energy.

It should be noted that in Slovakia the Crimea crisis disturbed the "long-existing domestic political consensus as to the foreign policy", as two priorities of Slovak foreign policy—i.e. 1) good political and economic relations with Russia and 2) constructive participation in European integration—now stand in direct conflict. Robert Fico's government has been forced to balance the domestic and European pressures. After 2014, the general public's opinion on how to react to the developments between Ukraine and Russia has become polarized. While the government in Bratislava pledged 'commitment to the rules of respect for the international law, and to promote a peaceful resolution of the crisis while maintaining Ukraine's sovereignty and territorial integrity' (Ministry of Foreign and European Affairs of the Slovak Republic 2015a), a significant part of the public and the opposition demanded the restoration of pragmatic relations with Moscow. This dualism was reflected in the fact that the government approved the sanctions that the EU proposed against Russia, but at the same time was "highly interested in searching for appropriate forms of communication with the Russian Federation on the European level and even more on the bilateral level" in order to preserve the basis for cooperation in the energy sector. In the domestic discourse, Slovak politicians often stressed the pointlessness of sanctions against Russia. Prime minister Fico himself described the conflict in Ukraine as the 'geopolitical struggle between Russia and the USA' (Marušiak 2015: 41). However, his government did not attempt to block the imposition of sanctions by the Union (European Council 2016)—be it initially, or when they were later extended and broadened. Talks at the EU level also led to Slovakia starting a "reverse gas flow to Ukraine, which covered three-quarters of Ukraine's imports and a third of its total gas consumption" (Ministry of Foreign Affairs of the Slovak Republic 2015b: 5) in September 2014. Such willingness to assist the EU's efforts created favorable conditions for political dialogue with Poland. In essence, it signaled not only socialization brought about by EU membership, but also a learning process that happened through intense contacts with other MS (the cross-loading dimension), including other V4 countries. In turn, these processes seem to have been both the cause and effect of growing conviction among the participants of the European system and its Visegrad subsystem (Poland and Slovakia included) of the advantage of cooperation over rivalry or even confrontation.

In conclusion, it should be noted that reaching a common position on the Ukraine crisis did not happen without obstacles, but represented a thus far unprecedented case of the Visegrad Group acting essentially as a single entity and joining the discourse in superpower politics. Moreover, it was the first time when Russia and its policies have entered the agenda of the Visegrad cooperation—a development that took the V4's common work beyond the confined of the "low politics" domain (Dangerfield 2012: 967). However, it is too early to tell if the situation described here signifies a new, permanent trend in development of the Visegrad Group, including Polish-Slovak relations in a multilateral perspective.

An important and, recently, most prominent area of Visegrad cooperation is the issue of managing the migration crisis that has emerged in Europe since 2014. 2015 and 2016 saw a rapid increase in the number of migrants attempting to enter the UE MS. Faced with an escalating problem, in June 2015 the Commission presented a proposal envisioning the relocation of refugees landing in Greece and Italy, complete with quotas allocated for each MS. The concept was vetoed by the Visegrad countries and several other Central and Eastern European states, Spain, Austria and Finland. As the crisis deepened, the pressure from Brussels increased, leading to the V4 being effectively isolated in their opposition to the proposal. Nonetheless, criticism expressed by Western European leaders did not dent the four governments' resolve on the matter. The Czech Republic, Hungary, Poland and Slovakia remained opposed to compulsory quotas and demanded that the EU's external borders be sealed. Interestingly, the campaign before the 2015 parliamentary election in Poland produced several occasions when various candidates distanced themselves from Warsaw's uncompromising rhetoric, possibly to avoid accusations of a lack of solidarity with those MS that were most affected by the influx of refugees. However, immediately after securing a victory in the election, the new Law and Justice government proceeded to consolidate the Visegrad coalition against the Commission's project (Grodzki 2015). The alliance was to be based on a firm opposition against the liberal migration policy and an active participation in dialogue at the European level. As is typical for political processes within the EU, over the next months all sides gradually softened their rhetoric and signaled readiness to seek a compromise. In a sense, Slovakia acted as a facilitator of this process when holding the Presidency in the EU Council in the second half of 2016. The summit held in Bratislava on 16th September 2016 was particularly important in this context. The Visegrad leaders used this opportunity to issue a joint statement declaring that the EU's migration policy should be based on the principle of "flexible solidarity". Such approach, they argued, would enable MS to decide on specific forms of contribution, so that each country would be allowed to take its potential and experience into account. They also maintained that any possible distribution mechanism should be voluntary. Moreover, the Visegrad countries offered to delegate more staff to secure the EU's external borders and increase funding for supporting the refugees remaining outside the EU. At the same time, the statement underscored the need to improve the relations between European institutions and MS, preferably by strengthening the role of national parliaments. The stated objective was to restore the trust in the European project and its institutions, and reinforce the position of the MS (Ministry of Foreign Affairs, Republic of Poland 2016). This alliance among the V4 partners has since remained stable, as evidenced by further joint declarations and positions, e. g. the 'Statement of V4 Interior Ministers on the Establishment of the Migration Crisis Response Mechanism' (Visegrad Group 2016b), adopted at the summit in Warsaw, November 21, 2016. Unexpectedly, the changing circumstances within the Union strengthened the V4's position at the European level with regard to the migration crisis. After several terrorist attacks across Europe (especially those in France and Germany), the pressure to enact the Commission's original proposal visibly lessened.

With regard to Polish-Slovak bilateral relations, their cooperation under the aegis of the Visegrad Group had a varying dynamic and was mainly functional in character. It was only towards the end of the time period analyzed here that it has become a project aimed at achieving goals related to superpower politics. Joint stance on the situation in Ukraine and its conflict with Russia was a partially successful attempt to transform V4 into a sub-regional political alliance. Recent cooperation on issues pertaining to the migration crisis that the V4 undertook as a political alliance have been somewhat more effective. Thus, it can be said that even when the V4 countries were able to jointly create an agenda of political issues of the highest priority, they could not maintain a complete unity in the long term and, in most cases, were not prepared to employ assets and resources required to attain political objectives adequate to their potential.

This lack of consistency and determination had various causes. First of all, each V4 member experienced a major change on its domestic political scene. Secondly, the V4's unity represented a genuine threat to powers—both regional (Germany and France) and global (United States and Russia)—interested in having a decisive influence on the situation in Central and Eastern Europe. While the United States and Germany were crucial to Poland's and Slovakia's foreign policies, Russia was far more relevant for Hungary and Slovakia. Thirdly, all four Visegrad countries were versed in the role of followers much more than that of creators and leaders. By seeking a significant place in the EU's decision-making process, Poland attempted to break free of these constrains—a decision that proved hugely important for the development of Polish-Slovak relations. Curiously, being the largest of the Visegrad states did not always facilitate Warsaw's effort to achieve its goals concerning relations with its V4 partners. In some areas, the asymmetry of potential and capabilities put a noticeable strain on the political dialogue. The resulting lack of consistency with regard to mid- and long-term objectives and foreign policy concepts should be considered as one of the biggest obstacles hindering the V4's functionality and effectiveness as a political body. Unfortunately, this particular problem does not have any apparent solution. This statement is true even for these areas of mutual cooperation which were jointly defined by the Group as matters of the highest priority, especially the issues of the European eastern policy. (Sobják 2012: 124).

At the same time, it should be noted that, on more than one occasion, the structured mechanisms and methods of cooperation typical of V4 helped optimize the outcomes of contacts and political activities undertaken by the Group's members. Regular consultations between Czech, Hungarian, Polish and Slovak representatives of various levels, the objective of which was to publish joint declarations, were not the only form of dialogue. An important instrument here was also the rotating presidency status.

As the countries of the Visegrad Group embedded themselves in structures of the EU and learned to articulate their interests at the European arena, the Group's functionality as a regional integration formula gained a new dimension. When the EU worked on issues important to individual Visegrad countries, they tried, with varying degrees of success, to form intra-EU coalitions. This fact justifies the thesis that "Visegrad confirmed its role as a consulting mechanism within the EU framework" (Marušiak 2006: 97).

The increasing importance the V4 cooperation held in operationalizing foreign policies of its member states may be linked to several factors. Firstly, despite the relatively low level of institutionalization, the Group became a quasi-actor in the European system. The „external recognition that the V4 tends to receive" (Dangerfield 2014: 80) was, in the mid-term perspective, as asset of foreign policy, but at the same time constituted a challenge for the diplomatic services. On the one hand, the V4's position strengthened as the Group was granted substantial attention by other European actors. On the other hand, when transferring their domestically formulated preferences to the international level, the decision-makers were forced to be ever more mindful of their V4 partners' interests and opinion (see: Table 1).

The analysis of the frequency, character and course of the Visegrad summits—especially those held after its member had acceded to the EU—reveals that the meeting formula shifted in several respects. The summits now frequently included participants from outside the V4, e.g. other EU MS or the Union's high-level officials. The toolbox of instruments pertaining to V4 cooperation on European affairs also expanded. The practice of seeking a common positon within the Group became more regular and often resulted in joint declarations or statements, especially regarding the developments in EU policies.

To reiterate: even if the initiatives brought to the sub-regional V4 forum by one of its members were not supported by other partners (or failed due to reasons unrelated to the Visegrad cooperation), this did not automatically indicate the dysfunction character of the Group. By confronting their approaches and preferences with other V4 members, governments in question were engaged in a gradual process of adaptation, socialization and learning. This, in turn, strengthened the cross-loading dimension of Europeanization. It can be assumed that thanks to the Visegrad cooperation, Europeanization itself became more intense and richer in form and content—a circumstance that also allowed national decision-makers to manage the international interdependence.

Polish-Slovak relations in the light of global system dynamics (between US and Russia) Pan-Slavism vs. Euro-Atlanticism

Throughout the period discussed here (2004-2016), the state of Polish-Slovak relations was affected by the perception of foreign policy issues in both countries. Relations with Russia on the one hand and with the United States on the other were important both for Warsaw and Bratislava. In fact, policies that the two superpowers adopted towards Europe can be seen as factors affecting Polish-Slovak dynamics in both bi- and multilateral context.

It should be pointed out that both Moscow and Washington preferred bilateral relations with countries of the European system, since they obviously found it easier to negotiate or exert influence in one-on-

one contacts. Accordingly, the Russian Federation tended to deal only with those multilateral bodies that were relevant to its foreign policy goals, or those it simply could not ignore (Dangerfield 2012: 967). Despite the support it stated for the idea of multilateralism, the United States also sought support from individual governments rather than international organizations when pursuing its vital foreign policy goals.

In the following section we shall examine a few selected issues that were affected relations between Poland and Slovakia, in all of which Russia and the United States proved strongly influential. The problems were chosen according to several criteria. First of all, all were clearly articulated in the domestic discourse on foreign policy held in Poland and Slovakia. Secondly, they had multiple implications for the dynamics of changes in the European system and the approach both countries took to positioning themselves as part of this system.

When analyzing the time period adopted for this book, one should start by the strategies adopted by Bratislava and Warsaw in their relations with the Russian Federation and the United States, as they were understood in the first decade of the 21st century. At first glance, the transatlantic orientation in foreign policies of both countries was markedly different—put simply, Slovakia positioned itself towards Russia and the United States in a manner different from Poland. For Warsaw, the strategic dialogue with the Americans was supposed to result in obtaining security guarantees, particularly in the political dimension. Slovakia, while it generally did not question the very idea of the Euro-Atlantic alliance, established "cooperation with US aimed at supporting economic and scientific and research cooperation including opportunities for the transfer of technologies" (Minister of Foreign and European Affairs of the Slovak Republic 2009: 5). Although Bratislava declared interest in certain issues of international politics that were the subject of the Euro-Atlantic dialogue, in bilateral relations with Washington it "has been focusing on cultivating relations with existing US investors and attracting new ones, with IT and cyber security being promising areas of cooperation" (Ministry of Foreign Affairs of the Slovak Republic 2014b).

Such approach did not necessarily imply that Slovakia's stance was incompatible with that of other V4 countries. To the contrary— Bratislava often made substantial efforts to take a moderate position that would not disrupt the Visegrad cooperation. For instance, it was the only V4 government not to sign "The letter of the eight" in January 2003, thus distancing itself from Washington's plan for overthrowing the Saddam Hussein régime. However, the following month it signed the so-called "Vilnius letter" and sent a company of sappers (who served under the command of the Polish contingent) as a part of the military mission to Iraq. The soldiers were withdrawn in 2007, with Poland following suit shortly afterwards. Naturally, the dynamics of Slovak-American relations were very sensitive to the developments on domestic political scenes. It is not possible to explain Bratislava's approach towards the intervention in Iraq and the alliance with the US without considering election results. The decision to join the anti-terror coalition was made by the government of M. Dzurinda—the same cabinet that also led Slovakia to becoming a full member of NATO. The withdrawal from Iraq and Afghanistan was triggered by Dzurinda' successor, R. Fico, who not only believed Slovakia's involvement in these particular operations should end, but also had far broader misgivings about any endeavors of such nature. In general, Fico's cabinet wanted to frame the relations with the US in a different manner—by emphasizing the value of cooperation under the auspices of NATO and the UN. In addition, the main factor in Slovak policy towards the US was to be its membership in the EU. Its Minister of Foreign Affairs repeatedly stressed (in years 2006 through 2009) that "Slovakia will support the position of the European Union, not that of the United States" (Ukielski 2009: 302). These words should be interpreted in the context of intra-EU conflicts and tensions between so-called old (especially France and Germany) and new (especially Poland, Czech Republic and Romania, Baltic republics to a lesser degree) members concerning the US policy on international security, including the plans to build missile defense sites in Central and Eastern Europe (i.e. in Poland and the Czech Republic). Slovakia remained opposed to the idea of deploying the components of the missile defense system not only on its own territory, but also in its neighboring countries. Fico reiterated on several occasions that as long as he remained the prime minister, his country would not join the US missile defense project. Additionally, he expressed understanding for Kremlin's concerns that deploying the system would escalate tensions between Washington and Moscow and, in consequence, lower the level of security in Europe. In his opinion, the plans conjured up by Washington with the support of Prague and Warsaw would have actually represented a threat to Slovakia's security (Hodor 2008: 384). The statement he made in January 2008 before the Parliamentary Assembly of the Council of Europe was particularly poignant: "I reject the assumption that these bilateral talks [between the US and Poland and Czech Republic] are not a cause for concern for other, especially neighboring, countries. We do not see any reasons for transferring the defense shield to Europe" (Gazeta Wyborcza 2008). Both in Poland and his homeland, Fico's words were interpreted as „a diplomatic gesture against Poland, the Czech Republic and the United States" and a signal of Slovakia's disloyalty towards its allies (Lesná 2007).

As established before, Poland and Slovakia differed in their approaches to relations with the United States and had divergent views of their role in Europe. The Slovaks believed that in the context of strictly political (including geostrategic) goals, their country was not a particularly attractive partner for the United States. Public opinion made its own pragmatic conclusions as to the assessments made by Washington—a development that translated into a steadily declining approval ratings for the US foreign policy (GMF 2012). Poles, on the other hand, considered themselves, and were occasionally considered by other actors of the European system, the "most loyal allies" of the United States.

Contrary to what political calculations might have suggested, it was Slovaks (along with Hungarians, Czechs, Lithuanians, Latvians, Estonians, and Cypriots) who became the beneficiaries of a no-visa tourist traffic agreement announced in 2008, with Poland perhaps the most notable omission. There can be no doubt that Slovakia's success in this regard was a simple consequence of a new, liberalized visa regulations adopted by the US. The new law stated that a country could apply for no-visa traffic if the percentage of rejected visa applications in cases when applicants had been suspected of attempting to illegally extend their stay did not exceeded 10% (and not 3%, as in the previous regulations). Unlike some of its neighbors, Poland simply did not meet the new numerical criterion, with the percentage consistently hovering above the 20% mark. The logic of this arithmetic was not convincing for the Polish public and parts of the political scene, visibly disappointed by the actions of the American administration.

In this context, one should also note Bratislava's and Warsaw's reactions and attitudes towards the so-called "reset" in American-Russian relations. The attempt to rebuild bilateral ties with Moscow was undertaken by president Obama's administration in late February and early March 2009 (Kaczmarski 2011). The main component of the concept was to be America's legitimization of Russia's new, more substantial role in European politics. To signal its good intentions, the United States decided to freeze the deployment of the missile defense system in Central and Eastern Europe. The move was announced by the White House on 17th September 2009. Another consequence of this American strategy was a more inclusive stance toward Russia in its relations with NATO. The scaled-down version of the concept envisioned solid relations maintained through the NATO-Russia council. The best-case scenario, however, went as far as trying to entice Moscow to join the alliance. It was the latter idea that was referenced by Polish minister of foreign affairs, Radosław Sikorski, as early as March 2009 (Gazeta Wyborcza 2009). Washington's altered stance towards Russia was a signal for Central European countries. Slovak diplomats expressed their satisfaction with the rapprochement, seeing it as a chance to redefine transatlantic relations in a manner neatly aligned with their preferences—that is, to develop the transatlantic dialogue „within the EU-RF-US triangle" (Minister of Foreign and European Affairs of the Slovak Republic 2010). Donald Tusk's government was also supportive of the idea, believing that a more active cooperation with Moscow could lead to a gradual Europeanization of Russian politics.

During Barack Obama's tenure, the Euro-Atlantic dialogue waned and lost some of its importance, both in the bi- and multilateral dimension. Correspondingly, foreign policies of the new EU MS shifted their focus away from the USA and towards the Union (or, from transatlanticism to continentalism). Additionally, the EU-Russia relations became increasingly vital in the minds of many European leaders. The catalyst for these changes was provided by the events beyond the EU's eastern borders, as Moscow once again attempted to regain more control over what it has always seen as its natural sphere of influence.

Russia began to voice its superpower aspirations and demand respect for its international political interests with a renewed vigor. Kremlin criticized, in rather sharp words, the West's attempts to expand its influence over South-eastern Europe. Such uncompromising stance was illustrated in the case of Kosovo. When the republic proclaimed its independence in February 2008, Moscow refused to recognize it and condemned all governments that have done so. At the same time, Kosovo's split from Serbia caused a rift among EU MS. While most of them, including France, Germany and Poland, formally acknowledged the independence of the new country immediately after the proclamation, Slovakia and some other EU members (Spain, Romania, Greece) adhered to Russian demands. For Slovak decision-makers, the decision made sense for several reasons: pro-Serbian sympathies resulting partly from historical (the presence of ethnic Slovaks in northern Serbia) and partly from geopolitical considerations, as well as domestic concerns. Specifically, given the very strained Slovak-Hungarian relations, Bratislava was afraid that supporting Kosovo would encourage pro-autonomy sentiments among ethnic Hungarians living in southern Slovakia. By contrast, Poland's decision may be seen as a result of intra-member Europeanization and the strategy of mimicking the positions of the most influential European actors. The stance taken by Tusk's cabinet was criticized by the domestic opposition, particularly the Law and Justice party and the President Lech Kaczyński. On 16th February, the day before Poland was expected to unilaterally recognize the independence of Kosovo, Law and Justice leader Jarosław Kaczyński argued that "recognizing Kosovo may result in Russia taking very aggressive actions, e.g. against Caucasian countries" (Wprost 2008)[7]. While the opinions expressed by the Kaczyński brothers seemed similar to Bratislava's position on the matter, the arguments behind them were distinctly different from those used by the Slovaks, who were not afraid of Russia's neo-imperial policy and saw the Kosovo issue as an opportunity for a rapprochement with Moscow.

---

[7] The issue of Kosovo returned after Russian annexation of Crimea in February 2014. President Putin said immediately after the Crimean incident that the secession of Crimea from Ukraine was identical to the secession of Kosovo from Serbia, accusing the governments that supported Kosovo's independence of hypocrisy.

To continue and expand on this topic, one should note that the Slovaks strongly supported Serbia's efforts to accede to the EU (Bilčík 2010: 15). The activities of Slovak diplomats aimed at supporting Serbia's prospective membership in the EU were especially intensive in the period before the country was granted the status of a candidate in 2011. Simultaneously, Polish politicians in Brussels loudly articulated their concerns about a possible negative political consequences of Serbia's membership in the EU. They argued that "Moscow has too much influence on Belgrade and Serbia" (Rettman 2012). The conflict of interests evident here emerged in an area deceptively distant from what was usually seen as crucial for the development of bilateral relations. However, the peculiar context of the European system acted as a defacto binding that increased the level of interactivity, not only between its elements (i.e. countries and EU institutions), but also between particular issues driving the intra-system processes and the relationship between the system and its surroundings. The problems of Kosovo's independence and Serbia's prospective EU membership became entwined within a complex web of relations and interests represented by Poland, Slovakia, Russia, European institutions and other relevant actors.

A similar pattern transpired when Europe considered pro-integration aspirations expressed by Georgia and Ukraine. While Bratislava generally approved the notion of the two countries cooperating with the Union, it remained ambivalent (or downright skeptic) towards the possibility of bringing them into NATO. Meanwhile, in bi- and multi-lateral contacts (including the EU and V4 platforms), Poland advocated their full integration with the transatlantic structures. When NATO organized a summit in Bucharest in 2008 to decide on its plans for the possible inclusion of Georgia and Ukraine, Prime Minister Fico simply refused to attend the meeting and, if that was not clear enough, made a gesture of hosting the Russian Prime Minister, Viktor Zubkov. András Rácz described Russia as "the greatest common divisor" (2012) when it comes to the V4 countries' approach to processes of international politics. Historically, Poland has always treated the Kremlin's foreign policy as a threat, while Slovakia did not voice any such concerns and supported the idea of strengthening economic cooperation and political dialogue with Moscow, even in times of crises in European-Russian relations. This was clearly illustrated by Poland's and Slovakia's reactions to the outbreak of the Russo-Georgian war in August 2008. Slovak representatives blamed Georgia for instigating the conflict and called for restrained reactions at the European arena, but went short of recognizing the independence of South Ossetia and Abkhazia. In an interview with Russian media, Prime Minister Fico stated he was convinced that "the war in the Caucasus was provoked by Georgia" (Bútora, Kollár, Mesežnikov 2011: 113). Even more radical sentiments, originating from SMER's coalition partner, the Slovak National Party (Slov. Slovenská národná strana, or SNS), began to surface in Slovak domestic discourse. SNS's deputy leader, Anna Belousovová, demanded that the Georgian president, Mikheil Saakashvili, be indicted by the International Criminal Court (Ukielski 2010b:352). Meanwhile, Polish politicians (particularly the incumbent president Lech Kaczyński and his advisors) not only condemned Russia for escalating the situations, but also pushed European institutions to engage in conflict resolution.

There were some occasions when Bratislava and Warsaw presented a seemingly convergent stance on preferred EU policy towards Moscow. Such was the case with the joint EU-Russian initiative, Partnership for Modernization, inaugurated at the Rostov-on-Don summit in 2010. However, a closer look into the arguments put forward by Slovak and Polish politicians in support of the project reveals that, once again, the motivations were markedly different. Polish representatives hoped that the initiative would Europeanize Russian political values (i.e. democratize the country). Meanwhile, "Slovakia pays less attention to these issues and strives for pragmatic, primary business oriented cooperation" (Rácz 2012: 50). The Slovaks were reasonably consistent in their position on how relations between the EU and the Russian Federation should develop. „The focus has been given to pragmatic relationship, aimed at: participation in the Partnership for Modernization and on continuing the dialogue on gradual visa liberalization, fulfilling WTO membership commitments, and encouraging a constructive dialogue between NATO and Russia" (Ministry of Foreign Affairs of the Slovak Republic 2014b). "Slovak diplomats wish to develop bilateral relations which will be concentrated on energy issues, such as stable supplies of energy resources and exploiting fully Slovakia's potential as a transit country as well as developing economic relations" (Ibidem).

Events and incidents described here clearly show that bilateral relations of neighboring countries (in this case—Poland and Slovakia) may be influenced by complex connections which are both cause and effect of international political interdependence. Fairly constant preferences and directions of Poland's and Slovakia's foreign policies had historical, social, geopolitical, and geo-economic determinants. Russia and the United States have remained the major reference point for both countries, but the roles, aspirations and influence of both superpowers have been perceived by Warsaw and Bratislava in different ways. This hindered cooperation between the two governments when it came to issues critical for the political situation in the region. Such assessment should not be interpreted as a statement that the aforementioned difficulties made political cooperation impossible. The phenomenon whereby a government refrains from blocking initiatives of other actors in cases when their interests are not fully aligned is explained by the theory of liberal intergovernmentalism. Firstly, rational actors of international relations, Poland and Slovakia included, were ready to compromise in bi- and multilateral relations to maximize benefits and minimize losses. Intra-state processes (or those resulting from interactions between the system and its surroundings) were managed based on the mechanism of negotiated policy coordination. Moreover, the preference for cooperative stances and readiness to compromise have been a constant feature of the European system. Moreover, the actions of Polish and, to an even greater extent, Slovak decision-makers can be explained by the concept of a two-level game, which is prominent in liberal intergovernmentalism. In Slovakia, the government's foreign policy narrative has shown a characteristic dualism, where information for the domestic audience and for foreign audiences was formulated differently, even inside the government itself. Accordingly, even though the opinions of the prime minister (especially when the government was helmed by Robert Fico) differed from positions publicly voiced by Slovak diplomats (including the minister of foreign affairs), this did not result in tensions inside the government (Duleba 2011: 60). This was so because prime minister's statements were made for the benefit of the domestic society, while those made by the diplomatic service were addressed at foreign partners. This way, both the domestic and foreign audience received the expected message at the same time. Such balancing act resulted in a seemingly paradoxical, but rationally explainable phenomenon, where on the one hand "Slovak political class has formed a relatively stable attachment to the EU" and on the other hand "the notion of the EU (...) in terms of everyday political struggle is still an alien concept in Slovakia" (Gabrizová 2014: 69-70). It seems as though the political elites were purposely utilizing "certain nostalgia among the Slovak public related to the times when the Russians were 'our best friends' and the Americans were 'enemies'", knowing where and how to use such sentiments (Bútora, Kollár, Mesežnikov 2011: 113). However, maintaining some elementary level of cohesion so as to enjoy the legitimization from both domestic social groups and international partners remained a constant challenge for the government.

Final summary of the political cooperation between the Slovak Republic and the Republic of Poland

Despite many seemingly important differences in their approaches to issues of international politics, Poland and Slovakia maintained functional, reasonably good relations. It seems both governments were calculated them so as to reap pragmatic benefits. If political alliances were formed, they were temporary and usually concerned the dynamics of European integration (e.g. negotiations over the EU's long-term budgets and climate policies). Regular bilateral relations were focused predominantly on issues such as the development of roads and railroads, as well as tourism and cross-border cooperation. The areas in question remained essentially unpoliticized (unlike the ethnic issues in Slovak-Hungarian relations or the shared history of Poland and Germany)—a circumstance that, to a large extent, protected the bilateral relations against excessive impact of changes that occurred at domestic political scenes. As both sides were well aware of the disproportion in their political and economic potentials, this unalterable aspect also proved fairly neutral. The combined effect of all this was that Polish-Slovak relations, especially in the bilateral context, developed somewhat independently to issues that both governments found critical in their foreign policies. For Poland, ties with Bratislava did not have a strategic value and were accordingly afforded less attention when compared to relations with other neighboring countries. Instead, they were often considered in the multilateral context of the Visegrad Group, the EU and, in a broader perspective, NATO. While both parties assumed the possibility of cooperation on strategic issues, the analysis of political processes does not corroborate any such declarations.

Poland and Slovakia found the meaning of foreign policy—including the issues broadly classified within the realm of European politics—to be different. In Polish domestic socio-political discourse, issues of international politics traditionally held a prominent spot and absorbed the public to a large degree. Moreover, the debate was often emotional and accompanied by arguments referring to values in international politics. It also encompassed Poland's ambitions to co-create the EU's political reality. Meanwhile, Slovak decision-makers believed that issues of so called 'hard politics' were secondary to the needs of the domestic society, which explains the manner in which Bratislava's policies were clearly economized. Moreover, Robert Fico's *modus operandi* assumed that "in foreign policy there is no room for values themselves and therefore Slovak diplomacy's fundamental priority, as well as task should be the strengthening diplomacy's dimension that may bring practical positive effects to the citizens of the Slovak Republic" (Vlček & Kaščáková 2012: 103). Understanding their position as takers, Slovaks preferred to present a moderate stance on key political problems in order to maintain beneficial relations with all major European and global powers. Fico's cabinet also chose to let domestic issues dictate the country's position on international matters. In addition, the government in Bratislava believed that Slovakia "as a small country with very limited possibilities of influencing the international scene should only concentrate on activities that bring concrete, pragmatic (economic and social) benefits to the citizens of the country" (Vlček & Kaščáková 2012: 100-103).

Poland's preferences as to key directions of foreign policy were markedly different. Warsaw saw the West as its crucial partner and when it looked to the East, it was with the hope of Europeanizing (or perhaps westernizing) its neighbors. This was in stark contrast to Fico's statement that "the world has four cardinal directions, and not only the 'western' one". Slovak experts from the Institute for Public Affairs rightly pointed out that in Bratislava's foreign policy all "projects and goals have a rational economic background without any specific 'ideological links'—one cannot find any hints at 'maintaining Slavic unity'" (Bútora, Kollár, Mesežnikov 2011: 122).

With regard to European policies of both countries and the impact of their activities in the European system on their bilateral relations, it should be noted that Polish-Slovak cooperation in the European system was aided by their similar view on the Union's potential growth. In general, the two countries shared the belief that EU membership was crucial to their security and growth. Especially the cabinets led by Donald Tusk, Iveta Radičova and Robert Fico saw deeper integration as a response to social and economic challenges, and consequently accepted the primacy of Germany and France as the main driving forces behind the EU. That is why it comes as no surprise that both countries supported, among other projects, the ideas of creating supranational banking supervision institutions.

In conclusion, the analysis conducted in this section clearly shows that relations between Poland and Slovakia, whether bilateral or multilateral, were strongly influenced by processes of European integration. Functioning inside the European system, with institutions, regulations, politics, and sociology organized in its peculiar manner changed the existing patterns and mechanisms of mutual relations. As an example, one can look at the changes to the functioning of the Visegrad Group, regarding both the manner and contents of cooperation. Moreover, after their accession to the EU in 2004, both countries gained new instruments, communication channels and mechanisms that could be used to mold bilateral relations: e.g. interactions within European institutions or participation in EU-funded programs.

Furthermore, as was argued above, some areas saw the Poland's and Slovakia's interests converge enough to spur substantial cooperation or, at the very least, affect the positioning strategies that both governments adopted within the European system or towards other global actors. The areas defined as key to Polish-Slovak relations included: the EU's CFSP, especially ENP and energy policy, and efforts towards energy security in national, sub-regional and European dimensions. As Poland and Slovakia's interests on the level of the international system crossed ever more often, this resulted in an increasing interdependence within the broader European and international context. The process of

European integration implied the necessity of taking into consideration the positions and actions of other relevant actors of the system and its surroundings.

The multilateral cooperation, which obviously dominated the political relations between Poland and Slovakia, generally had a positive impact on the two partners' effectiveness in pursuing individual and common goals, not only in bilateral relations but also with regard to their activities as EU members.

Several factors can be identified as key to shaping Polish-Slovak bilateral relations. First of all, one needs to consider the role of historical, cultural and social experiences, along with geopolitical and geoeconomic aspects that stem from their status as neighbors. Secondly, both countries' membership in the EU proved to be vital for building a broader, multilateral context in which they interacted. Thirdly, both bi- and multilateral relations were sensitive to stimuli, expectations and foreign policies pursued by actors outside the European system—most notably, the Russian Federation and the United States.

Jaroslav Ušiak

Chapter three
Slovak-Polish cooperation in the field of defense and security

Introduction

The Slovak-Polish relations in the security area are defined by mutual relations between both states and their membership in international organizations. In the context of selected methodology, i.e. A. Moravcsik's theory of liberal intergovernmentalism, it can be presumed that security and defense aspects are subject to national decision-making which, in turn, is reflected in mutual cooperation within international organizations also on the supranational and, hence, international level. Yet on the other hand, the liberal intergovernmentalism assumes that no member state can avoid interactions between its internal and external environment. Therefore, it cannot be considered as entirely isolated (Juncos & Reynolds 2007). Thus, it is problematic to utilize this model in its pure form in the field of security and defense, as the EU defense and security policy is created not merely as a direct consequence of its MS' national interests (Smith 2004: 754), but rather as a common interconnected structure.

In the following text, we will observe to what extent national interests of both states shaped their joint attitudes and positions on the bilateral as well as multilateral level during the analyzed period of 2004-2016. The process emerged in the wake of the collapse of the bipolar system, as the dissolution of the Soviet Union and the break-up of the communist bloc changed the quality of the Slovak-Polish relations. During the 1990s all countries were in search of their own identity in the international environment fundamentally affected by the dissolution of the USSR and the end of the Cold War. Until the middle of 1991 the territory of Central Europe, and especially that of (Czecho)Slovakia, was occupied by allied troops of the Warsaw Pact, whose retreat anticipated national self-determination within a new security environment (Bureš 2014). Preliminary discussions in both states dealt with the issues of their future policy direction and defense capabilities. At this stage Poland, in contrast to (Czecho)Slovakia, opted for a strict pro-Western orientation in terms of its foreign and security development, declaring its intention to incline towards Euro-Atlantic thinking (Nowakowski & Protasowicki 2008). At the same time, Polish authorities perceived engagement within regional organizations as one of the main pillars for building relations with its neighbors and reinforcing its regional status. Meanwhile, (Czecho)Slovakia leaned more towards the idea of neutrality, whose main proponents were V. Havel and J. Dienstbier (Mazalová 2006). Subsequent Slovak-Polish discussions, however, brought about the idea of common development towards ensuring their security and defense by means of integration with Euro-Atlantic structures, which seemed to both states as the most favorable alternative.

Mutual relations between the two states were specified for the first time by the 1993 agreement on military cooperation, concluded by the Ministry of National Defense of the Republic of Poland and the Ministry of Defense of the Slovak Republic. The document pointed to the fact that this cooperation concerned primarily the coordination of procedures in relation to external environment—in this context, it implied mutual support and cooperation in fulfilling criteria for admission to NATO, as joining the Alliance was considered a strategic goal of both states. Yet, as the analyzed period of 2004-2016 demonstrates, the cooperation between both states has always been linked rather to multilateral context than to the bilateral one, especially when it comes to security and defense. Various forms of inter-regional cooperation proved their significance. Common pro-integration ambitions resulted in the establishment of common mechanisms facilitating accession to NATO and the EU. After the dissolution of the USSR and the Soviet bloc, the institutional instruments of cooperation among the Central European states also fell apart. Both states' membership in Central European Free Trade Agreement (CEFTA) and Central European Initiative (CEI) enabled them to begin economic and political integration (Kosír 2010). The proclaimed strategic interest of both states to become NATO members gained real contours through the Partnership for Peace program which, in turn, stimulated the establishment of the Visegrad Group—an important project of regional cooperation aimed at helping all involved states to enter Euro-Atlantic structures by encouraging their integration tendencies.

Both states became NATO members at different times. Slovakia was admitted in March 2004, while Poland, having been much more active in the area of integration, became its member as soon as March 1999. Poland had participated in the North Atlantic Cooperation Council since 1991, which was a unique opportunity for the state to get involved in NATO's activities (Zięba 2011). Between 1995 and 1997 Poland underwent all required transformation processes. In the meantime, in 1996 Polish government submitted the Individual Discussion Paper outlining its arguments to be admitted to NATO (Nowakowski & Protasowicki 2008). Afterwards, at the 1997 Madrid Summit, Poland was officially invited to NATO together with Hungary and Czechia. It joined the Alliance on 12th March 1999. The foremost reason behind the delay of Slovakia's accession procedure was its domestic situation—during V. Mečiar's government's term in office the country experienced international isolation due to its perceived insufficient compliance with democratic criteria (Kmec & Korba & Ondrejcsák 2005). Although Slovak political elites made declarations in favor of Euro-Atlantic integration, their actions contradicted official rhetoric. Slovakia began to be presented increasingly often as a bridge between the East and the West (Asmus 2002). This checkered period in Slovakia's Euro-Atlantic integration process ended in 1998, with the induction of a new cabinet. Led by Prime Minister M. Dzurinda, the new government managed to complete all the necessary procedures and in March 2004 Slovakia joined NATO (Tarasovič 2011).

Until late 1998, Polish-Slovak relations were rather strained and largely symbolic. The first official visit of the Slovak Prime Minister to Poland was yet to happen. Poland, the then OSCE presiding country, initiated the presence of observers in Slovakia during that year's general election. At the same time, Polish authorities adopted something of a double-track approach, criticizing the direction of policies pursued by Bratislava but simultaneously emphasizing the need to build a stable Europe with Slovakia as its integral part (Lukáč et al. 1999: 34). In November 1998, the newly appointed Prime Minister Dzurinda visited his Polish counterpart in Warsaw. Thereafter, the Visegrad Group played an important role as a platform allowing Poland, Hungary and the Czech Republic to support Slovakia in its ambitions to integrate with Euro-Atlantic structures (Vlček & Kaščáková 2012). While Slovakia was seeking to re-launch and accomplish its integration goals, concepts of Polish foreign policy and security policy had to be adapted to the needs of collective defense and responsibility for the entire organization. In its statement, Polish Ministry of National Defense declared that 'Poland will keep solidarity with NATO not only in political issues but also through concrete actions' (SME 1999). Poland intended to prove that its admission to NATO really did have a strategic meaning. To successfully complete their consistent efforts at integration, both states became full members of the European Union in May 2004.

In terms of practical steps, a specific example of the emerging cooperation between Poland, Slovakia and the Czech Republic was the Multinational Brigade in Topoľčany, which operated between 2001 and 2005. It was dissolved after Slovakia acceded NATO, as it then lost its original significance (Koziej 2010, Světnička 2005). Thus, successful accomplishment of both states' pro-integration ambitions confirmed the importance of the Visegrad Group as a non-institutionalized discussion forum which helped to coordinate joint efforts, but at the same time, triggered both states' genuine integration within Euro-Atlantic structures. The time period analyzed here indicates clearly that the integration process contributed to the achievement of several important landmarks in Slovakia and Poland's quest to ensure their security.

Dynamics of the relations in the bilateral context

The aim of this part is to examine the development of bilateral relations between the Republic of Poland and the Slovak Republic. To do so, it is essential to outline main evolutionary tendencies of both states' security environment and undertake a detailed analysis of their strategic documents, which will point out their main security problems in the period from 2004 to 2016. These strategic documents constitute the cornerstone of the framework for cooperation and, when placed in the practical context of undertaken steps, can reveal the main similarities and differences in the attitudes adopted by both states. This enables the identification of areas with potential for cooperation. Afterwards, the chapter proceeds to the presentation of contractual agreements establishing mutual bilateral cooperation in the area of security and defense, as well as meetings at various levels between the representatives of both states. Both of these aspects have had a significant impact on developing common projects that have been successfully launched during the relevant period.

Brief assessment of the development of the security environment between 2004 and 2016

Before proceeding to the analysis of strategic documents (which will enable us to identify shared priorities) it is useful to present basic developments after Slovakia's accession to NATO in March 2004 and the admission of both states to the EU in May 2004. The following paragraphs concentrate on key events that have influenced the evolution of both states in the field of security and defense. The aim is not to describe all these events in detail, but rather to highlight those turning points that predetermined the framework of options for bilateral cooperation. In other words, it is to point out issues shared by Slovakia and Poland.

At first, both countries sought to work out the details of their attitudes in the context of newly acquired competences within the framework of the EU and NATO. The developments in the Slovak Republic reflected the political orientation adopted after the election of September 1998, when the Slovak political representation perceived the United States of America as its strategic partner (Duleba, 2011). In the post-accession period (in relation to both NATO and the EU, in case of Slovakia) both countries had to take a clear position on the processes emerging in these international organizations. At the same time, they had to clearly define their priorities with regard to the changes that were taking shape in the area of EU security and defense policy (the development of what today is CSDP as a part of the CFSP). They also had to take a stand on various disagreements among individual NATO MS, especially in the context of the Iraq crisis after 2003 (where Slovakia and Poland participated together in military operations). The reinforcement of the EU's defense instruments (for instance, the idea to establish the „EU Battlegroup") provoked questions of enhanced participation in the processes of co-decision and shared responsibility for steps taken by both organizations. All of these developments characterized the first post-integration years in both counties.

Apart from the above-mentioned issues, Poland faced yet another dilemma. Having considered the USA and NATO as its strategic partners[8], it now had to take a position with regard to the concept of building and supporting the EU's own capabilities. While initially Warsaw refused to build European Security and Defense Policy (ESDP) instruments at the expense of the European Security and Defense Identity[9], the process had already started taking place while Poland had been negotiating its accession to NATO, and continued after the creation of the ESDP (Pomorska 2011). For Slovakia, the question of strengthening military structures for the needs of the EU was not particularly substantial. Nonetheless, the concept gradually increased pressure and requirements on resources, material and personnel that was to be available for the benefit of both NATO and the EU defense/military structures (Pawlas 2014). NATO's Istanbul Summit in 2004 resulted in further demands on the Slovak and Polish Armed Forces, such as reinforcing contingents in Afghanistan or assisting NATO candidate countries. Warsaw warmed to the idea of EU defense mechanisms with a significant delay, only after its partnership with the USA had faltered when the much-anticipated establishment of missile defense system clements on Polish territory had not materialize. This awareness of the EU defense and security dimension, combined with increasing NATO demands, provoked greater engagement of both Slovakia and Poland within the EU structures.

In case of both countries, the second period is characterized by the U.S. initiative to establish a missile defense system, as well as a gradually increasing awareness of the Visegrad Group's importance in the de-

---

[8] The practical implementation of security policy and strategic documents pointed to the Polish security policy as being clearly oriented towards NATO and the USA. Some sources refer to this trend as the „militant Atlantism" (Ondrejcsák 2005: 194).

[9] Compared to the initial proposal on ESDP, the concept of European Security and Defence Identity (ESDI) advocated closer connections with NATO in assuring security and defense within the European Union. The issue was finally solved after the EU and NATO concluded an agreement on strategic partnership in crisis management (known as Berlin Plus) that granted the EU access to NATO logistical and planning capabilities, including intelligence.

velopment of foreign and security policy. In Slovakia, a significant change in the orientation of these policies occurred after the 2006 election. The newly formed coalition government, led by R. Fico, decided to shift away from the previous focus on transatlantic security and an exclusively pro-American approach, and move towards the idea of strengthening the European security model (Majer 2013). The then political elite did not realize that ongoing developments and parallel membership in both organizations did not allow any significant change. Only certain slight corrections were acceptable, bearing in mind each state's co-responsibility for the collective defense. For Poland, meanwhile, a major milestone came in the shape of the proposal to locate elements of the missile defense system on its territory. Official negotiations on the matter began in 2007, although the first unofficial talks between the USA and the Czech Republic—the other candidate to "host" the system—were held as far back as 2002. Poland perceived the construction of the missile defense system on its territory as a means of acknowledging and strengthening its long-lasting cooperation with the USA. Thus, the strategic partnership between Poland and the USA continued to be reinforced. Moreover, it would have assured the presence of U.S. forces in Poland (O'Donnell 2012). However, Poland's clear orientation towards the USA as its strategic partner changed in the aftermath of the 2007 parliamentary elections, when D. Tusk replaced J. Kaczyński as the Prime Minister. Tusk utilized the general public's negative opinion on the idea to locate the missile defense system on Polish territory, and demanded certain benefits (particularly US financial support for the purpose of modernizing Polish army) in return for his government's consent to its establishment (Mix 2016). When the USA and NATO offered Slovakia to join the project in 2009, Fico's cabinet strictly rejected the proposal. Only when the USA withdrew from the plan to establish the missile defense system in Central Europe (due, in part, to the pressure from the Russian Federation)[10], the government in War-

---

[10] Poland did, however, manage to obtain some compensation in the form of the presence of U.S. Armed Forces on its territory, pursuant to the Agreement on the Status of the Armed Forces of the United States of America in the Territory of the Republic of Poland (O'Donnell, 2012). This agreement enabled the Polish army to use the Patriot system during its own exercises, thus leading to the acquisition of airspace defense capabilities.

saw recognized that its partnership with Washington was not as strong as it had been in the past, and that Poland's ability to pursue its national interest within NATO effectively depended on the decisions of major actors. Thereafter, Polish government started to perceive the EU defense capabilities as one of the options to implement its power policy simultaneously to its engagement within NATO. Consequently, Poland acknowledged its position at the regional level as well as within the entire EU by means of practical steps and strategic documents[11]. It realized that the EU enabled it to command certain operations (e.g. the establishment of its own camp within the operation EUFOR (European Union Force in Bosnia and Herzegovina) in the Republic of South Africa, etc.) and that its real partner in the field of security and defense should be other EU MS (Germany, in particular). Within the EU, Poland had a chance to become an equal partner to other MS (Mitrache 2011) and to directly and efficiently influence the contemporary CSDP (ESDP) and CFDP. By contrast, its previous reliance on the partnership with the USA left it as Washington's only ally deprived of any substantial influence within NATO. In this period, the importance of cooperation within the V4 was already apparent. It acquired a particular significance for the four countries' effort to support the candidacy of individuals or national bodies to hold various functions in Euro-Atlantic structures. Simultaneously, Poland gained more confidence as the Central European leader, becoming convinced that its ability to drive and direct the efforts of the Visegrad Group (and command the V4 EU Battlegroup) would be beneficial for the entire region.

The third period followed the above-mentioned failure to build the missile defense system in Central Europe, when both Poland and Slovakia faced a new question regarding the future development of their security. In this period, the crucial events were the gas crisis of 2009 that affected Slovakia in particular, as well as the global financial and economic crisis that influenced both countries and their economies. In the context of relative peace prevailing in Europe, the financial crisis imposed an increased strain on the level of their security and defense

---

[11] The strategic documents of this period begin to emphasize the ESDP and the European Defence Agency as one of the key instruments and pillars of European security. They also stress the need for Poland's increased involvement and engagement within these structures.

expenditures. In the Slovak Republic the issue was tackled by the government of I. Radičová. In order to alleviate the negative impact of the crisis and manage problems related to defense spending, Radičová decided to launch the process of strategic defense assessment. The procedure eventually revealed that the extent of resources allocated for defense should be better adapted to the country's political ambitions, and pointed out the need to reform Slovakia's Armed Forces. The decline in spending was inevitable—it lasted until 2011 and was halted at 1,1% of GDP. Poland, however, in 2001 adopted an act according to which the level of defense expenditure could not fall under 1,95% of the previous year's GDP. This way, it has succeeded in maintaining its defense budget at between 1,8 and 2,2% of its GDP—a fact that produced a substantial disproportion between Poland and Slovakia in terms of financial outlays on security (Pawlas 2014). Nonetheless, the failed negotiations on the missile defense system, the historically driven perception of Russia as a major threat, as well as Poland's determination to prevent the repeat of past experiences when others decided its fate (Ozbay & Aras 2008) suggest that Warsaw should seek its genuine partners in the area of security and defense among other EU MS.

The outbreak of conflict in Ukraine and the migration crisis in Europe are among the most recent events that influenced Poland and Slovakia's policies. After Radičová's cabinet was dissolved over a European, rather than a domestic issue (specifically, voting on the European bailout funds), R. Fico assumed the position of the Prime Minister. The professional community expected his government to reform the security and defense policy and to update strategic documents (Ondrejcsák 2014). However, the process was slow and a number of highly-anticipated outcomes—such as the establishment of Slovakia's Security System and the revision or adoption of a new constitutional law related to security—failed to materialize.

2013 saw the adoption of the White Paper on the Defense of the Slovak Republic. The document, updated in 2016, initiated the long-awaited reform of Slovak Armed Forces. At the same time, Prime Minister Fico changed his personal approach in dealing with foreign partners—a calculated move that allowed Slovakia to gain more recognition within international organizations. Fico emphasized international crisis management operations in which his country was participating (ISAF in

Afghanistan and others). Polish political elite also benefited from EU membership status, as it was aware of the opportunity to influence and co-decide the Union's future orientation. Poland's ambitions as a regional leader explain its involvement in the Ukraine crisis in February 2014, when it became one of key actors representing the EU. In this particular case, though, Warsaw's aspirations met with little sympathy from Germany (Buras 2014; Dempsey 2014).

Last but not least, the development of both Slovak and Polish security policy has been affected by the conflict in Ukraine that the current political representation needs to deal with (Devlin 2015). Slovak elite's ambivalent attitude towards the crisis, its root causes and resolution does not always correspond with the attitude of other European representatives—a fact that reminds us of the influence of the pro-Eastern orientation. Poland, on the other hand, adopted a clear stance on this matter and was the first among the Central European states to update its National Security Strategy[12] (signed by President B. M. Komorowski in October 2014). This reflects Poland's urgent efforts to resolve the crisis. The Strategy encompasses several key approaches which will determine the future security policy: aspirations to return to the original rationale behind NATO's establishment (i.e. collective defense and deterrence) (Madej 2015: 134), the importance of the EU and Poland's position within it (CFDP and CSDP that Poland had previously persistently ignored, emphasizing instead the importance of NATO and the position of the USA), strategic presence of American soldiers in Europe (especially on the territory of Poland) and restoration of future relations with Russia in compliance with the principles of international law. The latter issue reflects the fear of Russian expansion and its confrontational policy (which can be illustrated by the annexation of Crimea to the Russian Federation) (Machnikowski 2015). Official documents of the Slovak Republic suggest its elite's preference for political solution at any stage of the ongoing conflict in Ukraine. Moreover, Slovakia adopt-

---

[12] The White Book on the National Security of the Republic of Poland adopted in 2013 proclaimed that Poland was not directly threatened by any military conflict. The subsequent events in Ukraine accelerated the adoption of the National Security Strategy of the Republic of Poland which withdraws from such view. Moreover, it points to the fact that experts all across Central Europe failed to predict such a rapid development of events and the emergence of a potential threat in the proximity of their countries' borders.

ed an ambivalent attitude towards sanctions imposed by the EU against the Russian Federation (Ministry of Foreign and European Affairs of the Slovak Republic 2015c: 14). One particularly serious problem is the neglect of security policy on the part of Slovak political representation. If it is to be solved, the authorities have to change their position with regard to defense funding, take a clear stance on the crisis in Ukraine and its root causes, and determine security priorities. Most of all, though, President A. Kiska and the government led by R. Fico have to reach a common position on the desired orientation of foreign and security policy. Declarations made by the highest constitutional representatives influence not only the public opinion towards the crisis, but also the country's ability to define a clear attitude in the European and Central European context. Differences in the Polish and Slovak approaches towards the crisis in Ukraine have a negative impact on the security situation in the Central Europe. Poland (as the only country within the Visegrad Four) unequivocally named the Russian Federation[13] as the 'villain' (Devlin 2015), while positions taken by political representations and the public opinion in Slovakia, the Czech Republic and Hungary were not so definite.[14]

The last of the foreign and security policy-related issues relevant to these considerations is the migration crisis emerging in Europe. Similarly to the conflict in Ukraine, this problem also revealed vague attitudes of both states. While the Slovak political representation strictly rejected measures adopted by the EU, the Polish elite supported them despite the previous agreement reached within the Visegrad Group and

---

[13] The survey of Centrum Badania Opinii Społecznej concluded that the Poles are interested in the situation in Ukraine. As many as 78% of respondents care about the problem, while 69% of them believe that this situation threatens the security of Poland (CBOS 2014: 1, 4). At the same time, 57% of respondents assume that the Russian Federation will further increase its territorial claims and that Moscow will provoke conflicts also in other states with Russian minority.

[14] The discussion over the position towards Russia and the interpretation of events in Ukraine occurs mainly at the political level, and for a random Slovak the issue is quite obscure. Vague political statements lead to unclear opinions among the general public (Gyárfášová 2014). The survey conducted by FOCUS agency for the *Hospodárske Noviny* newspaper investigated whether the public opinion inclines rather towards the EU or Russia in the context of the Ukrainian crisis. However, as many as 65% of respondents were unable to express their opinion or they did not incline to either of the sides (Agentúra FOCUS 2014), which proves the above-mentioned antagonism.

the public's disapproval. This was also due to the fact that, as the President of the European Council, D. Tusk promoted these measures among Polish decision-makers. Ultimately, the issue became a vital topic in the run-up to the parliamentary election that was held in the Autumn of 2015 and led to the induction of a less pro-European cabinet. Just a couple of months later, at the beginning of 2016, parliamentary election took place in Slovakia. R. Fico kept his post and formed a government which now states the European policy and NATO membership as the main sources of its foreign policy orientation.

As a consequence of the recent events described above, the Central European states have become more aware of the significance of their position and their ability to influence the decision-making process within the EU. This was confirmed during the migration crisis, when all states took more or less the same stand and approach in relation to the adopted measures and their acceptability. Towards the end of the period analyzed here, the position of the USA diminished compared to that of the EU. However, the fear of Russian expansion (in the context of the Ukrainian crisis and its potential escalation into an armed conflict of greater magnitude) provoked both countries to reconsider the importance of Euro-Atlantic relations (i.e. with NATO and the USA in case of Poland, and just NATO in case of Slovakia), particularly with regard to territorial defense.

Analysis of the strategic documents of the Slovak Republic and the Republic of Poland

Over the analyzed period both countries endorsed several conceptual strategic documents. Slovakia adopted the Security Strategy of the Slovak Republic and the Defense Strategy of the Slovak Republic (both in 2005), as well as the White Paper on the Defense of the Slovak Republic (in 2013, with an update in 2016). In case of the Poland, documents that can be analyzed include the 2007 National Security Strategy of the Republic of Poland, the Defense Strategy of the Republic of Poland from 2009, the White Book on the National Security of the Republic of Poland from 2013 and the National Security Strategy of the Republic of Poland adopted in 2014. The following part will be focused on examining the contents of these documents, especially in the context of threats and risks to national security anticipated by both countries. The following analysis will lead to identification of both shared and divergent attitudes, as well as common issues in the area of security and defense.

The Slovak Republic

The 2005 Security Strategy of the Slovak Republic was the first strategic document in the area of security and defense adopted after Slovakia's accession to the EU and NATO. This document was created partly in reaction to the 2003 European Security Strategy. It presents Slovakia's position on the issues of transatlantic cooperation and security. It also introduces the following main security problems: terrorism; failed states; proliferation of weapons of mass destruction and their carriers; vulnerability of information and communication channels (this can be perceived as an attempt to define the problem of information security); activities of foreign intelligence services; illegal and unregulated migration; increasing influence of non-state actors; state´s dependency on resources, including food; organized crime; radical nationalism and intolerance; natural disasters, accidents and catastrophes; spread of infectious diseases and ecological changes (National Council of the Slovak Republic 2005a: 4-7). The security interests of the Slovak Republic declared in 2005 include: strengthening the transatlantic partnership; co-guaranteeing security of all allies; reinforcing efficiency of those international organizations which Slovakia is a member of; further EU and NATO enlargement; developing good partnerships and all types of mutually beneficial cooperation with states sharing common interests with Slovakia. A significant change that occurred in this period concerned a shift of perspective—from one focused exclusively on Slovakia's own territory to a broader outlook on protecting interests of the entire EU and NATO (and, hence, to an approach towards security in a global environment). That change might have been the reason why the 2005 Security Strategy was inspired by the framework presented in the 1999 NATO's Strategic Concept and the 2003 European Security Strategy.

The Defense Strategy of the Slovak Republic issued in 2005 became one of the first documents reflecting Slovakia's conceptual adaptation to the realities of its membership in NATO and the EU. Its aim was to replace two earlier documents: the Defense Strategy of the Slovak Republic and the Military Strategy of the Slovak Republic, both adopted in

2001. The Strategy of 2005 was, similarly to its previous version, drawn up by the Ministry of Defense of the Slovak Republic. It introduced much-anticipated changes, especially in the field of defense, and defined new challenges that the Armed Forces of the Slovak Republic had to cope with upon joining NATO, as the country had to shift its focus from purely national security to the collective defense of the whole Alliance (National Council of the Slovak Republic 2005b). In the figurative sense of the term, we can regard this commitment as the declaration that Slovakia would only develop capabilities pre-defined by NATO and the EU, so that its Armed Forces would be compatible and could be deployed in multinational missions and operations. At the same time, however, Slovakia reserved its right to determine how its military would be deployed in overseas missions. The document contains defense requirements and outlines methods of future transformation of the Slovak Armed Forces. Both the Defense Strategy and the Security Strategy of the Slovak Republic laid basis for the transition from individual to collective security, and for the principles of further development of security policy within NATO and the EU. However, one of the first deficiencies to become apparent was an insufficient reaction to the double-track security system in Europe. This shortcoming has so far not been overcome.

The White Paper on the Defense of the Slovak Republic presented in 2013 suggested an overall restructuring of the security sector that would enable Slovakia to fulfill its commitments and ambitions (expressed, for instance, in the Model of Development of the Armed Forces of the Slovak Republic 2010, 2015, or the forthcoming one, encompassing the time horizon of 2020). However, the political elite has so far not supported these ambitions. Quite to the contrary—it has continued to decrease defense spending. Moreover, the period discussed here has not seen any major modernization project in the field of defense (Ivančík 2012). It is beyond doubt that, at that time, there was a significant disproportion between Slovakia's security commitments, political and military ambitions on the one hand, and the level of financial resources allocated for defense on the other hand. The White Paper from 2013 proposed the so-called 'Model 2024', i.e. long-term modernization of the Armed Forces (planned for until 2024, as the name suggests) in a newly defined environment and within a revised financial framework.

However, it can be argued that the 2013 White Paper failed to envision adequate funding for the initiative. It stated that budget allocation would not drop below 1,0% of GDP (Ministry of Defense of the Slovak Republic 2013) and called for additional investments for modernization, all the while assuming that the process would be completed within the suggested timeframe. Unfortunately, such shortcomings with regard to specifying the financial aspect mean that decision-makers responsible for implementing the reform may fail to comply fully with the stipulations of the Paper. It can only be hoped that the current attempt at reform will prove more successful than the previous ones. In response to the Ukraine crisis and other developments in the international environment (among other, the so-called Arab spring, with its impact on Europe), the White Paper was updated in October 2016. The amended version reshapes the framework for the security and defense policy. It establishes mid-term (until 2030) objectives and envisions an increase (up to 1,6 per cent of GDP) in annual defense budgets. The additional funding is to be allocated primarily to the modernization of combat technologies and armaments (Government Office of the Slovak Republic 2016b). The updated White Paper also opens up more possibilities for reacting to terrorism, cyber and hybrid threats.

The Republic of Poland

The National Security Strategy of the Republic of Poland adopted in 2007 came as a reaction to the new environment and the country's accession to the EU. It provided an official interpretation of Polish government's approach to security. It enumerated the threats and risks to Poland, specific measures that it intended to implement, as well as roles of particular public bodies. Poland is perceived as a sovereign and democratic state located in Central Europe, with a significant demographic, political, military and economic potential. It views itself as an equal partner to other NATO and EU MS and assumes responsibility for security in the region (National Security Bureau 2007). The 2007 National Security Strategy of the Republic of Poland corresponded with the NATO Strategic Concept and the European Security Strategy. This was clearly a positive development, particularly given Poland's sense of responsibility as a NATO and EU member state, as well as both organizations' role as Europe's stability providers. In the document, Polish government sought to define means and possibilities of achieving its declared national interests. The main instruments of Poland's engagement included effective cooperation with NATO and the EU, as well as a partnership with the USA. The Strategy emphasized that ensuring international security called for closer cooperation and coordination among the above-stated actors. It also mentioned the need for cooperation within the Visegrad Group. It confirmed Poland's commitment to active participation in the effort to maintain global and regional security, both through NATO and the ESDP.

The Defense Strategy of the Republic of Poland issued in 2009 followed trends stemming from cooperation within the EU. The document acknowledged the existence of asymmetric threats to the Armed Forces and to the state, but it also stressed the need to build and maintain an effective military force. The latter consideration reflected concerns that arose in the aftermath of the conflict in Georgia in 2008. Besides typical goals, such as protecting sovereignty and independence, or defending the population, Poland's strategic ambitions focused on improving its readiness to handle crisis management tasks stemming from NATO and EU membership. The 2009 Strategy ranked the ESDP and the European Defence Agency among the main instruments and pillars of European security and highlighted the need for greater participation and engagement in these structures (Ministry of National Defense Republic of Poland 2009: 7). Furthermore, it defined key prerequisites for efficient national defense and stipulated the tasks and structure of the defense system. The system, as presented in the document, consisted of three main components: 1) the defense management subsystem, 2) the military subsystem (the Armed Forces, tasked with securing sovereignty and independence and, if necessary, with assistance in the aftermath of natural disasters, crisis management or search and rescue operations) and 3) the non-military subsystem (reserve force, economic mobilization, protection of critical objects and infrastructure, enhanced health care provisions, communication and education—all in all, measures concerning primarily civil defense). Over the recent years, Poland has focused on establishing and improving a crisis management system that could be applicable at all levels of state administration. However, while the 2009 Defense Strategy discussed the matter at considerable length, several experts (see e.g. Bieniek 2012) point out that the implementation of such a system remains problematic due to unclear division (and occasional overlap) of competences.

In 2013, Polish government issued another important defense-related document—the White Paper on the National Security of the Republic of Poland. The Paper deals with the current state of Poland's security, as well as with prospects for the next 20 years. It is based on conclusions from the strategic assessment prepared by the Committee for National Security over the course of almost two years (2010-2012) with the help of more than 200 experts. In identifying main risks and threats to national security, the Paper points to the trend of widening the entire security agenda. Hence, it defines security very broadly and is not restricted to the analysis of Polish Armed Forces. It encompasses issues such as the state of the health care system, road infrastructure and even the sense of national identity. The authors agree that, while Poland is not directly threatened by a military conflict, authorities must pay attention to non-military threats, e.g. low birth rate or inadequate road and energy infrastructure (National Security Bureau 2013). The White Paper consists of four chapters containing key recommendations on, for instance, the integration of currently fragmented security system management. The authors suggest the establishment of a National Security Committee that would coordinate all activities as directed by the presidential National Security Council. They also call for professionalization of all components of the security system. Finally, the Paper is aimed at disseminating knowledge about security and emphasizes the link between contemporary security-related research the practice of ensuring national security.

The last document to be analyzed here is the National Security Strategy of the Republic of Poland adopted in 2014. In this document, Poland intended to define itself as a regional (i.e. Central European) power among the post-soviet countries. The reason behind its adoption and, at the same time, the source of its importance, was the crisis in Ukraine. The 2014 Strategy seeks to define Poland's perception of the Russian Federation as the main threat to its external security. It points to Moscow's efforts to restore its sphere of influence over its neighboring countries and regain its status as a global superpower (Kutěj 2015: 50). Nonetheless, the document identifies other security threats, e.g. international terrorism and the prospect of weapons of mass destruction being used by terrorists, as well as failed states that are the breeding ground for organized crime. It goes on to highlight the development of information and communication systems and the need for protection against cyberterrorism. It also refers to issues such as extremism, food security, natural or ecological disasters, corruption, activities of foreign intelligence services, internal security and civil unrest, economic competitiveness and financial security, as well as energy security. Since oil and gas dependence is also considered a significant threat, Polish government stresses the need to find alternative supply sources and transport routes (National Security Bureau 2014: 17-26).

Summary of the analysis of strategic documents
The above analysis of strategic documents reveals why identifying priorities, risks and threats to both states in question was important for the formulation of their defense policies. Security priorities (along with their practical reflection in security policies) were updated in response to ideological and procedural changes that occurred throughout the time period considered here. First of all, both governments' perspective on the issue of ensuring security changed as Poland and Slovakia progressed from candidate to full membership status in NATO and the EU. Assuming responsibility for wider, European security brought about the need to reorganize their armies and adjust competences of various bodies and departments operating in the area of defense. Participation in political decision-making within the Euro-Atlantic structures, which in the pre-accession period had been seen as an additional benefit of the integration process, became a permanent obligation. This provoked a shift of orientation towards common systems and structures and raised the question of Polish and Slovak Armed Forces' compatibility with their European and American counterparts. Moreover, with relative peace prevailing in Central Europe, the two governments redirected their attention from direct to indirect threats: problems stemming from economic instability, the rise of radicalism and, most recently, migration (along with its accompanying question of human rights). After the outbreak of the crisis in Ukraine, Poland and Slovakia have been forced to face a new challenge of how to deal with indirect military threats in the vicinity of their region. This particular situation re-

vealed the first of the currently evident differences in their attitudes and positions.

Similarities and differences in the two governments' perception of threats are presented in table 1. Areas that both countries consider as security risks represent potential for cooperation.

Table 8. Key similarities and differences in the perception of threats by Poland and Slovakia.

Threat	Slovak Republic	Republic of Poland
terrorist attacks and terrorism	X	X
proliferation of WMD and their carriers	X	X
Cyberattacks	I	X
instability and regional conflicts	I	I
activities of foreign intelligence services	X	X
emergence of conflicts on the periphery of the Euro-Atlantic area	0	X
failed states	X	I
influence of non-state actors	X	I
negative aspects of international migration	X	I
organized crime	X	X
Corruption	X	X
threats to critical infrastructure	X	X
interruption in the supply of strategic and energy resources	X	X
dependence on resources, including food	X	I
disasters with natural and anthropogenic cause	X	X
radical nationalism and intolerance	X	0
extremism	I	X
ecological changes	X	X
ensuring financial security	0	X
hybrid war	0	X

Legend: X—entirely identical perception; I—partially identical perception (threats defined somewhat differently); 0—absence of similar perception.
Source: adapted by the author, based on: (National Council of the Slovak Republic 2005a: 4-7; National Security Bureau 2014: 17-26).

As the table above indicates, both governments have identified a number of non-military threats emanating from their internal or external environment. The nature of these threats means they cannot be eliminated solely by means of military defense. As a result, Polish and Slovak decision-makers are faced with several questions, some of which are related to stability and economic well-being rather than to security in the traditional, narrow sense of the term. In quest for adequate security, both states rely to a large extent on their status as NATO and EU members, hoping to provide their citizens with a sense of protection guaranteed by collective defense measures and initiatives. However, statements about taking responsibility for dealing with global threats notwithstanding, strategies adopted by the two states are not always specific about how to achieve the security goals. It should be noted that, in general, Poland has been taking its obligations somewhat more seriously than Slovakia. While Poland has been consistently able to meet commitments arising from its membership in organizations of collective defense, Slovakia, having gradually decreased its defense spending, has struggled to comply with its obligations. Reacting to the altered security environment, both states revised their strategies (in case of Poland, on more than one occasion) after their accession to NATO and the EU. Global threats identified by Warsaw and Bratislava are very similar and closely mirror the European Security Strategy (including its updated version), as well as NATO's Strategic Concept for the period of 1999-2010. However, when it comes to internal and regional security, some threats and their sources are assessed differently (as is the case with the Ukraine crisis). Still, certain regional threats are formulated roughly identically in all strategies—these include organized crime, energy security, corruption and environmental changes. The shift of focus toward non-military aspects constitutes a trend that is also reflected in the theoretical understanding of security and is clearly visible in strategies adopted by both states.

At present, one can point out two problems that will determine future development of Poland and Slovakia's security and foreign policies. The first one concerns cuts in defense budgets, while the second one refers to the crisis in Ukraine. The decrease in defense expenditures has been characteristic for many countries of Central and Eastern Europe and can be explained by their exhaustion after years of instability (the conflict in the Balkans) and systemic transformation. The strain of the global financial crisis has also contributed to governments' unwillingness to allocate more funds for defense. However, as illustrated in figure 1, while Slovakia has followed the trend and systematically cut its expenditures, Poland has pursued a more ambitious goal set by its Act on the Level of Defense Spending adopted in 2001.

Figure 1. Comparison of Poland and Slovakia's defense spending (as percentage of GDP).

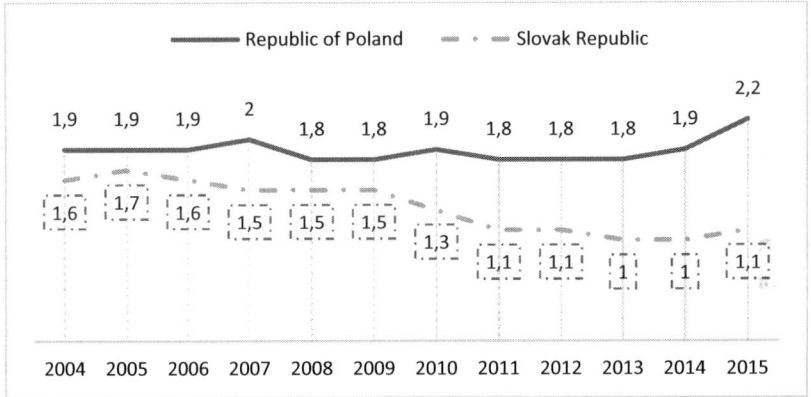

Source: adapted by the author, based on data provided by the Stockholm International Peace Research Institute (SIPRI 2016).

As has been suggested above, the global financial crisis cannot be considered as the only cause triggering the reduction of defense budgets—in the case of Slovakia, the trend had emerged even before the outbreak of the crisis. It can be safely assumed that it had been driven also by other political and economic factors, including the diminishing danger of an East-West military confrontation. Although upon acceding to NATO Slovakia made a commitment not to decrease it defense expenditures below 2 per cent of its GDP, the lack of immediate threats to national security made it difficult for the government in Bratislava to sustain such level of funding. Consequently, in contrast to Poland, Slovakia has slipped into comfortable complacency and started to rely on the fact that its missing contribution would be covered by other members of NATO (Ivančík & Ušiak 2013). The second milestone that will determine the future cooperation between Warsaw and Bratislava is the conflict over Crimea that flared up in the winter of 2014. The two governments differ substantially in their evaluation of the conflict's root causes and essence, as well as their approach to sanctions against the Russian Federation, with Poland being much stauncher in its criticism of Vladimir Putin's policy.

Poland's and Slovakia's security policies and strategic interests have been, and will continue to be, determined by ideas rather than a succession of battles and wars. While they do genuinely share some of these ideas and values, their current cooperation is based primarily on much more down-to-earth factors, such as geographical proximity, strategic considerations and active membership in the same international organizations.

The overview of bilateral cooperation between the Slovak Republic and the Republic of Poland

This part of the chapter calls firstly for an overview of bilateral meetings at various levels that led to the initiation of common projects. Bilateral cooperation between the two countries is formally based on the Agreement between the Ministry of National Defense of the Republic of Poland and the Ministry of Defense of the Slovak Republic on cooperation in the military area, signed on 9th of June, 1993. The document was focused around Poland and Slovakia's strategic goal to become integrated with NATO. It formalized bilateral relations and created the foundation for cooperation in the area of security (particularly defense) over the next two decades. It was followed by several narrower, more specific agreements and memoranda. At that time bilateral negotiations between the representatives of Poland and Slovakia were held at various levels, from Prime Ministers, Ministers of Defense and Foreign Affairs to regular officers. The meetings tackled a number of issues related to the development of the security environment: common air defenses, support for the defense industry and cooperation in this area, regional cooperation within the Visegrad Group, as well as other questions arising from the state of affairs in the EU, NATO and around the world. However, many of the security and defense initiatives were managed at the multilateral, rather than bilateral, level. The Visegrad Group proved to be a particularly convenient consultations forum, where all partners could develop common positions toward emerging issues. The formal framework for Polish-Slovak cooperation was reshaped by a new bilateral agreement on the cooperation in the area of defense, signed on 16th of May, 2014, during the Security Forum GLOBSEC 2014 held in Bratislava.

The following paragraphs present the outline, development and outcomes of bilateral cooperation from 2004 to 2016. The first meeting between Polish and Slovak Prime Ministers took place as late as 1998—five years after the creation of the independent Slovak Republic. Afterwards, the cooperation was gradually intensified to reach its current stage, when in 2015 alone there were 10 meetings between the Presidents of both states (Ministry of Foreign and European Affairs of the Slovak Republic 2015d). An important impulse for the development of closer relations came in 2013, after Poland's very active Presidency in the Visegrad Group. The following year, however, the process stagnated, particularly due to differing positions on the crisis in Ukraine. Nonetheless, many common projects (e.g. the EU Battlegroup, as well as a number of initiatives related to the defense industry and military cooperation) have survived the setback and are continued.

When it comes to the period analyzed here (2004-1016), the foundations of bilateral cooperation were built in 2004 and 2005, in the immediate aftermath of Poland and Slovakia's accession to the EU (and in Slovakia's case, also to NATO). Their newly acquired status as full members of these organizations redefined the framework for their needs and mutual relations. For Bratislava, the partnership with Warsaw has been crucial to the orientation of its foreign and security policy, particularly toward Western Balkans, Ukraine and Russia, but also with regard to counter-terrorism and transatlantic cooperation. Practical steps taken at that time included the decision to form a common EU crisis management battlegroup to be led by Poland, as well as the deployment of Slovak soldiers to Iraq under Polish command (Ministry of Foreign and European Affairs of the Slovak Republic 2005). Meanwhile, Poland did not direct its security policy solely towards the cooperation within the Visegrad Group. Instead, it often chose to emphasize its presence in the so-called Weimar Triangle, alongside France and Germany. While this cooperation format may not be particularly attractive to Paris and Berlin, the government in Warsaw sees it as a tool to be perceived as a major actor on the international scene (Interview, 2016). In 2006, the three partners began a dialogue on the idea of establishing a common Weimar Battlegroup. Although the unit was eventually formed (and put on stand-by in the first half of 2013), further cooperation gradually withered away, later to be revitalized during the crisis in Ukraine.

In 2006 and 2007 the mutual cooperation between Slovakia and Poland deepened due to their joint participation in the operation Iraqi Freedom. Communication between the Armed Forces of both states was bolstered as common units were established, personnel was prepared for overseas deployments and armies underwent modernization (Ministry of Foreign and European Affairs of the Slovak Republic 2006).

One of the first official meetings at the level of Defense Ministers was held in May 2007 when the Minister of Defense of the Slovak Republic, F. Kašický, and the Minister of Defense of the Republic of Poland, A. Szczygło, met in Warsaw. Their negotiations concerned primarily the intensification of bilateral military cooperation, including that within NATO and the EU. At that time, Slovak authorities was finalizing a project to set up a military training area in Lest, where an abandoned residential complex was converted into a site for carrying out counter-terrorism exercises. Bratislava offered to make the facility available to Polish Armed Forces—a gesture that triggered a long-term cooperation that has lasted until today. The training site is also used to simulate response to an attack on a NATO member state and is often utilized by a tank division operating closely with Slovak-Polish mechanized units (Ministry of Defense of the Slovak Republic 2014a). The two ministers discussed the possibility of closer cooperation in the area of defense industries. The Slovaks offered Poland their demining kit ('Božena') that had already been used by Polish soldiers during their deployment with the ISAF mission in Afghanistan (Ministry of Defense of the Slovak Republic 2007).

Cooperation was further strengthened as a result of negotiations between Defense Ministers, J. Baška (Slovakia) and B. Klich (Poland), that took place in September 2008 in Bratislava. The two delegations debated issues stemming from both countries' NATO and EU membership, particularly the need to reform NATO's command system so as to give it a simpler structure and organization. Both parties agreed that all MS should be able to contribute more proportionately to the composition of NATO headquarters' staff (Ministry of Defense of the Slovak Republic, 2008). The talks touched on options to bolster cooperation in military education and training (e.g. the possibility of granting Polish soldiers access to simulators of Mi-17 and Mi-24 helicopters), as well as cooperation in technical areas with military applications (Interview 2016). Furthermore, Poland invited Slovakia to join the project of an international military integration battalion in Bydgoszcz.

Another milestone came in February 2009, when the two Ministers met again, this time in Kraków. On that occasion, Polish government offered its southern neighbor a prospect of joint involvement in the ISAF mission (Interview 2016).

The next impulse to deepen cooperation resulted from the 2009 gas crisis. In July 2010 Prime Ministers I. Radičová and D. Tusk met in Warsaw to discuss the construction of a gas interconnector between the two countries (Ministry of Foreign and European Affairs of the Slovak Republic 2010d).

In August 2011, the State Secretary of the Slovak Ministry of Defense, R. Ondrejcsák, met in Krakow with the Undersecretary of State for defense policy in the Polish Ministry of National Defense, Z. Włosowicz. Once again, talks were focused on the multilateral level of cooperation, including the reform of command structures, establishment of an EU Battlegroup of Visegrad countries, as well as Slovakia's support for Polish Presidency in the Council of the European Union (Ministry of Defense of the Slovak Republic 2016).

Negotiations between the Slovak Defense Minister, M. Glváč, and his Polish counterpart, T. Siemoniak, that took place in September 2012 in Wisła constituted another step in the development of bilateral relations. The most significant outcome of the meeting was the establishment of common working groups that would be tasked with identifying areas for future cooperation. Other, previously debated topics—i.e. common interests within NATO and the EU, strengthening ties within the Visegrad Group, common training exercises to be held in Lest and cooperation between defense contractors—were also touched on (Ministry of Defense of the Slovak Republic 2012). Since 2012, the two countries' cooperation has significantly intensified thanks to the creation of the first Polish-Slovak discussion forum dealing with issues of energy security (particularly with the need for a gas interconnector that would be prepared as a part of the North-South pipeline) and common initiatives related to the defense, industry (Ministry of Foreign and European Affairs of the Slovak Republic 2012b).

When Prime Ministers R. Fico and D. Tusk met in Poprad in March 2013, they confirmed both governments' long-term intention to work together to enhance energy security (Government Office of the Slovak Republic 2013). Subsequent meeting held throughout 2014 confirmed the resurgence of cooperation in the area of defense. In April, Defense Ministers M. Glváč and T. Siemoniak discussed the preparation of a new framework Intergovernmental agreement on the development of cooperation in the area of defense (Ministry of Defense of the Slovak Republic 2014b). The document was finalized and signed in May. However, toward the end of the year and in the first months of 2015, the outbreak of conflict over Crimea produced a stumbling block in bilateral relations, as positions taken by Warsaw and Bratislava on how to resolve of the crisis were incompatible.

In 2015, bilateral meetings, be it between Defense Ministers or Secretaries of State in Defense Ministries, were even more frequent. The key negotiated issues were common air space defense (Cross-Border Operations), cooperation between entities of defense industries, regional cooperation within the Visegrad Group, as well as matters related to current situation in the EU, NATO and around the world (Interview 2016). The last important meeting up to date was held in February 2016, when Defense Ministers M. Glváč[15] and A. Macierewicz conferred about the problems of defense industry, as well as military intelligence capabilities and NATO's Counter Intelligence Center of Excellence—a newly formed structure that faced certain problems toward the end of 2015, after the new Polish cabinet took over the duties from its predecessor.

The practical aspects of bilateral cooperation can be divided into several areas concerning armed forces, defense and, in some cases, border control, as presented below:
    a) Common involvement in international crisis management operations—operation Iraqi Freedom was the first significant common contribution of both states to crisis management ac-

---

[15] After the elections in Slovakia in March 2016 P. Gajdoš became the Minister of Defense and, as of May 2016, he has not met officially with his Polish counterpart.

tivities. Their involvement lasted from 2003 to 2007 (although Poland pulled its soldiers out of Iraq the following year). Poland was put in command of the Center-South multinational division. Slovakia's initial contribution to the unit comprised 85 troops, mostly from the 5th Special Forces Regiment, while Poland sent 2 500 soldiers (Lorenz 2015). The division's task was to ensure the security in the Center-South zone and support Iraqi state structures.

b) Common training and education of soldiers—Slovakia provides the Lest facilities, as its best and most modern training center. The facilities are used by Slovak and other allied NATO troops, since Lest is one of the top military training centers across Central Europe. It allows armed forces to practice reacting to different kinds of threats: from terrorist attacks, through resolution of crisis situations to defending against a full-scale invasion. One of the most important joint exercises, the Slovak Shield, involved Czech, Hungarian, American and Polish forces (Dušička 2015). Poland's best facility is the Joint Force Training Center in Bydgoszcz, opened in 2004. Since then, it has held numerous exercises relates to crisis situations, many of which saw the participation of Slovak armed forces. The base of the Multinational Corps North-East, headquartered in Szczecin, is also worth mentioning. Slovak troops have been present there since 2005. Both Polish facilities constitute integral parts of NATO's structure (Interview 2016).

c) Establishment of the Visegrad EU Battlegroup—while this concept belongs more to the multilateral sphere, documents prepared as a result of bilateral meetings reiterated its importance to both countries. The V4 Battlegroup, as it was named, was certified during a NATO training exercise, Common Challenge, that took place in November 2015 in Poland. It was on stand-by from 1st of January 2016 to 30th June 2016. Its establishment is, in general, considered as a success of the Visegrad cooperation.

d) Common projects within defense industry—after the dissolution of the Warsaw Pact—an entity on which both Poland and Slovakia were dependent, also in terms of military technology—their armed forces required modernization. While Poland opted for a systematic transformation toward the Western type of equipment, in Slovakia modernization was undertaken rather as an ad hoc reconstruction (Goda, 2015, Lorenz 2015). The first step concerned aviation technology and the purchase of multirole fighters. In 2002, Poland decided to acquire American F-16s. Slovakia selected MIG-29A/UB, taking this opportunity to settle a part of its long-standing debt to Russia (Mihálik 2012: 47). These moves indicated different perceptions of armies and their roles. 2009 saw the development of several concepts of cooperation within the Visegrad Group ('Soldier of the 21st century', 'Modernization of air and missile defense') that dealt with the function of armed forces (Gotkowska & Osica 2012: 59). Over the past few years, common purchase of military technology and equipment (e.g. helicopters) was also suggested. However, so far none of these ideas have come to fruition, primarily due to the lack of political will on both sides. A possible turning point occurred in 2015, when Poland and Slovakia agreed upon two joint projects related to the arms industry. The first one envisions the production of the 'Rosomak-Scipio' armored personnel carrier, with the chassis to be supplied by Polish companies and the turret to be manufactured in Slovakia. The second project concerns the use of Slovak know-how to modernize self-propelled howitzers ('DANA') which have been used by the Polish Army (Wilk 2015). The result of the overhaul—a model of an entirely new version of the howitzer (to be named 'Diana')—was unveiled in Slovakia in 2016 as the first product of cooperation between Polish and Slovak arms manufacturers (HNonline 2016). Unfortunately, in the second half of 2016 both initiatives hit a roadblock when the two governments failed to resolve their disagreements regarding detailed terms of cooperation. As a result, the 'Rosomak-Scipio' project was terminated, while the work on 'Diana' was suspended (Kováč 2016a; Kováč 2016b).

e) Sharing intelligence within NATO's Counter Intelligence Center of Excellence established in Kraków. As Poland and Slovakia were co-founders of this body, its creation played an important role in the development of bilateral cooperation. The Center's main goal is education and training in the field of counter-intelligence capabilities, tactics and use of technical facilities, as well as preparation to combat hybrid threats (NATO 2015a). In December 2015 a serious dispute arose as the new Polish government unexpectedly replaced one of the Center's directors, K. Dusza (PRAVDA.SK 2015b). As a result of this development, subsequent bilateral meetings of Defense Ministers were devoted to the issue of military intelligence.

f) Common air defense and Cross-Border Operations (CBOs)—this initiative emerged as a direct result of Poland and Slovakia's accession to NATO and their participation in the NATO Integrated Air Defense System (NATINADS). The CBOs were initiated so as to enable cross-border use of aircraft put on standby by the two countries, as well as allow the use of airspace for training exercises (Matejko 2015). The legal aspects of cooperation between Polish and Slovak air forces are regulated by a bilateral agreement on the air traffic of military aircraft of the Slovak Republic and the Republic of Poland in the airspace of both states, concluded by Defense Ministries in 1998 (Interview 2016). Expert groups formed by the two governments have been working on a new legal framework for bilateral Cross-Border Operations since 2015.

g) Energy security—discussions about reducing dependence on deliveries of strategic resources from Russia intensified all across Central Europe after the 2009 gas crisis. One of the most prominent initiatives of the Visegrad Group was the establishment of the North-South transit corridor. The proposal became one of priorities also in Polish-Slovak bilateral cooperation. Strategic documents prepared by the two governments point to energy security being one of the crucial issues in non-military security—a sentiment echoed during meetings between various government officials. In this perspective, the bilateral initiative simply followed on the idea of creating an infrastructural link that would enable the transport of gas from countries other than the Russian Federation.

In final remarks to this part of the chapter, it should be emphasized that Slovakia is only a minor partner for the Polish government. Even though many common concepts and undertakings have had a bilateral basis, most of them have been shaped outside the framework of strictly bilateral cooperation. In many cases, they resulted from both states' involvement in multilateral bodies. It can be said that relations between Poland and Slovakia, although not inadequate, are hampered by certain unanswered questions and unresolved issues: for instance, the situation concerning the Counter Intelligence Center of Excellence in Kraków, the implementation of cooperation between defense industries or the new agreement on CBOs. Regular meetings of Defense Ministers, Secretaries of State and Chiefs of General Staffs often take place within the framework of the Visegrad Group. In this particular area, communication between Poland and Slovakia's armed forces[16] is actually above-standard. Bilateral contacts were intensified particularly in 2012 and 2013, partly due to the creation of a common discussion forum and the organization of first intergovernmental meeting on 27th of March 2013 (Government Office of the Slovak Republic 2013). They have ultimately turned into regular consultations, attended by Prime Ministers, Ministers and Secretaries of State responsible for sectors deemed particularly important for the development of Polish-Slovak relations. The meetings deal with all relevant questions related to bilateral cooperation, from project proposals to monitoring ongoing initiatives. As regards a broader security perspective, the discussions have dealt most of all with the construction of gas interconnection within the South-East corridor (Ministry of Foreign and European Affairs of the Slovak Republic 2015d). However, while expert groups are well capable of reaching agreements on most issues, these agreements are not always approved by top decision-makers in Warsaw and Bratislava. The need for

---

[16] It is important to compare the position and size of Polish and Slovak armed forces. Slovakia has approximately 13 500 soldiers (GlobalFirepower 2016a), 22 tanks, 478 armoured vehicles, 17 missile systems and 42 aircraft (including a modest number of 12 fighters) (GlobalFirepower 2016b). Meanwhile, Poland boasts 120 000 troops (GlobalFirepower 2016a). Its ground-based equipment comprises 1009 tanks, 2068 armoured vehicles and 240 missile systems. Air Force possesses 461 aircraft, including 99 fighters. Unlike Slovakia (for obvious geographical reasons), Poland also has a naval force that features 5 submarines, 5 frigates and a number of other vessels (GlobalFirepower 2016c). These numbers illustrate a strong asymmetry between Poland and Slovakia's military positions.

endorsement on the part of political elites often proves the biggest hindrance in the development of bilateral relations.

Dynamics of Polish-Slovak relations in the multilateral context

This part of the chapter outlines Polish-Slovak cooperation within the framework of international organizations. The effective multilateralism introduced into regional cooperation by these bodies constitutes the basis of Poland's and Slovakia's foreign and security policies. Key strategic documents produced by the two governments suggest that the multilateral context is built around the Visegrad Group, NATO and the EU. They also mention the role of other international entities, such as the Organization for Security and Cooperation in Europe (OSCE), as well as the United Nations (UN)—major actors engaged in ensuring regional and global security. Altogether, the aforementioned organizations constitute a framework that allows countries to pursue their national interests by means of international law, crucial in regulating inter-state relations, particularly between small and mid-sized states (such as Poland and Slovakia). The following section analyzes the position, cooperation and achievements of the two governments within selected groupings.

Cooperation within the Visegrad Group

The Visegrad Group is, historically, the first major documents example of Central European states seeking common approaches and effective multilateral cooperation. On 15th of February 1991, ten days before the dissolution of the Warsaw Pact, governments of the original V3[17] (the Czech and Slovak Federal Republic, Poland and Hungary) signed a common declaration on coordinated integration with the European Communities and NATO. The document was conceived as an instrument that would accelerate post-communist states' transformation into

---

[17] The Visegrad Group does not have any organs—it is more of a consultation forum than an international organization in the real sense of the term. The only related institution is the International Visegrad Fund, which serves to support grants, scholarships or mobility (Rosputinský 2011).

members of the Euro-Atlantic political community. Nonetheless, after all four of them joined NATO and the EU, the platform remained in place and the cooperation has continued. Between 1999 and 2004, the Group focused on assisting Slovakia in its quest to prepare for NATO membership. After 2004, common efforts of the V4 have somewhat stagnated (Paulech & Urbanovská 2014), but overall, the quad-lateral bond forged between Prague, Budapest, Warsaw and Bratislava is still reasonable potent, as the four partners try to coordinate their defense and security policies through various projects (e.g. the establishment of an EU Battlegroup). The Group also encourages joint military operations, training exercises and education. Furthermore, it helps the governments to harmonize their policy approaches and positions within other international organizations, so as to reflect their shared attitudes toward particular security issues. Many areas for cooperation are still only proposals, waiting to be implemented (Ušiak 2013).[18]

The most important document created during the period analyzed here is the Declaration of Prime Ministers of the Czech Republic, the Republic of Hungary, the Republic of Poland and the Slovak Republic on cooperation of the Visegrad Group countries after their accession to the European Union. As the four states joined NATO and the EU, the original purpose behind the existence of the Group was achieved. This raised the question about the contents and sense of future cooperation. The governments in question recognized that the importance of their cooperation warranted its continuation (Visegrad Group 2004b). The intention was confirmed in a new document entitled Guidelines on the Future Areas of Visegrad Cooperation. It was agreed that a summit of the Group would be held at least once a year. The document identified several areas for cooperation: supporting the EU CFSP in order to enhance relations between the Union and NATO; consulting common approaches to the issue of NATO's defense capabilities; strengthening cross-border cooperation; combating organized crime and illegal migration; contributing to crisis management and the protection of the EU's external borders; enhancing cooperation between national de-

---

[18] There are several examples of successful regional cooperation in the area of security, for instance: Baltic cooperation, Nordic cooperation, cooperation among the states of the Benelux, and several others.

fense industries (Visegrad Group 2004b). The framework created by the Guidelines, with minor amendments made over time, remains valid today.

Milestones in the development of cooperation throughout the analyzed period are represented by the adoption of joint declarations and communiqués, rather than by examples of practical actions. The actual implementation of common statements was most significant in 2009 and 2010, in the context of the gas crisis and the EaP initiative which represented an important point in the process of seeking common interests and areas suitable for cooperation. Another notable step came in 2011, when the Group declared its will to establish an EU Battlegroup (Paulech & Urbanovská 2014). The Visegrad countries' readiness to cooperate has seemingly further strengthened during the subsequent years, as illustrated in table 8.

Table 9: Selected joint Visegrad group (V4) declarations related to defense and security.

Document	Date / Place	Highlights
Joint Statement on the Eastern Partnership of the Foreign Ministers of the Visegrad Group	4th May 2016 / Prague	The V4 Ministers reaffirmed their strong support to the EaP as a strategic dimension of the European Neighborhood Policy. They called for full implementation of the Minsk Agreements.
Bratislava Declaration of the Visegrad Group Heads of Government for a Stronger CSDP	19th June 2015 / Bratislava	The V4V4 supports the elaboration of a new European security strategy and acknowledges the importance of cooperation between the EU and its partners for handling specific threats. The V4 will enhance security dialogue and practical CSDP cooperation with countries of the EaP, the Western Balkans and the Union for the Mediterranean.
Joint Communiqué of the Visegrad Group Ministers of Defense	23rd April 2015 / Tomášov	The V4 agrees to establish the V4 Military Educational Platform to pursue new forms of cooperation (Senior Body, the V4 Planning Group) and dialogue about the V4 EU BG 2019. Cooperation shall include: training and exercises; logistics; support group; chemical, biological, radiological and nuclear (CBRN) defense capabilities; joint terminal attack controllers; special operations tactical training.
Bratislava Declaration of the Visegrad Group Heads of Government on the Deepening of V4 Defense Cooperation	9th December 2014 / Bratislava	Defense Ministers are tasked with: 1. finding common V4 solutions to meet the commitments made at the NATO Summit in Wales; 2. working on establishing the permanent V4 modular force for NATO and EU rapid response formations and operations.

Budapest Declaration of the Visegrad Group Heads of Government on the New Opening in V4 Defense Cooperation	24th June 2014 / Budapest	Defense Ministers should: 1. prepare an Action Plan of the V4 defense cooperation; 2. develop a Training and Exercise Strategy; 3. strengthen cooperation among national defense industries; 4. explore options for a common project of developing and procuring a universal modular tracked platform and wheeled armored personnel carrier; 5. explore possibilities of forming a permanent V4 modular force.
Long-Term Vision of the Visegrad Countries on Deepening their Defense Cooperation	14th March 2014 / Visegrad	Practical cooperation shall focus on: 1. capability development, procurement, defense industry; 2. multinational units and cross-border operations; 3. education, training and military exercises.
Framework for an Enhanced Visegrád Defense Planning	14th March 2014 / Visegrad	Capacity development projects could encompass the pooling and sharing of assets, joint procurement of equipment, research and development. Countries have agreed to regularly attend each other's bilateral meetings, hold joint consultations with NATO and conduct defense planning experts' exchange.
Budapest Joint Statement of the Visegrad Group Heads of Government on Strengthening the V4 Security and Defense Cooperation	14th October 2013 / Budapest	Defense Ministers should: 1. draft a long-term vision for a Visegrad defense cooperation strategy; 2. strengthen training and exercises of the armed forces in the V4 format; 3. explore the possibility of creating a framework for enhanced defense planning cooperation.
Joint statement of the V4 ministers of defense	4th June 2013 / Brussels	Future cooperation should concern the V4 EU BG, education, training, joint exercises, development of defense capabilities. Visegrad cooperation will be focused on: CBRN capabilities, logistics, countering cyber threats, armament, air and missile defense.
Declaration of the Visegrad Group Foreign Ministers "For a More Effective and Stronger Common Security and Defense Policy"	18th April 2013 / Bratislava	The V4 reconfirms its commitment to strengthening the EU's ability to react to security challenges by increasing the effectiveness, visibility and impact of CSDP, enhancing the development of military capabilities and strengthening Europe's defense industry.
Joint Statement of Defense Ministers of the V4 Countries, the Federal Republic of Germany and the French Republic	6th March 2013 / Warsaw	All parties to the talks held in Warsaw remain committed to strengthening European defense capabilities that will contribute to the development of CSDP and strengthening NATO.

Joint Communiqué of the Ministers of Defense of the Visegrad Group	4th May 2012 / Litoměřice	Cooperation should be intensified in the following fields: air controllers' training; chemical, biological, radiological and nuclear defense; helicopter pilots' training; logistics; medical treatment facilities; multinational research and development; training in handling improvised explosive devices and explosive ordnance devices.
Declaration of the Visegrad Group — Responsibility for a Strong NATO	18th April 2012 / Prague	The V4 supports further implementation of the 2010 NATO Strategic Concept, in particular: dedicated NATO capabilities, interoperability of national defense capabilities, balance between conventional, nuclear and missile deterrence and defense, Smart Defence Initiative and NATO enlargement.
Joint Communiqué of the Ministers of Defense of the Visegrad Group Countries	12th April 2007 / Bratislava	The V4 countries state their support for NATO transformation, development of EU capabilities, crisis-management and stability in the Western Balkans and Afghanistan. They welcome the agreement reached on the establishment of the V4 EU BG beyond 2015.
Guidelines on the Future Areas of Visegrad Cooperation	12th May 2004 / Kroměříž	The V4 supports cooperation within the V4 area, EU, NATO, as well as cooperation with other international organizations and partners in the field of defense and security.

Source: Adapted by author on the basis of Visegrad Group declarations.

2009 and 2010 provided another important point in the history of Visegrad cooperation. The global economic crisis spurred sharp decreases in defense spending. At the same time, however, some new joint programs and initiatives (e.g. Smart Defense) were launched within NATO and the EU, while others were continued despite financial constraints. The end of 2013 and the first months of 2014 brought the outbreak of the Ukraine crisis. Both the economic crisis and the events in the Crimea affected the development of relations among the V4 states and can be regarded as crucial, as they revealed how fragile this cooperation can be, all declarations notwithstanding. Today, just as in the past, the times of great challenges tend to verify the extent to which cooperation in the area of security is prioritized by the four partners—especially when the emerging threats affect them directly (Šuplata 2013a). It is important to remember that the Visegrad Group has also served to develop broad political, economic and cultural cooperation (Visegrad Group 2011). It has been a communication channel for coordinating various policies, including, of course, security and foreign policies. While culture and education have proven the most fruitful and visible areas of cooperation, the foreign and security dimension has been much more challenging. On the one hand, the four governments have issued joint declarations that present a common approach to certain issues (e.g. the decision to not recognize the annexation of Crimea and the consensus on the illegal nature of Moscow's actions) (Visegrad Group 2014a). On the other hand, the reality has shown that the positions adopted by the V4 countries are not as uniform as the declarations would suggest.

Recommendations from experts seem to present a wide range of possibilities for cooperation among the Visegrad states. The Long Term Vision of the Visegrad Countries on Deepening their Defence Cooperation—a document adopted in March 2014—defines three areas of particular potential: 1) capability development and procurement; 2) establishment of multinational units and cross-border activities and 3) common education and training (Visegrad Group 2014b).

The following paragraphs focus primarily on security and defense policies. The greatest success in this area has been the establishment of the Visegrad EU Battlegroup that became operational in the first half of 2016. However, as some authors point out, from the historical perspective, 'Poland, the Czech Republic and Slovakia already had a common brigade over 10 years ago' (Bednár 2014, Lukášek 2010). The more recent project was suggested as early as 2007, when a joint communiqué (Visegrad Group 2007) put forward the idea of creating an EU Battlegroup of the V4 countries. The consensus on the implementation of the concept was somewhat difficult to achieve. There have, however, been some examples of successful cooperation in the field of non-military security. One major achievement, spurred largely by the 2009 gas crisis, has been the construction of the link in the North-South corridor. The section connecting Hungary and Slovakia is already finished, while the link between Slovakia and Poland is to be completed in 2018/2019 (EUSTREAM 2016). The second success concerns meetings of committees for European affairs, which have been held on a regular basis since 2005. Communiqués and other products of the meetings are sometimes presented to relevant European institutions. Still, the process of preparing joint statements within the Visegrad Group is substantially easier that the practical implementation of their stipulations.[19] It can be argued that proposals related to non-military aspects

---

[19] This issue results from the form of cooperation adopted by the Visegrad Group and the absence of institutionalization. The latter circumstance is actually advantageous in

of security (various forms of support for common policies, nominations, positions toward specific problems) are easier to implement than those strictly connected to defense policies.

As far as military security is concerned, the most significant contribution of the Visegrad Group is, again, the EU Battlegroup. It is composed of three components: 1) Force Headquarters, located in the Polish city of Kraków (Šuplata et.al 2013b); 2) the 'core' and 3) operational and strategic facilities. The Battlegroup has over 3 700 soldiers, of which 560 are contributed by Slovakia, 728 by the Czech Republic, 640 by Hungary, while 1 800—a number reflecting its leadership position within the unit—by Poland. It should be noted that the numbers may change slightly depending on current capabilities of each partner. When put on standby in the first half of 2016, the Battlegroup, placed at the EU's disposal, was able to deploy as far as 6 000 km from Brussels for up to 30 days. The deployment could be extended to 120 days, provided supplies were adequately replenished (Český rozhlas 2015). It is planned that the unit will be on standby again in the first half of 2019 (Visegrad Group 2015). One should remember that, so far, none of the EU Battlegroups have ever been activated at the EU's request. Apart from holding command of the unit, Poland is responsible for its communication and information systems, while Slovakia's role is providing protection against radiation, chemical and biological weapons (Interview 2016).

When assessing the potential for future cooperation among members of the Visegrad Group, one needs to consider two issues that are likely to prove decisive. The first one concerns the decrease in resources allocated by states for security and defense capabilities. This tendency needs to be adequately reflected in policy priorities if national interests are to be pursued efficiently in today's demanding economic environment. The V4 countries attempted military cooperation immediately after their systemic transformation—albeit with a varying degree of success. After 2008, the global financial crisis put governments under ever more pressure to economize, effectively forcing them to work together for the sake of limiting costs. Such situation constitutes

---

some aspects, as it allows a more leeway in the framework for cooperation. However, it also causes certain inconveniences, particularly with regard to compliance with procedures agreed on through negotiations.

an opportunity to expand common efforts in the future.[20] Hence, having formed the Visegrad EU Battlegroup, the Czech Republic, Hungary, Poland and Slovakia are now engaged in the discussion about the possibility of creating a common Czech and Slovak aviation unit or establishing common airspace (the Common Sky project), in which Hungary and Poland could also participate, at least in terms of common purchase / rental of new aviation technology. The V4 states are also considering cooperation in non-military aspects of security: efforts to ensure energy security (the North-South transit link), mutual assistance in resolving crisis situations, managing societal (migration, extremism) and economic (corruption, organized crime) security issues.

The second key determinant revolves around the ongoing crisis in Ukraine and the divergent positions adopted by the Visegrad states with regard to the nature and causes of the situation. In terms of attitudes toward Russia, the V4 governments differ widely, occupying roughly the entire scale from cooperation to conflict (Gawron-Tabora 2015). While Hungary's orientation is considered by many analysts as essentially pro-Russian, Poland perceives Moscow as the aggressor and the root cause behind the conflict. Sitting somewhere between, the Czech Republic and Slovakia move slightly toward one pole or the other, depending on their current situation and policy priorities. The situation is further complicated by the lack of agreement among domestic political elites in each country, as well as divergence of opinions among the general public (Majer & Schneider & Šuplata 2016).

Areas that offer significant potential for future cooperation include energy security, combating extremism and countering Russian propaganda, creating new EU and NATO strategic documents, military and civilian intelligence, crisis management as well as research and development, particularly in the defense industry (Naď, Šuplata 2016). The

---

[20] This, however, is not to imply that one side's failure to meet its commitments releases other partners from their responsibilities. For such cooperation to work, all parties have to contribute proportionately. England and France proceeded along these lines when they were exploring options for joint efforts. This enabled them to limit security-related spending in favour of other areas. In the case of Central European states, any savings generated this way could be invested in military research or any number of other fields. There are several possibilities for cooperation—e.g. Pooling and Sharing or the concept of Smart Defence—that have emerged since Poland and Slovakia joined NATO and the EU. It is crucial that the two governments continue to examine all possibilities and utilize them to enhance both external and internal security of the Visegrad Group members.

Visegrad EU Battlegroup has contributed considerably to the development of military cooperation and joint deployment capabilities. It can be used not only for various purposes designated by NATO or the EU, but also for joint actions undertaken by all Central European states.

Polish-Slovak cooperation within international organizations (NATO, EU, OSCE, UN)

Participation in various important projects and operations initiated within the framework of international organizations such as NATO, the EU, OSCE and the UN constitutes another important element in multilateral cooperation involving Poland and Slovakia. Both countries partake in crisis management operations, thus proving their readiness to accept responsibility for global stability. Their contribution to such undertakings, however, necessarily reflects the disproportion in the size of their respective armed forces—this is clearly visible when one takes a closer look at several past or current operations conducted under the auspices of international bodies (see tables 9 and 10).

In case of the most inclusive international organization—the United Nations—active participation of all states is natural, as members consider themselves to be a part of the solution to certain problems. Despite doubts and criticism surrounding the effectiveness of the Security Council and the functioning of the organization as a whole, the UN is still regarded as the most important body dedicated to guarding world security. The principles it has introduced over the last 70 years have become a symbol of the global political system. Poland and Slovakia are well aware of the UN's importance and wish to be involved in its functioning by engaging with its structures to handle specific issues (see table 9). The issues in question are not confined to military security—these days, they refer more and more often to non-military aspects. Slovakia's greatest success came in 2006 and 2007, when it was elected a non-permanent member of the Security Council. In February 2007, while holding the rotating post of the presiding country, it opened the debate about a possible reform of the security sector. In 2011 and 2012, Slovakia served—also for the first time in its history as an independent state—as a member of the Economic and Social Council. Finally, between 2011 and 2014 was a member of the Office of the Contracting States to the Rome Statute of the International Criminal Court (Ministry of Foreign and European Affairs of the Slovak Republic 2015c).

While Poland did not hold a post as a non-permanent member of the UN Security Council in the period encompassed here, it had previously had that privilege on as many as five occasions (1946-47, 1960, 1970-71, 1982-83, 1996-97) (Permanent Mission... 2016a). Recently, it has announced its intention to apply for a non-permanent seat once again, for 2018-2019, as a representative of the Eastern European Group (Permanent Mission... 2016b). Moreover, several UN institutions, including the UN Information Center, WHO and UNHCR, are represented in Poland through permanent offices (Organizacja Narodów Zjednoczonych 2016). In 2015, the country allocated 0,5 billion USD for humanitarian aid (Lorenz 2015), proving its involvement with the UN is more significant than Slovakia's. Nonetheless, both countries reciprocally support their nominations for any important posts (including, of course, that on the Security Council). Areas of common activities encompass human rights, counter-terrorism and participation in UN peacekeeping operations, although after their admission to NATO and the EU, both Poland and Slovakia have operated more under the auspices of these two organizations than as UN members (compare Table 10 and Table 11).

As for the OSCE, Slovakia was a very active member from 1999 to 2005, when the post of the Secretary General was held by a Slovak diplomat, J. Kubiš. Thereafter, in 2005 and 2006, Bratislava presided over the OSCE's Committee for non-military aspects of security. More recently, in 2013-2014, it headed the economic and environmental committee (Ministry of Foreign and European Affairs of the Slovak Republic 2015d). Poland's participation in the OSCE also included a number of areas. Its representatives have occupied important posts within the organization. One particularly worth mentioning is A. Kobieracki, the director of the Conflict Prevention Center—a body that constitutes a focal point for coordination and development of OSCE's tasks in the political and military area (Ministry of Foreign and European Affairs of the Slovak Republic 2016c). Notably, Warsaw provides the seat for the OSCE Office for Democratic Institutions and Human Rights (ODHIR) (Ministry of Foreign and European Affairs of the Slovak Republic 2015d).

Both countries share a number of areas when it comes to participation and support for the OSCE's agenda, especially with regard to certain geographically delimited regions, such as the Western Balkans or Eastern Europe. They actively take part in human rights actions and ODIHR election observation missions.

Table 10: Overview of current and completed UN crisis management and other international operations in which Poland and Slovakia have been involved.

	Operations	Slovakia (period/staff/description)	Poland (period/staff/description)
UN missions	United Nations Stabilization Mission in Haiti (MINUSTAH)	June 2015–present / 6 people / supporting recovery, reconstruction and stability efforts in the country	–
	United Nations Mission in the Republic of South Sudan (UNMISS)	–	2011–present / 2 people / protecting civilians, monitoring human rights, supporting the delivery of humanitarian aid and the implementation of the Cessation of Hostilities Agreement
	United Nations Organization Stabilization Mission in the Democratic Republic of the Congo (MONUSCO)	–	July 2010–present / 2 people / protecting civilians, humanitarian personnel and human rights defenders, supporting the government in its stabilization and peace consolidation efforts
	United Nations Operation in Côte d'Ivoire (UNOCI)	–	2004–present / 1 person / protecting civilians, supporting the government in disarmament, demobilization and reintegration of former combatants, promoting security sector reform and human rights
	United Nations Mission in Liberia (UNMIL)	–	2003–present / 4 people / implementation of the ceasefire agreement, protecting the UN staff, facilities and civilians, supporting humanitarian activities and national security reform
	United Nations Assistance Mission in Afghanistan (UNAMA)	–	2003–present / 1 person / providing political assistance, supporting peace and reconciliation, monitoring and promoting human rights and protection of civilians, encouraging regional cooperation

United Nations Peace-keeping Force in Cyprus (UNFICYP)	May 2001–present / 159 people / preventing violence, monitoring the ceasefire, improving communication between hostile parties	–
United Nations Truce Supervision Organization (UNTSO)	August 1998–present / 2 people / monitoring the ceasefire in the Golan Heights	–
United Nations Mission for the Referendum in Western Sahara (MINURSO)	–	1991–present / 1 person / monitoring the ceasefire, reducing the threat of mines, supporting the confidence-building measures, ensuring a free and fair referendum and proclaiming results
United Nations Mission in the Sudan (UNMIS)	–	2005–2011 / 40 people / supporting the implementation of the Comprehensive Peace Agreement, humanitarian aid and human rights
United Nations Organization Mission in the Democratic Republic of the Congo (MONUC)	–	1999–June 2010 / 3 people / supervision of the implementation of the Ceasefire Agreement
United Nations Mission in the Central African Republic and Chad (MINURCAT)	–	June 2008–November 2010 / 2 people / protecting civilians, promoting human rights, rule of law and regional peace
United Nations Observer Mission in Georgia (UNOMIG)	–	1994–2009 / 7 people / verifying compliance with the ceasefire agreement
United Nations Interim Force In Lebanon (UNIFIL)	–	1992–2009 / 491 people / monitoring the cessation of hostilities and helping ensure access of humanitarian aid to civilian population
United Nations Disengagement Observer Force (UNDOF)	May 1998–June 2008 / 96 people / monitoring and patrolling in order to detect potential violation of international treaties	1974–2009 / 356 people supervising ceasefire and disengagement of the Israeli and Syrian forces in the Golan Heights

			November 2000–2008 / 124 people / promoting security, stability and respect for human rights in Kosovo
	United Nations Interim Administration Mission in Kosovo (UNMIK)	–	November 2000–2008 / 124 people / promoting security, stability and respect for human rights in Kosovo
	United Nations Missions in Ethiopia and Eritrea (UNMEE)	December 2000–June 2004 / 197 people / demining, reconstructing and building roads, engineering	2000-2008 / 6 people / maintaining liaison with the parties, monitoring cessation of hostilities
	United Nations Operation in Côte d'Ivoire (ONUCI)	–	2005–2006 / 2 people / protecting civilians and supporting the government in disarmament, demobilization, reintegration and SSR
	United Nations Mission in Sierra Leone (UNAMSIL)	August 1999–December 2005 / 2 people / collecting, processing and assessing operational intelligence, full assessment of military threats	–
International coalitions	Operation Iraqi Freedom	July 2003–February 2007 / 100 people / demining, pyrotechnical work, eliminating weapons and ammunition on Iraqi territory	September 2003–October 2008 / 2500 people / command of the Central-South Zone
International coalitions	Enduring Freedom, Afghanistan	August 2002–December 2005 / 40 people / maintaining and reconstructing airports	March 2002-2004 / 2500 ensuring security in Ghazni province, providing combat engineers and logistical support

Source: Adapted by the author on the basis of the official UN data.

The next organization to be considered is NATO. Its meaning for both counties stems from the principle of ensuring collective security for all its members. Several documents of political, strategic and general character adopted after 2000 declare NATO's intention to adapt to the new security environment. During the 2002 summit in Prague, the Alliance proclaimed readiness to cooperate with the EU—a process that is still considered as one of the challenges most important to the future of the organization. NATO's governing bodies have had to consider trends of the last two decades, particularly the possible emergence of institutional alternatives available to its European members (Duffield 2012). After their admission as full members, Poland and Slovakia have reaped benefits of being under the umbrella of collective security, but have also assumed certain obligations. NATO's key principle is cooperation and indivisibility of its members' security. This solidarity means that individual countries do not have to rely only on their own forces, but, at the same time, they share their partners' problems and should contribute to their solution.

Strategic Concepts are important documents that delineate NATO's operational engagement. So far, the Alliance has adopted three Concepts—the first one in 1991, then in 1999 and, most recently, in 2010. The 1991 document expanded the scope of NATO's activity and introduced enlargement as an instrument of stabilization in the post-Cold War Europe. The second Concept confirmed the Alliance's open door policy, acknowledged reinforcement of defense capabilities and again endorsed enlargement as a stabilizing instrument (Krokosová 2013). The document adopted in 2010 presented a new vision which has since become an integral part of Polish and Slovak security policies. It declared the establishment of a missile defense system, strengthening the Smart Defense program and opened the space for new security-related topics, such as counter-terrorism and protection against cyber-attacks (NATO 2010).

Both countries are involved in the development of NATO's doctrine and capabilities through active participation in international crisis management operations (see table 10). One of the strongest impulses for cooperation was the establishment of NATO Response Forces (NRF), initiated in 2002. NRF was formed to provide the Alliance with the option of reacting to any changes in the security environment, as well as to strengthen the collective defense. In 2014, the initiative was further enhanced by the formation of Very High Readiness Joint Task Force. Early in 2015, it was decided that the Task Force would comprise 5000 soldiers (NATO 2015b), with Poland placed in command of the Multinational Chemical Biological Radiological Nuclear Defense Battalion. Later that year, it was announced that a new headquarters would be established for the NRF in the Slovak territory (RT 2015). However, the evolution of the conflict in Ukraine remains the unresolved issue. Poland expects (as was evident during NATO summit which took place in Warsaw in July 2016) that NATO will further strengthen its presence in Central and Eastern Europe, while Slovak authorities—particularly the Prime Minister, R. Fico—warn that stationing more divisions in the region could lead the escalating the already tense relations with Russia.[21] Arguably, both Poland and Slovakia could utilize their experience with the V4 EU Battlegroup if they were to host a major NRF base. The political feasibility of implementing the idea, however, remains questionable (Bodnárová 2013). One of the major recent contributions on the part of both countries is the establishment of the Counter Intelligence Centre of Excellence in Kraków, ran under their joint leadership. The Centre will serve all NATO members, supporting education and development of counter-intelligence capabilities.

NATO offers Poland and Slovakia a wide range of opportunities for cooperation. Warsaw wishes to be seen as a reliable partner within the transatlantic framework and to strengthen its position as the leader in Central and Eastern Europe. To do so, it is willing to build a coordinated approach within the Visegrad Group and work with the Central European Defence Cooperation. The issue that can hinder cooperation between Warsaw and Bratislava is the discrepancy in their positions toward Russia.

The impact of the European Union on defense cooperation is much broader that than of NATO. The last major change concerning the security and defense dimension occurred in 2009, following the adoption of the Lisbon Treaty. The Treaty introduced a new concept of building external relations, proposed evolution toward common defense (sub-

---

[21] It might be useful to point out that the difference in attitudes toward both the U.S. and Russia has a somewhat longer history. It first emerged on the occasion of discussing the establishment of a missile defense system. It flared up again during the Russo-Georgian war, and has now culminated with the advent of the Ukraine crisis. When the missile defense system was preliminarily discussed by the American, Czech and Polish governments, Prime Minister R. Fico categorically rejected the notion that Slovakia could be involved in the project (even though no such offer was ever made). During the Russo-Georgian conflict in 2008, Warsaw claimed that Russia was clearly the aggressor, while Bratislava described the situation as ambiguous. Moreover, Slovakia remained entirely passive towards Polish initiative to create a Central European coalition to assist Georgia. Recent developments in relation to the conflict Ukraine suggest that the divergent attitudes evident in 2008 would re-emerge (Goda 2015; Lorenz 2015).

ject to unanimous decision of the European Council) and revised obligations with regard to the deployment of armed forces and police for the purpose of peacekeeping and conflict prevention outside the EU territory (European Union 2009). Its stipulations demand that the MS should agree on common attitudes toward future developments within the internal or external security environment. It also broadens the competences of the European Defense Agency (including the EU Military Staff and Satellite Centre), as well as improves coordination of military and non-military aspects of common EU operations. Finally, the Treaty widens the scope of the Petersberg tasks and the EU's defense-related responsibilities (Danics 2012). As for non-military aspects of cooperation, the most relevant ones were outlined in the Internal Security Strategy adopted in 2010. The Strategy discussed several dimensions, including preventing terrorism and organized crime, dealing with natural disasters and cyber security (European Union 2010). Finally, it defined a framework and procedures for future cooperation.

Interests shared by Poland and Slovakia (as indicated by strategic documents) include active participation in initiatives launched within CSDP and CFSP. Going beyond the scope of what is explicitly stated in its key documents, Polish government endeavors to influence the EU's future development, particularly since the missile defense system discussed in 2010 did not come to existence. Slovakia is aware of the fact that by partaking in the EU's security-related efforts it can promote its own interests that it would be unable to pursue otherwise. As they are not ranked among Europe's strongest actors, both countries attempt to build their position through the wider framework of the Visegrad Group, where Poland has been acting as the regional leader. Slovakia recognizes its position in the Union and the possibilities that come with it. Consequently, it regards its involvement within the EU as both a commitment and opportunity to enhance its own credibility.

Areas where Poland's and Slovakia's interests meet include the Western Balkans. Recently, the two governments encouraged the establishment of a network of experts on the region and the Western Balkans Fund (Ministry of Foreign and European Affairs of the Slovak Republic 2015b). Both Warsaw and Bratislava support the V4+ format and share a keen interest in the developments across Eastern Europe, as indicated by their participation in various operations (see Table 4). They wish to influence their eastern neighbors with the ultimate goal of stabilizing the region. To do so, they utilize opportunities provided by the EaP initiative, initiated in 2009. They also provide Eastern European governments with knowledge and experience stemming from their own political and economic transition (Ušiak 2013, Duleba 2011). Both states endorse further EU enlargement in the Eastern and South-Eastern direction (Ministry of Foreign and European Affairs of the Slovak Republic 2015d; Ministry of Foreign and European Affairs of the Slovak Republic 2016b). Another important chance to strengthen cooperation is the fact of holding the Presidency in the Council of the European Union. Poland's Presidency took place from July to December 2011, while Slovakia is currently leading the Council (its tenure encompasses the second half of 2016). Moreover, in August 2014, D. Tusk, then Polish Prime Minister, was elected to be the second President of the European Council. This brief comparison demonstrates that Poland and Slovakia's bilateral cooperation in the multilateral context of the Union is focused primarily on reaching a consensus and supporting candidacies to the EU's institutions and agencies. Still, Poland's overall position in the EU structures is obviously a lot stronger than that of Slovakia.

The priorities shared by the two countries include the establishment of the Energy Union, as well as the issue of controlling illegal migration and quotas for accepting refugees (that both states refused to agree to). As part of supporting the EU, both Poland and Slovakia engage with the European Defense Agency established in 2004 and participate in building European defense capabilities through the concept of Pooling and Sharing (Tarasovič 2011). Based on the notion that by sharing resources all members will be able to limit their defense expenditures, Pooling and Sharing was initiated at the meeting in Ghent in 2010, in the aftermath of the global financial crisis. For Poland and Slovakia, its practical implementation has come in the form of an EU Battlegroup established in parallel to the Visegrad cooperation. The Battlegroup was put on standby in the first half of 2016. As for substantial differences in opinions, the major questions concern relations with and sanctions against Russia. Poland has firmly stressed the need for multilateral coordination of the approach toward the Ukraine crisis, so as to keep the EU actively engaged in the process of resolving the conflict. It has also repeatedly stated its readiness to support the Union's efforts on that front in case EU institutions request assistance (Gromadzki 2015).

Polish-Russian relations have in recent years been consistently tense. Already before the Ukraine crisis, Warsaw's priority was to enhance Eastern Europe's independence and pro-Western stance in foreign policy. Polish governments have considered the re-emergence of Russian influence over former Soviet bloc states as a major security risk. Throughout the conflict in Ukraine, Poland's policy toward Russia has been unerringly consistent—it has been in favor of EU-imposed sanctions and has agreed to host NATO bases on its territory (or support the establishment of such bases in other Central and Eastern European states). Meanwhile, when referring to its bilateral relations with Russia before the crisis, Slovakia stressed positive aspects of their shared history and the cultural affinity among Slavic nations. Although after the outbreak of the conflict Bratislava has provided assistance to Ukraine, it disagreed with the EU's move to impose sanctions. The Slovak government has warned that it would veto any sanctions that could harm Slovak national interests. Moreover, Prime Minister R. Fico has stated that his cabinet would not agree to admit Ukraine to NATO (Marušiak 2015).

Table 11: Overview of current and completed NATO and EU international crisis management operations in which Poland and Slovakia have participated.

	Operations	Slovakia (period/staff/description)	Poland (period/staff/description)
EU	EU Police Mission in the Palestinian Territories / EU Police Coordinating Office For Palestinian Police Support (EUPOL COPPS)	2012-2015 / 1 person / reconstruction of order, police training	September 2015–present / 1 person / combating corruption, training police forces
	EU Military Advisory Mission in RCA (EUMAM RCA)	–	April 2015–present / 2 people / training and expertise in the military and security sector, supporting the rule of law
	EU Advisory Mission for Civilian Security Sector Reform	–	July 2014–present / 1 person / supporting the government

Ukraine (EUAM Ukraine)		in the planning and implementation of the reform of security sector
EUNAVFOR Med Sophia	–	2015–present / 1 person / identifying trafficking routes, conducting rescue operations
EUNAVFOR ATALANTA Somalia	–	2010–present / 2 people / protecting the transport of humanitarian aid, escorting ships, helping vessels attacked by pirates
EU Training Mission Mali (EUTM)	March 2016–present / 2 people / restoration of constitutional order, fight against terrorist threats and organized crime	February 2013–May 2014 / 20 people / advisory-training tasks
EU Police Mission in Afghanistan (EUPOL Afghanistan)	June 2010–December 2015 / 2 people / supporting human rights, internal reforms, capacity building, improving long-term planning, implementation of policies, combating corruption	2008–present / 5 people / supporting human rights, internal reforms, capacity building, improving long-term planning, implementation of policies, combating corruption
EU Monitoring Mission in Georgia (EUMM)	January 2009–present / 1 person / supervising military and police units, ensuring compliance with the Memorandum of Understanding	September 2008–present / 20 people / supervising compliance with the adopted agreements, conflict prevention, monitoring security situation, stabilization, confidence building and promoting EU policy
EU Rule of Law Mission in Kosovo (EULEX Kosovo)	2008–present / 6 people / monitoring and advising local police on management systems and developing professional standards at regional police HQs, preparing and implementing EU projects on reorganization of police forces	2008–present / 135 people / protecting convoys and minorities, crowd control during riots, supporting the reform of the security sector and the bodies responsible for security and public order, developing and strengthening multi-ethnic police
EU Force in Bosnia and Herzegovina (EUFOR ALTHEA)	December 2004–present / 37 people / situational awareness, strengthening contacts with local authorities, representatives of NGOs and international organizations	2004–present / 190 people / guarding security, capacity building, training, supporting state authorities in handling redundant weapons and ammunition

Mission	Period / People / Task	Period / People / Task
EU Border Assistance Mission to Moldova and Ukraine (EUBAM Moldova/Ukraine)	2005–present / 5 people / border management, increasing operational capabilities of border guards, strengthening cross-border cooperation	2005–present / 18 people / border management, increasing the operational capabilities of border guards, strengthening cross-border cooperation
EU CSDP mission in Mali (EUCAP Sahel-Mali)	–	2015 (until September) / 1 person / training, providing advice and expertise for Mali security forces, improving the effectiveness of law enforcement and the work of the legal system
The European Union Integrated Rule of Law Mission for Iraq (EUJUST LEX Iraq)	–	2005–2013 strengthening the rule of law, providing expertise and assistance related to police, justice and human rights
EU Police Mission in Bosnia and Herzegovina (EUPM/BiH)	2003-2012 / 4 people / assisting with the fight against organized crime	2003–2012 / 6 establishing sustainable policing arrangements in accordance with best European and international practice
EUFOR Chad/CAR	–	July 2008–December 2009 / 400 people / protecting civilians and UN personnel, facilitating the delivery of humanitarian aid
EUFOR RD Congo	–	June 2006–December 2006 / 130 people / securing the region during elections
EU supporting action to African Union Mission (AMIS II) in Sudan/Darfur	May 2006–November 2006 / 2 people supervising the ceasefire	–
EU Rule of Law Mission to Georgia (EUJUST THEMIS)	–	2004–2005 / 1 person supporting, mentoring and advising Ministers, senior officials and other bodies of the central government
EU Police Mission in the former Yugoslav Republic of Macedonia (EUPOL Proxima)	–	March 2004–December 2005 / 3 people / monitoring, mentoring and advising police forces, helping to fight organized crime and promoting European policing standards

	Mission		
NATO	Resolute support (RS)		January 2015–present / 130 people / consultancy, training and assistance to the ANSF	January 2015–present / 150 people / consultancy and training related to the administration and security issues
	Baltic Air Policing Mission	–	2006–present / 100 people / protecting the airspace of Lithuania, Latvia and Estonia
	NATO HQ Sarajevo	December 2004–present / 1 person logistics	–
	Operation Active Endeavour	–	2005–present / 39 people / patrolling the Mediterranean basin, monitoring the safety of navigation on the main communication routes, detecting any irregularities in the maritime traffic, preventing illegal migration and smuggling
	Kosovo Force (KFOR)	September 1999–November 2010 / 135 people / patrolling and monitoring local objects, reconstructing transport infrastructure, demining, ensuring the continued and safe return of Kosovar Serbs, protecting the Serbian minority, assisting humanitarian organizations	June/July 1999–present / 230 people / monitoring the situation in border areas, supervising compliance with international agreements, assisting with the creation and maintenance of living conditions which provide essential safety to inhabitants, ensuring public order and transport of humanitarian aid
	International Security Assistance Force (ISAF)	May 2005–December 2014 / 343 people / reconstruction and stabilization, training the ANSF, monitoring the key objects	2004–2014 / 2600 people responsibility for the Ghazni province, stabilization tasks (including mobile patrols), training the ANSF, facilitating information sharing
	NATO Training Mission—Afghanistan (NTM-A)	–	2009–2014 / 70 people / supporting the development of capable and self-sustaining ANSF, mentoring of the Afghan National Army, developing professional Afghan National Police

NATO Training Mission—Iraq (NTM-I)	February 2005–December 2007 / 5 people / training and mentoring, helping Iraq to create effective armed forces	2004–2011 / 17 people / training and mentoring, helping Iraq to create effective armed forces
SFOR HQ Bosnia and Herzegovina	June 1998–December 2004/ 10 people / deterring hostilities and preserving peace	–
Stabilization Forces (SFOR)	August 2002–December 2003 / 21 people / contribution with one helicopter unit	January 1996–December 2004 / 500 people / deterring hostilities, preserving peace, contributing to a secure environment
Essential Harvest / Amber Fox / Allied Harmony in Macedonia	–	September 2001–April 2004 / 25 people / disarming ethnic Albanian extremists, ensuring the protection and continued support for international observers

Source: Adapted by author on the basis of official NATO and EU data.

Together, NATO and the EU cover a wide spectrum of activities, thus creating space for their members to participate in addressing security problems. They also serve the purpose of developing a cooperative approach to security and allow non-MS to get involved in the process through various partnerships. The cooperative security developed within NATO is based both on the security of its individual members and the collective approach to internal and external challenges. The European Union also enjoys the competence to conduct its own operations and other stabilizing activities, as defined in the 2003 European Security Strategy (and updated in its 2008 version) or the 2010 EU Internal Security Strategy. Thus, both organizations exhibit progression toward the next stage—i.e., cooperative security.

NATO and EU membership influences the security environment of their MS. Poland and Slovakia became integral parts of NATO's collective defense system. They have also contributed to the EU's CFSP and CSDP. Their status as full members brings about certain inevitable implications—be it the obligation to support joint operations or the need to assume responsibility for commonly made decisions and manage their implementation in national security policies. Today, it is NATO that is perceived as a decisive actor in the quest to guarantee the safety of Central European countries. However, one cannot exclude the possibility that in the future the EU's security architecture will be enhanced at the expense of the Alliance. Poland's active engagement within both organizations demonstrates its aspiration to a more prominent role in European structures. It is also the key to Warsaw's ambition to become a regional leader.

Final summary of Polish-Slovak cooperation in the area of security and defense

When examining cooperation between the two countries, one needs to take account of differences in quantifiable aspects such as size, economic and human potential, the composition of armed forces or access to natural resources. A quick glance at numbers reveals asymmetry in their positions. Nonetheless, the shared historical experience ultimately led to the creation of the Visegrad Group as an instrument of regional cooperation in Central Europe. The time that has elapsed since the Group was formed allows us to evaluate its members' initial intentions: pursuing compatibility, cooperation and mutual assistance in the process of integration with Euro-Atlantic structures. It seems that over the first decade of the Group's existence, the concerned governments differed in their perceptions regarding the essence of integration. Still, if one compares how the four states managed the process with how it went in case of other countries applying for NATO and EU membership (or association status), it becomes apparent that the Visegrad formula, despite its non-institutionalized character, had a positive impact. Keeping in mind their historical, geographic, ideological and strategic affinities, the Czech Republic, Hungary, Poland and Slovakia used it to evaluate domestic political developments. Such sub-regional cooperation also helped to overcome the pitfalls of a non-structured security policy that could not possibly work without proper coordination. The need to coordinate security policies was particularly strong in the context of NATO membership. The developments up to date suggest that in the future, the Visegrad countries may form new types of common policies and strategies, even when acting as fully involved members of the EU and NATO.

The Visegrad Group virtually guarantees the absence of serious tensions in Central Europe in the near future. Its presence will also help avoid major discrepancies between integration policies adopted by its members. As for now, Poland and Slovakia share an identical (or, at least, a very similar) perception of European security, partly due to being situated on the borders of the Schengen area, in the vicinity of Ukraine, Russia and the Western Balkans. Their most recent security strategies reveal a lot about their values, similarity of which prompts them to react the same way to contemporary threats and risks. The analysis presented earlier in this chapter leads to several conclusions. First of all, the increase in defense spending could become an important accelerator of bilateral cooperation, particularly given current changes in the international security environment. One factor that could hinder cooperation is the differing outlook on the origins of risks and threats emanating from the immediate surroundings—this refers to perceptions of Russia, as well as of the position and role of the USA (possibly also NATO) in ensuring the security of Central Europe. One needs to remember that Polish-Slovak cooperation in the area of defense is, to a significant extent, dependent on political decision-making. Hence, multilateral agreements often have to be approved also at the bilateral level. Moreover, due to the disproportion in defense budgets, as well as the size and capabilities of Polish and Slovak armed forces, many security-related projects implemented at the bilateral level have been conceived as a reaction to the requirements stemming from NATO and EU membership. Cooperation has been fairly advanced particularly with regard to the process of modernizing both countries' armed forces (although the future of projects Diana and Rosomak remains uncertain at the moment). Its success owes much to state-owned arms manufacturers and factories operating in Poland. If one tries to estimate the potential for future cooperation, one factor worth emphasizing is the possibility of joint participation in international crisis management operations. For Slovakia, given its rather limited capacity to engage individually, the joint approach opens up a much wider range of options (as exemplified by successful cooperation in Iraq).

If security cooperation is divided into the military and non-military aspects, then the latter is dominated by the European Union, which coordinates activities designed to eliminate identified threats. In some instances, the Visegrad Group also acts to that effect, although the overall framework is dictated by EU policies—a fact that leaves the Visegrad states no choice but to implement supranational regulations to deal with specific regional threats. In military aspects, the Union acknowledges that decision-making (including that related to cooperation) is the exclusive competence of individual nation states. As for NATO, the scope of cooperation is partly dictated by the Article 5 of the Washington Treaty. Any coordinated actions of two or more states can constitute a functional contribution to NATO and the EU's security and defense sub-system. All in all, majority of Polish-Slovak cooperation occurs within the multilateral format of the Visegrad Group, which ultimately prevails over strictly bilateral cooperation.

In the light of these considerations, it may be argued that areas holding most potential for further development are those covered by international organizations, such as migration, energy security, common projects related to the defense industry or enhancing military capabilities (air space protection, joint crisis management operations). These, however, still require individual approaches on the part of the MS when it comes to implementing specific concepts. The remaining thorny issue is the differing attitude toward relations with Russia, as well as divergent views on NATO's role in Central and Eastern Europe (albeit the latter problem is broader and resonates also across other EU and NATO MS). The areas of agreement and disagreement are not defined solely by national interests, as stemming from the position and structure of national parliaments and cabinets (particularly after the last parliamentary election in Poland that brought a slight change in the orientation of foreign and security policy). They are also shaped in reaction to events that affect whole integration organizations—the proposal to strengthen military presence in Central and Eastern Europe in case of NATO, and migration or the so-called 'Brexit' in case of the EU. These events and ideas are among key factors affecting how strategic problems and policy topics are formulated and considered. Therefore, both states have to take these issues into account when devising their own policies. Their admission to NATO and the EU means the integration process has also had a significant impact on their policies' direction, spurring bilateral and multilateral cooperation within the Visegrad Group—a grouping that both Poland and Slovakia perceive as a platform for developing common positions, making their voice heard in the Union, and (particularly for Poland, acting as its leader) pursuing their national interests. Finally, it can be argued that both states, their governments and bodies responsible for security and defense policy should be more consistent in the implementation of joint declaration—be it those adopted within international organizations, those agreed on by the Visegrad Group, or those negotiated by the Polish-Slovak discussion forum. Such consistency would provide these initiatives and ideas with a bilateral framework useful not only in garnering domestic political support or employing instruments from the supranational level (such as the Presidency of the EU Council), but also in searching for areas of common interest. As for now, the cooperation between Poland and Slovakia can be described as partial, with most of it being related with the institutional framework of NATO and the EU. Its practical expression can be found within the forum of the Visegrad Group. Examples not covered by these multilateral formats are much harder to find. A more comprehensive cooperation could be achieved through small successes in specific, narrow areas and activities. Such step-by-step approach should serve to build and strengthen mutual trust, which has always been and will continue to be the basis of any international cooperation.

Sebastian Jakubowski

Chapter four
Economic relations between Poland and Slovakia

Introduction

Central Europe's contemporary economic reality has been and still is shaped by three phenomena. The first one was the collapse of the Soviet bloc and the economic transformation of the post-Soviet countries. The second one was the successful EU enlargement that inducted the majority of Central European states into the EU and accelerated their convergence with the well-developed Western economies. The third one came in the shape of the global financial crisis that has brought back the old economic division between the North and the South of Europe. While economic relations between Slovakia and Poland have been naturally shaped by these macro-phenomena, the factors most important to their development are business activity in both countries and economic policies of the two governments.

The main goal of this chapter is to analyze economic relations between Slovakia and Poland. The first part of the analysis is focused on their direct bilateral economic relations. The second part examines the importance of strong economic ties between Germany, Slovakia and Poland. German dominance in Central Europe has been the most important factor shaping Polish-Slovak cooperation at the sub-regional level. The analysis is then concluded with consideration of the European context of Polish-Slovak cooperation.

Each part of the analysis has its specific nature and demands different methodological approaches. The first two parts of the study are based on the analysis of academic literature, supplemented with statistical methods. The third part, while also rooted in the secondary sources, refers to A. Moravcsik's theory of liberal intergovernmentalism. It should be emphasized that applying the model of liberal intergovernmentalism to the analysis of economic relations presents serious difficulties and is partially possible only with regard to the European context of Polish-Slovak cooperation.

Poland and Slovakia—economic relations in bilateral context

Economies of Slovakia and Poland are different. The first and most basic factor is simply the size of the two countries. Poland has a territory of 312,685 km² and 38.5 million citizens. Meanwhile, Slovakia covers only 49,035 km², and is inhabited by a population of approximately 5.4 million people. Naturally, the scales of their economies reflect this disparity. Slovakia's $161 billion GDP in purchasing power parity pales in comparison to Poland's $1.005 trillion. The fact that Slovak economy is much smaller means it is less diversified in commodity production but much more open to the external environment (Fitzová & Žídek 2015). The share of exports in Slovak GDP reaches 93%, while in Poland it amounts to only 49.4% of GDP (GUS 2014). This particular difference has a fundamental impact on economic performance and is one of the reasons why Poland was the only EU country to avoid recession throughout the 2008-2009 downturn. Meanwhile, Slovakia had to endure substantial travails along with all other European states.

Another significant dissimilarity is the employment structure. In Poland, a relatively large proportion of the population works in agriculture (12.6% of the entire labor force). Industry provides jobs for 30.4% and services for 57% of the working population. By comparison, Slovakia's employment structure resembles that in Western European countries, with low numbers for agriculture (4.2%), medium levels in industry (22.6%) and a very well developed services sector (73.2%) (GUS 2015).

Thanks to a better structure of the labor force by sector of occupation, Slovakia has a smaller population living below the poverty line (12.6%) and better income distribution (Gini index 26) (Banerjee & Jarmuzek 2010). The same indicators for Poland are slightly worse, with 17.3% of population living in poverty and the Gini index still at over 30 points (in 2012 it was at 32.4).

However, the two economies do share several important characteristics. Firstly, after the dissolution of the Soviet bloc, both Poland and Slovakia had to introduce significant reforms in the early 1990s (Lavigne 1999). Secondly, they enjoy the benefits of a relatively low-cost, highly-skilled labor force, reasonable tax rates, and favorable geographic location in the heart of Central Europe. Thus, trade and foreign direct investments are important factors of their development. In both countries, the manufacturing and financial sectors are dominated by foreign investors. Exports are directed mostly to other Euro-zone members. They also share strong economic ties with Germany (Popławski 2016; Wyżnikiewicz 2014). Industrial output accounts for a high proportion of their GDP: over 40% for Slovakia and over 30% for Poland.

The two countries face several common challenges. One of them is the problem of deficient road and rail infrastructure which, especially in the eastern regions, remains underdeveloped. Another is the outdated energy sector characterized by high costs, unpredictable regulatory oversight and growing governmental interference (Baláž & Margan, & Ružeková & Zábojník 2011). An additional long-term problem concerns the need to increase the spending on innovation, research and development (Ivanová & Masárová 2016; Zastempowski & Przybylska 2016). The two governments face the task of attracting further foreign investments—an effort that may be hindered by shortcomings in their business environment, such as a rigid labor code, slow dispute resolution, dysfunctional system of commercial courts, red tape and corruption (Guay 2016).

After their accession to the European Union in 2004 and before the global crisis broke out in 2008, both economies enjoyed a rapid growth, increasing foreign trade and investment activity. The trend was ubiquitous across Central Europe, with the notable exception of Hungary. Despite these positive factors, since the beginning of their economic transformation, Poland and Slovakia have faced problems of high unemployment and a relatively low GDP per capita when compared to the EU average (Berend 2009: 205).

Direct economic relations between Poland and Slovakia are shaped by two bilateral agreements:

- Agreement between the Republic of Poland and the Slovak Republic for the Avoidance of Double Taxation with Respect to Taxes on Income and on Capital of 18th of August 1994,
- Agreement between the Republic of Poland and the Slovak Republic on Reciprocal Investment Protection and Promotion of 18th of August 1994.

Mutual investments between Poland and Slovakia

Foreign direct investment (FDI) is an investment in a business by an entity from another country, which may take the form of either establishing business operations or acquiring business assets. According to the Organization for Economic Cooperation and Development (OECD), the criterion is the possession of at least 10% of the ordinary shares or voting rights at the general meeting of shareholders. If the criterion is not met, the investment is classified as a portfolio investment.

Numerous theories have sought to explain the determinants of FDI inflow. The most popular ones are associated with the OLI paradigm formulated by J. H. Dunning. He divided the motives behind making investments into four groups: market seeking, resource seeking, efficiency seeking and strategic asset seeking (Dunning 2000). In later studies (Dunning 2003, 2004, 2006) he also stressed the importance of the political framework and business environment, i.e., institutions.

Today, scholars differ in the focus of their analysis. Some of them concentrate on macroeconomic factors, while others emphasize institutional or geographical aspects. One group, with Mottaleb and Anyanwu among them, highlights market size (Mottaleb 2007, Anyanwu 2012). This perspective is followed by Busse and Hefeker, who also point to the significance of the market's growth rate (Busse & Hefeker 2007). The second group, including Carstensen, Toubal, Janicki and Wunnava, indicates the role of labor cost and quality (Carstensen & Toubal 2004; Janicki & Wunnava 2004). The third group points out the role of tax privileges (Clausing & Dorobantu 2005;). Some individuals within it, e.g. Guagliano and Riela, emphasize the role of special industrial parks (Guagliano & Riela 2005). Additionally, Owczarczuk analyzes the role of other investment incentives (Owczarczuk 2013). The fourth group of scholars indicates the role of infrastructure (e.g., Zhang 2001, Botrić &

Škuflić 2006). The fifth group highlights openness to trade (Anyanwu 2012). Finally, the sixth group argues that political risk should be also included in the analysis of FDI determinants (Busse & Hafeker 2007, Asongu & Kodila-Tedika 2015). The remaining groups emphasize the role of institutional conditions in countries trying to attract FDI.

It is necessary to note that statistical methodology for describing direct and portfolio investments has been modified in recent years, both by the International Monetary Fund (IMF) and OECD. The change and resulting lack of consistency with older data means it is not possible to analyze these phenomena over a long period of time. The introduction of the new methodology was spurred by several phenomena that called for adjusting the way we measure and describe international transactions. The most important among them were an intensification of cross-border economic ties, an increase of complexity of multinational enterprises, the creation of many new financial instruments and the rise in movement of capital between countries (IMF 2009).

The first of the changes indicated above took place in 2010. Some categories of portfolio investments between enterprises that belong to the same corporate group were redefined as direct investments. This created an apparent sharp discontinuity in mutual investments between Poland and Slovakia.

Another methodological amendment was introduced in 2014. Following the guidelines of international organizations, Polish National Bank started publishing data on direct investment based on the OECD methodology. Therefore, the data collected from 2010 to 2016 cannot be compared with that from previous years. Hence, by necessity, the analysis of FDI presented here is focused exclusively on the 2010-2015 period to guarantee comparability of statistical data. The OECD methodology will be used to examine both Polish investments in Slovakia and Slovak investments on Poland. Information developed by Polish National Bank is supplemented with the data from the Polish Central Statistical Office for a more detailed analysis of investments in Poland.

In modern economies, the circulation of capital between regions and countries has gained significant importance. Foreign direct investments are considered the safest and the most beneficial form of capital flow. From the host country's perspective, FDI generate multiple positive effects. The most important ones are the promotion of trade, financial stability, acceleration of economic development, technological modernization of the economy, improved living standards of societies, as well as international economic integration (OECD 2002). Moreover, FDI foster economic activity in less developed regions and improve economic efficiency (e.g., reduce unemployment as foreign investors create new jobs) (Dorożyński & Kuna-Marszałek 2016). Therefore, the states in Central and Eastern Europe have been trying to develop permanent mechanisms for attracting foreign capital (Estrin & Uvalic 2013, Subasat & Bellos 2013).

Poland and Slovakia have been successful in that respect over the last two decades. Their integration with the European Union further accelerated the inflow of capital to both countries. Advantages they offer to investors include a convenient location, solid human resources and relatively low operating costs. The region's rapid development has been facilitated by investments in infrastructure and social projects. In combination, all these elements made Poland and Slovakia attractive investment locations. The conditions in the two countries meet investors' expectations, as governments grant them various allowances and preferential tax solutions to enable faster business growth (Dorożyński & Kuna-Marszałek 2016).

Poland is still a country with a relatively limited domestic capital. Polish entrepreneurs are unable to spend much money abroad. Nevertheless, after Poland's accession to the EU, the value of Polish FDI was consistently increasing to reach €43.5 billion in 2013 (Gálová 2013). Thereafter, the introduction of a more restrictive EU policy towards tax avoidance and capital transfers resulted in a decreased FDI, limiting it to €22 billion in 2016 (see: Table 12). As for 2015, the largest Polish investments were located in Cyprus (€8.24 billion), Luxembourg (€4.53 billion) and the Czech Republic (€1.71 billion).

Poland and Slovakia's geographical closeness constitutes an opportunity for regional cooperation and establishing close economic relations. The afore-mentioned shared history, as well as similarities in political and cultural background are important elements that facilitate mutual investments between the two countries (Gálová 2013).

Although total Polish foreign direct investments in Slovakia remain relatively low, the size and importance of individual projects are notable. Factors such as the proximity of markets, continuing development of economic cooperation and growing investment potential are conducive to mutual investments. In fact, it can be argued that statistics do not fully reflect the investors' activity on both markets. This is so because after making initial investments, Polish and Slovak entrepreneurs often broaden their activity by creating new legal entities which, being registered locally, do not count as FDI even though their ownership remains foreign.

Table 12. Polish direct investments in Slovakia (end of year, in million EUR).

Year	Total Polish FDI globally	Polish FDI in Slovakia	Share
2010	33 264.0	177.7	0.53%
2011	40 887.6	151.6	0.37%
2012	43 492.2	238.1	0.55%
2013	22 265.7	292.5	1.31%
2014	22 839.4	292.7	1.28%
2015	21 959.6	306.4	1.40%

Source: Own calculation based on (National Bank of Poland 2016).

According to the Polish National Bank, after the end of the global financial crisis Polish direct investments in Slovakia have been consistently increasing, even as the total value of the country's global FDI has shrunk. In 2010, Polish enterprises invested only €178 million in Slovakia, which amounted to 0.53% of total FDI. Half a decade later, the annual value of investments made in Slovakia was at €306 million, accounting for as much as 1.4% of Poland's global FDI (see: Table 12).

As for sectoral distribution, Polish investments in Slovakia are focused primarily on consumer goods (furniture, food, textiles, footwear, household appliances), construction materials, as well as components for the automotive industry. The largest ones are associated with the production and distribution of beverages (Wadowice Group), production of cans (CanPack), IT services and software sales (Asseco Poland), as well as the distribution of construction and interior decoration materials (Mercury Market), as well as furniture (Nowy Styl Group, Black Red White). Several large Polish chain clothes and footwear stores (RESERVED, Gatta, Top Secret, Wojas, CCC, Bonprix, Cropp Town, House

Shop) have expanded their operations into Slovakia. Slovak market is also attractive for consulting companies (Accace Group, TGC Corporate Lawyers, ACARTUS) and debt collection agencies (Kruk).

Before the onset of the global financial crisis, both Poland and Slovakia enjoyed a steady influx of FDI. After 2009, the value of FDI made in Poland has stabilized at over €150 billion annually. At the end of 2015, the countries that invested most capital in Poland included the Netherlands (€30.3 billion), Germany (€27.3 billion) and Luxembourg (€19.2 billion). By comparison, Slovak investments have been minute in their scale, never exceeding €400 million in a single year.

Table 13. Slovak Direct Investments in Poland (end of year in million EUR).

Year	Total FDI in Poland	Slovak FDI in Poland	Share
2010	161 377.7	194.5	0.12%
2011	157 151.1	237.2	0.15%
2012	178 256.7	317.4	0.18%
2013	168 505.8	375.8	0.22%
2014	174 017.9	355.5	0.20%
2015	167 091.0	143.7	0.09%

Source: Own calculation based on (National Bank of Poland 2016).

Between 2010 and 2013, Slovak investments in Poland grew in value each year, peaking at €375.8 million—a number that constituted 0.22% of all FDI made in Poland in 2013. Thereafter, Slovak FDI in Poland decreased sharply: from 2014 to 2015 they shrank by as much as €212 million—the second biggest drop in any state's investments in Poland that year (the largest one coming from US businesses). As a result, in 2015 Slovakia's share in all FDI made in Poland was reduced to mere 0.09% (see: Table 13).

The annual publications of the Polish Central Statistical Office (GUS) on the economic activity of entities with foreign capital are based on information from statistical reports. Therefore, there is a significant divergence between the numbers published by the Polish National Bank and GUS. Data based on information from statistical reports is prepared only in Polish currency and includes foreign investments of small and medium-sized enterprises from other countries. This makes it particularly valuable for the analysis of mutual Polish—Slovak foreign investments.

According to the Central Statistical Office, year-to-year growth of FDI in Poland was fairly consistent from 2005 to 2014 and only slowed down once, in 2009, in the aftermath of the crisis. In 2005, total capital invested by foreign shareholders in Poland amounted to more than 111 billion PLN. 10 years later, it reached almost 200 billion PLN (see: Table 14). Data from GUS puts the Netherlands, France and Germany as the biggest providers of foreign investments in Poland. Entities from these three countries control over 50% of the entire foreign capital.

Table 14. Total foreign investments and Slovak investments in Poland.

Year	2005	2006	2007	2008	2009
Total foreign shareholders' capital in Poland (in million PLN)	111028.3	123196.6	131856.9	145996.9	153577.8
Total number of Slovak entities in Poland	80	92	88	98	112
Slovak shareholders' capital (in million PLN)	133.8	180.1	171.9	167.9	174.3
Slovak share in the whole foreign capital in Poland	0.12%	0.15%	0.13%	0.11%	0.11%

Year	2010	2011	2012	2013	2014
Total foreign shareholders' capital in Poland (in million PLN)	159267.2	164559.4	179372.3	188243.1	195796.8
Total number of Slovak entities in Poland	121	149	173	179	195
Slovak shareholders' capital (in million PLN)	178.7	257.3	284.5	309.7	272.1
Slovak share in the whole foreign capital in Poland	0.11%	0.16%	0.16%	0.16%	0.14%

Source: Own calculation based on "Economic Activity of Entities with Foreign Capital", (Główny Urząd Statystyczny 2005, 2006, 2007, 2008, 2009, 2010, 2011, 2012, 2013, 2014).

During the 2005–2014 period Slovak investments in Poland also significantly increased, but the growth was non-linear. The first spike came in 2006, when they jumped up by 34.6%, from 134 to 180 million to PLN. The next one happened in 2011: this time, investments increased by as much as 44%, from 179 to 257 million PLN. The record year was 2013, with 309 million PLN. Ever since then, Slovak investments in Poland have been slowing down.

While the value of Slovak investments in Poland has decreased over the recent years, the number of Slovak entities operating on the Polish market keeps growing. In 2005, there were 80 such companies. By 2014, there were almost 200. This is mainly because the majority of these entities are micro and small enterprises that employ less than 10 people and possess a capital no higher than $1 million. The number of larger companies (with a capital exceeding $1 million) has tripled, but remains very limited (see: Table 15). It is easy to spot that the record value of total Slovak investments in 2013 coincides with the highest annual value of investments from these large enterprises (285.2 million PLN).

Table 15. Enterprises with Slovak capital—over 1 million USD.

	Number of Slovak entities	Slovak shareholders' capital in million PLN
2005	6	118.6
2006	8	160.6
2007	7	156.4
2008	6	147.4
2009	8	152.2
2010	7	156
2011	8	238.4
2012	14	257.8
2013	14	285.2
2014	19	245.3

Source: Own calculation based on (Główny Urząd Statystyczny 2005a, 2006a, 2007a, 2008a, 2009a, 2010a, 2011a, 2012a, 2013a, 2014a).

The largest Slovak companies operating in Poland belong to several different sectors of economy. Asset Portfolio Servicing provides business support activities. Accace handles accounting, tax consultancy and auditing. Ekoservis Slovensko (through its Polish subsidiary,

Ekoservispol Sp. z o.o.) operates in waste management and recycling. ESET (Eset Polska Sp. z o. o.) is one of the most popular developers of antivirus and Internet security software. HB Reavis (HB Reavis Poland Sp. z o.o.) and Vahostav-SK (Vahostav-PL Sp. z o.o.) are construction and development companies. I.D.C. Holding (I.D.C. Polonia S.A.) is the largest Slovak producer of confectionary and pastry products. KOAM (KOAM Sp. z o.o.) manufactures plastic parts for the automotive industry. Trade Trans Invest owns and runs several transport companies, such as PKP Cargo Connect Sp. z o.o., Rentrans Cargo Sp. z o.o. and Trade Trans Log Sp. z o.o..

Table 16. Enterprises with Slovak capital by number of people employed.

Year		2007	2008	2009	2010	2011	2012	2013	2014
Entities with Slovak shareholders (10 and more persons employed)	Number of entities	40	44	40	40	46	49	45	47
	Slovak shareholders' capital (in million PLN)	169.6	162.0	165.3	169.0	214.4	235.0	258.1	207.2
Entities with Slovak shareholders (up to 9 persons employed)	Number of entities	48	54	72	81	103	124	134	148
	Slovak shareholders' capital (in million PLN)	2.3	5.8	8.9	9.7	43.0	49.5	51.6	64.9

Source: Own calculation based on (Główny Urząd Statystyczny 2007a, 2008a, 2009a, 2010a, 2011a, 2012a, 2013a, 2014a).

The most dynamic part of Slovak direct investments in Poland is based on small and medium-sized enterprises. In 2007, the number of companies employing 10 and more people was very close to the number of smaller investors, employing up to 9 people (see: Table 16). In 2014, the number of the latter exceeded the number of the former by over 100. As a result, small companies were three times as numerous as mid-sized and large enterprises combined. The dynamics of these small-scale investments were spectacular: between 2007 and 2014 they increased by an astonishing 2722%, from 2.3 to 64.9 million PLN. This was possible thanks to the low base effect and the emergence of several small, but very capital-intensive companies. Nonetheless, the highest-value investments were made by the biggest Slovak enterprises.

Mutual trade between Poland and Slovakia

The increase in trade between Poland and Slovakia has been enabled by several factors, including the EU accession, mutual FDI and the reorganization of global value chains. In 2004, Slovakia constituted the 16th largest market for Polish exports while in 2015 it ranked 11th. Since both countries joined the Union, Polish export to Slovakia has grown by 432%, from approximately €1 billion to almost €5 billion. Over the same period, import from Slovakia also grew, albeit by a smaller margin (274%, from €1.17 to €3.22 billion).

Immediately after the two countries acceded to the EU, the trade balance was tipped slightly in Slovakia's favor. That changed after 2006, with Poland recording only a small surplus at first. The major change in dynamics came in the aftermath of the crisis. Starting in 2010, Polish surplus rose sharply to reach almost €1.5 billion in 2015 (see: Table 17).

Table 17. Commodity imports and exports between Poland and Slovakia by CN/SITC/CPA/BEC section (in million EUR).

YEAR	2004	2005	2006	2007	2008	2009
IMPORT	1 175.20	1 495.20	1 781.90	2 190.30	2 700.50	2 190.90
EXPORT	1 065.80	1 367.80	1 838.80	2 219.90	2 851.60	2 244.50
BALANCE	-109.40	-127.40	56.90	29.60	151.10	53.60

YEAR	2010	2011	2012	2013	2014	2015
IMPORT	2 768.40	3 151.40	3 229.60	3 116.50	3 122.90	3 224.10
EXPORT	3255.2	3 356.70	3 725.10	4 090.60	4 203.60	4 612.20
BALANCE	486.80	205.30	495.50	974.10	1 080.70	1 388.10

Source: Own calculation based on (Główny Urząd Statystyczny 2004, 2005, 2006, 2007b, 2008b, 2009b, 2010b, 2011b, 2012b, 2013b, 2014c).

Slovakia's deficit was, for a while, somewhat limited due to the exchange of services between both countries—an area where Slovak companies maintained a small advantage even throughout the crisis.

However, since 2013 Poland has recorded a surplus also in this sphere (see: Table 18).

Table 18. Export and Import of services between Poland and Slovakia (in million EUR).

Year	2010	2011	2012	2013	2014	2015
Value of provided services	658.018	680.607	789.726	750.202	657.288	726.23
Value of acquired services	663.023	753.694	797.899	693.058	625.222	713.24
Balance	-5.005	-73.087	-8.173	57.144	32.066	12.99

Source: Own calculation based on (Główny Urząd Statystyczny 2004, 2005, 2006, 2007b, 2008b, 2009b, 2010b, 2011b, 2012b, 2013b, 2014c).

Slovakia is not the only Euro-zone country to experience trade deficit with Poland. Unlike Slovenia, Slovakia, Estonia, Latvia and Lithuania, Poland has not adopted the common currency yet (Li 2016). Moreover, Polish currency's rate against the Euro is not fixed. This provides Polish government with a unique chance to continue an independent monetary policy and benefit from the flexible currency exchange system. This is considered particularly useful during the periods of high economic and political risk (Acocella & Bartolomeo & Hallett 2016).

The global financial crisis caused a flight of capital from many emerging economies, including most Central European countries (with the Czech Republic being the sole exception). States whose currency had a flexible exchange rate faced a surge in the value of USD and the Euro. The depreciation of national currencies was especially painful for economies characterized by a high debt (be it sovereign, corporate or household) in foreign currencies (Allen 2009). Unlike in the case of Hungary or Ukraine, Poland's foreign debt was relatively low. Therefore, the depreciation of its currency brought certain positive effects that actually outweighed the negatives. Between July 2008 and February 2009, the EUR / PLN exchange rate changed from 3.2026 to 4.8999 (NBP 2016). This helped maintain the profitability of Polish exports throughout the time of the biggest economic turmoil. In the post-crisis era, the exchange rate has been more stable, oscillating between 4 and 4.5, with some experts predicting possible depreciation.

As Slovakia adopted the Euro in 2009, it was unable to replicate Poland's recipe for managing the effects of the crisis. Instead, it has been faced with the need to implement structural reforms in order to regain competitiveness (Toporowski 2015). These, however, require time and, for economic and political reasons, are more difficult to execute than the depreciation of national currency (Ćwikliński & Pawłowski 2015).

All in all, the global crisis has proven to be the one of the key factors that reshaped the structure of commodity trade between Poland and Slovakia. The latest data from GUS reveals that from January to September 2016, Poland recorded the largest surplus in food trade (+€289.8 million), including prepared foodstuffs (€147.9 million), live animals and animal products (€132.1 million), as well as fats and oil (€50.6 million). However, it also recorded a deficit of €40.8 million in vegetable products trade. The sector that brought Poland its second-biggest surplus was the chemical industry (€162.1 million). Transport equipment provided nearly as much: €161.6 million. The largest deficits came from mineral products (- €273.8 million), machinery and mechanical appliances, electrical and electrotechnical equipment (- €77.3 million), as well as base metals and articles produced from them (- €58 million).

Table 19. Polish import from and export to Slovakia of base metals and base metal-based articles (in million EUR).

Year	2004	2005	2006	2007	2008	2009
Import	412.60	498.00	563.90	647.10	791.10	551.80
Export	178.40	224.70	297.90	388.40	575.70	443.20
Balance	-234.20	-273.30	-266.00	-258.70	-215.40	-108.60

Year	2010	2011	2012	2013	2014	2015
Import	712.20	818.60	826.60	714.10	745.80	699.70
Export	739.1	577.70	633.50	672.40	675.60	691.90
Balance	26.90	-240.90	-193.10	-41.70	-70.20	-7.80

Source: Own calculation based on (Główny Urząd Statystyczny 2004, 2005, 2006, 2007b, 2008b, 2009b, 2010b, 2011b, 2012b, 2013b, 2014c).

The last category of the products has been the most important commodity in mutual trade between Poland and Slovakia since 2004. Base metals include iron, steel, copper, nickel, aluminum, lead, zinc and tin. They constitute some of the most common raw materials used in industrial production. Articles manufactured with their use are typically used as components and half-finished products.

When the two countries joined the EU in 2004, base metals and products made from them amounted to more than 35% of Polish imports from Slovakia, with the value of these imports estimated at €412.6 million. Record-high imports in that category were observed in 2012, when Polish industry bought Slovak materials and products worth €826.6 million (see: Table 19). While the value of imports in that category grew considerably (with a short interruption in the immediate aftermath of the crisis), their share in total imports from Slovakia dropped to 21.7% in 2015. This was due to the intensification of bilateral economic relations and the rapid increase in the total import value.

A similar pattern described Polish exports to Slovakia in the same category. In 2004, Poland exported far less than it imported (€178.4 million vs €412.6 million). Thereafter, the value of exports increased fairly systematically until the outbreak of the crisis. The 2008-2010 period was characterized by various perturbations, but since 2011 the exports have stabilized at well over €0.5 billion. Over the last couple of years, the value of exports and imports was similar, suggesting that the intra-industry trade between the two countries has matured. While Polish exports of base metals to Slovakia increased in value, the share of this category in total exports to Slovakia has remained around the same levels: in 2004, it was at 16.74% and in 2015 it was only slightly lower (approximately 15%).

Table 20. Polish import and export to Slovakia of machinery and mechanical appliances, electrical and electronical equipment (in million EUR).

Year	2004	2005	2006	2007	2008	2009
Import	176.9	206.5	269.9	367.8	509.5	546
Export	117.7	158.4	224.2	285.4	444.4	284.3
Balance	-59.2	-48.1	-45.7	-82.4	-65.1	-261.7

Year	2010	2011	2012	2013	2014	2015
Import	680.4	560.3	632.4	674.9	688	660.7
Export	621.4	453.1	535.4	569.7	563.5	598.5
Balance	-59	-107.2	-97	-105.2	-124.5	-62.2

Source: Own calculation based on (Główny Urząd Statystyczny 2004, 2005, 2006, 2007b, 2008b, 2009b, 2010b, 2011b, 2012b, 2013b, 2014c).

The fact that base metals and products made from them are the most important commodity in mutual trade between the two countries indicates that their economic relations are still based on intra-industry exchange (see: Table 20). This thesis is supported by the fact that the second key category of Polish imports from Slovakia includes machinery, mechanical appliances, electrical and electrotechnical equipment (both finished products and their components). In 2004, the value of these imports was estimated at €176.9 million, which constituted just over 15% of all Polish imports from Slovakia. In 2015, that share increased to over 20%, with the value exceeding €660 million. The effect of the crisis was visible also in this category, albeit with some delay—imports continued to grow until 2011. Thereafter, their value has remained stable.

Table 21. Polish import from and export to Slovakia of transport equipment (in million EUR).

Year	2004	2005	2006	2007	2008	2009
Import	71.50	63.00	83.00	175.60	213.50	172.50
Export	38.30	46.80	112.10	182.30	242.40	206.70
Balance	-33.20	-16.20	29.10	6.70	28.90	34.20

Year	2010	2011	2012	2013	2014	2015
Import	239.80	273.20	293.50	289.80	334.30	342.30
Export	250.3	337.10	417.70	464.00	468.80	601.10
Balance	10.50	63.90	124.20	174.20	134.50	258.80

Source: Own calculation based on (Główny Urząd Statystyczny 2004, 2005, 2006, 2007b, 2008b, 2009b, 2010b, 2011b, 2012b, 2013b, 2014c).

The same positive trend can be observed with regard to the import of transport equipment from Slovakia. This sector, ranked as the third most important in the mutual trade, includes products such as cars, motorcycles, railway and tram locomotives, as well as other machines and devices. When the two countries joined the EU, the import value was rather modest: approximately €71.5 million. Over the next 11 years it grew to €342.3 million. In terms of share in total imports, this category rose from just over 6% in 2004 to 10.6% in 2015. Here, the increase can be attributed largely to significant FDI in Slovak automotive industry that have been made over the last two decades and turned the country into one of the major automotive manufacturers in the entire Europe—a fact from which Polish consumers have undoubtedly benefited (see: Table 20).

The growth of Polish exports to Slovakia in the same category of commodities has been even more substantial, both in terms of value and share. In 2004, it accounted for only 3.6% of total exports to Slovakia and was estimated at merely €38.8 million. In 2015, the volume increased to €601 million and the share to 13%, making transport equipment the second largest category of export (see: Table 21). The fact that the balance from Poland's perspective shifted from a slight deficit to a reasonable surplus owed much to the change in the exchange rate of Polish currency against the Euro.

Table 22. Polish import from and export to Slovakia of plastics and rubber articles (in million EUR).

Year	2004	2005	2006	2007	2008	2009
Import	80.40	119.10	151.00	189.70	195.90	172.90
Export	66.50	104.10	159.60	196.20	242.00	201.40
Balance	-13.90	-15.00	8.60	6.50	46.10	28.50

Year	2010	2011	2012	2013	2014	2015
Import	227.20	270.40	248.50	274.40	242.20	276.70
Export	250.9	294.90	335.00	352.40	377.00	399.60
Balance	23.70	24.50	86.50	78.00	134.80	122.90

Source: Own calculation based on (Główny Urząd Statystyczny 2004, 2005, 2006, 2007b, 2008b, 2009b, 2010b, 2011b, 2012b, 2013b, 2014c).

Plastic and rubber products constitute a category of commodities that is partially linked to the automotive industry, as many of these items are used as components for vehicle production. It can be said that the exchange in this sector developed somewhat better than Polish-Slovak trade in general. In 2004 Slovakia exported €80.4 million in this category of products, while Poland's export was worth €66.5 million. In 2015 both variables were much higher: Slovak exports stood at €276.6 million, while Polish at €399.6 million, which corresponded to 8.5% and 8.6% of the total export respectively (see: Table 22).

Table 23. Polish import from and export to Slovakia of chemicals (in million EUR).

Year	2004	2005	2006	2007	2008	2009
Import	77.60	84.30	101.60	106.50	133.90	93.10
Export	71.10	97.00	134.60	149.40	171.00	128.20
Balance	-6.50	12.70	33.00	42.90	37.10	35.10

Year	2010	2011	2012	2013	2014	2015
Import	125.20	177.90	143.70	135.90	158.30	135.30
Export	157.2	205.60	206.30	257.80	310.20	323.70
Balance	32.00	27.70	62.60	121.90	151.90	188.40

Source: Own calculation based on (Główny Urząd Statystyczny 2004, 2005, 2006, 2007b, 2008b, 2009b, 2010b, 2011b, 2012b, 2013b, 2014c).

The chemical industry provided another vital sector of trade between Poland and Slovakia. Commodities that are included in this category encompass organic and inorganic chemicals, organic and inorganic compounds of precious metals, pharmaceuticals, fertilizers, inks, essential oils and resinoids, as well as perfumes, cosmetics, soap, cleaning agents, lubricants, waxes, glues, enzymes, explosive materials, pyrotechnic products and other miscellaneous chemical products. Before the financial crisis, Poland imported increasing amounts of chemicals from Slovakia: in 2004, it was €77.6 million and over the next four years the value of imports almost doubled (to €134 million). It peaked in 2011 at €178 million. As in other categories, the crisis put a dent in

Slovak exports, which have remained at below €150 million for the last several years.

Poland's success in dealing with the economic slowdown was apparent in how its export of chemicals was unaffected by the bleak financial landscape across Europe. Between 2004 and 2015, the value of chemicals exported to Slovakia almost quintupled, increasing from €71 million to €323.7 million. Prognosis for 2016 promised further growth (see: Table 23). Such a rapid development turned the chemical industry into one of the biggest exporters of Polish products to Slovakia.

Table 24: Polish import from and export to Slovakia of mineral products (in million EUR).

Year	2004	2005	2006	2007	2008	2009
Import	153.80	261.20	297.50	319.20	392.80	247.40
Export	271.90	277.90	343.90	296.20	292.70	242.60
Balance	118.10	16.70	46.40	-23.00	-100.10	-4.80

Year	2010	2011	2012	2013	2014	2015
Import	322.40	482.80	425.80	408.30	269.50	209.70
Export	347.9	469.40	317.00	312.90	287.20	322.70
Balance	25.50	-13.40	-108.80	-95.40	17.70	113.00

Source: Own calculation based on (Główny Urząd Statystyczny 2004, 2005, 2006, 2007b, 2008b, 2009b, 2010b, 2011b, 2012b, 2013b, 2014c).

Unlike all previously mentioned categories, mineral products have lost some importance as export articles between Poland and Slovakia. Products from this category include salt, sulfur, stone, plastering materials, lime and cement, ores, slag and ash, mineral fuels, oils and their distillates, bituminous substances and mineral waxes. Back in 2004, minerals were among the crucial trade commodities in Polish-Slovak economic relations. They accounted for over 13% of products imported by Poland from Slovakia and as much as a quarter of Polish export to its southern neighbor. In 2015, the respective percentages were far lower: 6.5% and 7%. Interestingly, though, the value of mutual trade in mineral products actually increased over the same period. Slovak export grew from €153 million in 2004 to a record high of €482 million in

2011, subsequently dropping below €300 million annually. Polish export in 2004 was worth €271.9 million and peaked at €469.4 million (also in 2011), only to decrease to €322.7 million in 2015 (see: Table 24). This strange pattern of increasing value and decreasing share indicates two things. Firstly, that both countries have advanced in the global chains of production from providers of raw materials and simple half-finished products to manufacturing machines, vehicles and other more complex objects. Secondly, it points to a quick development of intra-industry trade in numerous sectors.

Table 25: Polish import from and export to Slovakia of textiles and textile articles (in million EUR).

Year	2004	2005	2006	2007	2008	2009
Import	23.00	23.70	23.10	21.40	19.50	13.60
Export	26.90	39.10	51.00	70.10	85.00	62.60
Balance	3.90	15.40	27.90	48.70	65.50	49.00

Year	2010	2011	2012	2013	2014	2015
Import	15.60	17.30	18.40	48.70	76.60	203.70
Export	76.8	90.90	96.80	104.30	130.20	164.30
Balance	61.20	73.60	78.40	55.60	53.60	-39.40

Source: Own calculation based on (Główny Urząd Statystyczny 2004, 2005, 2006, 2007b, 2008b, 2009b, 2010b, 2011b, 2012b, 2013b, 2014c).

Textiles were one of the categories that enjoyed the fastest growth in Polish-Slovak trade after 2004, but have remained relatively less important overall than the previously mentioned sectors of minerals, chemicals or base metals. GUS classifies the following products as belonging to textiles: silk, cotton, wool, animal hair, woven fabrics, vegetable textile fibers, paper yarn, man-made staple fibers, lace, tapestries, trimmings, embroidery, as well as impregnated, coated or laminated fabrics and textile articles suitable for industrial use. Between 2004 and 2015 Slovak exports in this category increased from €23 million to €203 million, while Polish exports went up from €26.9 million to €164.3 million. This highly impressive growth can be attributed to mutual investments and the development of Polish furniture industry which uses various textiles as production materials (see: Table 25).

A separate part of the analysis should be devoted to trade in food. Although it has not attained the importance of some other categories of goods, the growth that occurred over the period examined here was extraordinary and deserves a closer attention (Rytko 2014). In international trade, various food products are divided into four different groups: 1) live animals and animal products; 2) vegetable products; 3) fats and oils; 4) prepared foodstuffs. Polish export has exploded in all four sub-categories, while Slovakia developed substantial export of vegetables.

Table 26. Polish import of food products from Slovakia (in million EUR).

Year	2004	2005	2006	2007	2008	2009
Live animals; animal products	2.50	4.40	7.50	12.80	17.40	20.30
Vegetable products	20.80	35.10	53.60	64.40	88.60	84.30
Fats and oils	2.10	0.70	0.60	2.50	0.80	2.10
Prepared foodstuffs	36.90	38.50	43.50	55.00	53.90	68.60

Year	2010	2011	2012	2013	2014	2015
Live animals; animal products	29.70	31.50	31.80	46.50	52.10	66.80
Vegetable products	97.30	118.80	125.00	112.90	108.10	117.40
Fats and oils	3.00	4.70	5.20	2.50	7.40	3.20
Prepared foodstuffs	88.00	109.70	148.50	119.10	102.20	114.00

Source: Own calculation based on (Główny Urząd Statystyczny 2004, 2005, 2006, 2007b, 2008b, 2009b, 2010b, 2011b, 2012b, 2013b, 2014c).

Upon joining the EU, both Poland and Slovakia faced several challenges regarding the restructuring of their agriculture sector (Bojnec & Fertő 2008). Nonetheless, thanks primarily to the low base effect, Slovak export grew by a huge margin in three of the four sub-categories. The value of live animals and animal products exported to Poland increased from a scant €2.5 million to €66.8 million between 2004 and 2015. Slovak vegetables also proved very popular with Polish consumers— the value of exports rose from €20.8 million to €117.4 million, making it the largest of the four sub-categories. Export of prepared foodstuffs more than tripled, reaching €114 million in 2015. Fats and oils remained the only sub-category of Slovak food exports characterized by negligible numbers (see: Table 26).

Table 27. Polish export of food products to Slovakia (in million EUR).

Year	2004	2005	2006	2007	2008	2009
Live animals; animal products	21.10	59.50	75.70	73.10	93.60	110.50
Vegetable products	21.80	21.80	24.10	29.50	53.40	40.30
Fats and oils	0.50	3.80	8.90	8.70	21.80	16.80
Prepared foodstuffs	53.00	83.70	106.30	140.50	173.10	156.70

Year	2010	2011	2012	2013	2014	2015
Live animals; animal products	155.9	177.30	206.80	235.60	240.60	245.70
Vegetable products	35.4	35.00	49.40	61.10	62.00	82.20
Fats and oils	17.3	23.10	11.90	105.30	89.80	92.00
Prepared foodstuffs	208.8	216.70	287.30	314.10	307.40	327.50

Source: Own calculation based on (Główny Urząd Statystyczny 2004, 2005, 2006, 2007b, 2008b, 2009b, 2010b, 2011b, 2012b, 2013b, 2014c).

While the development of Slovakia's food exports to Poland can be considered as solid, Polish food products enjoyed a truly spectacular success on the Slovak market. In comparative terms, the absolute record belongs to the goods from the 'fats and oils' sub-category: the value of their export increased by an astonishing 184 (sic!) times between 2004 and 2015, from a barely noticeable €0.5 million EUR to €92 million. Naturally, the growth is far more moderate when considered in terms of share in the entire Polish export to Slovakia (from 0.05% to just under 2%). The value of live animals and animal products export grew from €21 million to €245 million, while prepared foodstuffs went up from €53 million to €327 million. The latter sub-category's share in the entire Polish export to Slovakia reached 7.1% in 2015. In a complete contrast to Slovak exports, vegetable products were the only sub-category to record a decrease in the share of total export (although its value still increased substantially, from €21.8 million to €82.2 million) (see: Table 27).

Table 28. Polish import from and export to Slovakia of miscellaneous manufactured articles (in million EUR).

Year	2004	2005	2006	2007	2008	2009
Import	22.30	30.90	29.40	36.90	52.80	47.60
Export	86.10	106.20	125.80	165.00	176.70	133.90
Balance	63.80	75.30	96.40	128.10	123.90	86.30

Year	2010	2011	2012	2013	2014	2015
Import	41.70	49.30	50.40	51.50	64.00	88.80
Export	141.1	161.10	196.50	213.40	241.40	281.10
Balance	99.40	111.80	146.10	161.90	177.40	192.30

Source: Own calculation based on "Foreign Trade Statistics of Poland", Central Statistical Office.

It is also worth noting that Poland currently enjoys a significant surplus in the trade of various manufactured articles, including furniture, stuffed furnishings, lamps and lighting fittings, prefabricated buildings, toys, games and sports requisites. The largest contributors here are the furniture and construction industries. Their relative success (not only in Polish-Slovak economic relations, but also globally) has seen the value of export in this category grow from €86 million to €281 million between 2004 and 2015.

Polish import of miscellaneous manufactured articles from Slovakia enjoyed two periods of stable and fast growth. The first one came shortly after the two countries joined the EU and lasted until the onset of the financial crisis. It saw the value of import increase from €22.3 million in 2004 to €52.8 million in 2008. As signaled by statistics quoted above, the years 2009-2013 were characterized by a stagnation. However, since 2014 imports from Slovakia have regained some momentum and reached a record high of €88.8 million in 2015.

Poland and Slovakia—economic relations in the sub-regional context

In the post-crisis era Poland and Slovakia, together with the rest of the Visegrad region countries, have continued their fast economic growth. Their reasonably strong economic position, along with changes in the political environment across the European Union, has made them an even more attractive partner for the most important economy in Central Europe—Germany. As Poland and Slovakia were integrated into Germany's industrial export production and supply chain, these close economic ties with Berlin have shaped bilateral Polish-Slovak cooperation at the sub-regional level.

From Germany's perspective, Poland and Slovakia display a number of common features. Both are geographically close and culturally similar to German-speaking countries. Both have adopted uniform market rules which apply throughout the entire European Union. They also share long-standing industrial traditions and the substantial participation of industrial production in their GDPs. Moreover, their manufacturing and financial sectors are characterized by a significant presence of foreign capital. Both Poland and Slovakia strive to adopt an economic model based on exports, with foreign companies holding vital roles. Since their raw material resources are small or insignificant, they rely heavily on import in this crucial area of trade. Their energy systems are based on power plants using coal or nuclear energy—fuels which are gradually being replaced across the EU (Obadi & Korcek 2016). Both countries possess a solid reserve of highly-skilled workforce, with salary expectations noticeably lower than in Western Europe. Finally, both Poland and Slovakia recorded relatively good economic performance during the global financial crisis when compared to most other EU MS (Farkas 2016a).

All the above features made Poland and Slovakia an ideal area for the expansion of German trade and investments. Aiming to establish solid economic relations with the two countries, Berlin has supported their transformation since the beginning of the 1990s (Popławski 2016). After 2004, the ties between Berlin, Bratislava and Warsaw were further strengthened by the progressing modernization of Polish and Slovak economies, funded largely from the EU's Cohesion Policy. In fact, Poland was the biggest beneficiary of these funds. Slovakia also received significant support. Moreover, in the post-crisis era, both countries managed to maintain discipline in public finances and high levels of public investments (Stehrer & Stöllinger 2015). Resulting solid economic performance, coupled with lower (than in Germany) salaries, turned Poland and Slovakia into an industrial hub for German businesses (Farkas 2012).

The reasonably favorable economic landscape of the two countries survived the crisis surprisingly well, especially when considered against the background of increasingly difficult global situation. Consequently, their importance as Germany's partners has risen even further. The following section presents some data that illustrates their macroeconomic performance before, during, and after the crisis.

One of the obvious factors to be examined is gross domestic product (GDP), defined as the value of all goods and services produced less the value of any goods or services used in their creation. The calculation of the annual growth rate of GDP volume is intended to allow comparisons of the dynamics of economic development both over time and between economies of different sizes. A quick look at statistics reveals that after 2004 both Poland and Slovakia enjoyed a consistently faster GDP growth than the average for the Euro area (see: Table 29). It can be argued that, similarly to the increase in trade volume, the impressive growth rate was possible due to the low base effect. When the two countries started their transformation and undertook major reforms aimed at removing the remnants of the command economy in the early 1990s, their absolute GDP levels were very low. Over the next quarter of a century, they have made significant steps towards economic convergence with Western Europe, where the overall development level has made it much more difficult to maintain equally high growth rate.

Therefore, for analytical purposes it makes much more sense to compare Poland and Slovakia to other countries that have undergone a similar development process—namely, to other members of the Visegrad Group: the Czech Republic and Hungary. Such comparison shows that the post-crisis era became a turning point for both Poland and Slovakia, as the two states were able to maintain a growth rate exceeding that of not only the Euro-zone, but also of their Visegrad partners.

Table 29. Annual growth rate of gross domestic product in selected economies.

Year	2004	2005	2006	2007	2008	2009	2010
Euro area (19 countries)	1.8%	1.7 %	3.2%	3.0%	0.4 %	-4.5 %	2.1 %
Slovakia	5.1%	6.8 %	8.5 %	10.8 %	5.6 %	-5.4 %	5.0 %
Poland	5.3%	3.5 %	6.2%	7.0 %	4.2 %	2.8 %	3.6 %
Czech Republic	4.5%	6.4 %	6.9 %	5.5 %	2.7%	-4.8 %	2.3 %
Hungary	4.8%	4.4 %	3.9 %	0.4 %	0.9 %	-6.6 %	0.7 %

Year	2011	2012	2013	2014	2015	2016
Euro area (19 countries)	1.5 %	-0.9 %	-0.3 %	1.2 %	2.0%	1.7%
Slovakia	2.8 %	1.7 %	1.5 %	2.6 %	3.8 %	2.9%
Poland	5.0 %	1.6 %	1.4 %	3.3 %	3.9 %	2.8%
Czech Republic	2.0 %	-0.8 %	-0.5 %	2.7 %	4.5 %	2.4%
Hungary	1.7 %	-1.6 %	2.1 %	4.0 %	3.1%	2.1%

Source: own calculations based on: (Eurostat 2016).

Poland was the only country of the European Union that avoided recession during the global financial crisis. Meanwhile, Slovakia was hit quite hard (-5.4% in 2009), but managed to almost immediately rebound to the growth level resembling that from before the great tumble, recording an impressive 5% in 2010. Both countries continued their solid performance throughout the post-crisis era. As a result, the 2004-2016 period saw their economies increase by over 50% (see: Table 30), making them the fastest-growing economies in the entire European Union. The only European (but non-EU) country to outperform them was Turkey that recorded an increase of almost 80%. These statistics put them in sharp contrast to the Euro-zone and several other new EU MS (e.g. Hungary). The comparison of Visegrad Group members is particularly interesting, since in the aftermath of their democratic transition they were all targets of German business' expansion. Hence, they have long competed to attract the German capital (Orenstein 2014).

Table 30. Gross domestic product at market prices (chain linked volumes—index 2004 = 100).

Year	2004	2005	2006	2007	2008	2009	2010
Euro area (19 countries)	100.0	101.6	104.8	107.9	108.4	103.6	105.7
Slovakia	100.0	106.3	114.8	126.5	133.2	126.3	132.4
Poland	100.0	103.4	109.6	117.0	121.9	125.2	129.6
Czech Republic	100.0	106.1	113.0	118.9	121.9	116.3	118.9
Hungary	100.0	104.2	108.1	108.5	109.4	102.5	103.2

Year	2011	2012	2013	2014	2015	2016
Euro area (19 countries)	107.3	106.3	106.1	107.3	109.5	111.2
Slovakia	136.0	138.1	140.1	143.5	148.8	151.7
Poland	135.9	138.1	139.9	144.4	150.0	152.8
Czech Republic	121.1	120.2	119.7	122.7	128.0	130.4
Hungary	104.9	103.3	105.4	109.5	112.8	114.9

Source: own calculations based on: (Eurostat 2016).

However, their exceptional economic growth was not enough to solve the problem of a relatively low GDP per capita, which in both Poland

and Slovakia has remained well below the EU average. As presented below, the volume index of GDP per capita in purchasing power standards (PPS) is expressed in relation to the EU28 average set at 100. An index exceeding 100 means the country's GDP per capita is higher than the EU average. Basic figures are expressed in PPS, i.e. a factor that eliminates the differences in price levels between countries and allows for meaningful comparisons of GDP volumes.

Table 31. Gross Domestic Product per capita in purchasing power standards.

Year	2004	2005	2006	2007	2008	2009
Euro area (19 countries)	110	110	110	109	109	109
Slovakia	57	60	63	67	71	71
Poland	50	50	51	53	55	60
Czech Republic	78	79	79	82	84	85
Hungary	61	62	61	60	62	64

Year	2010	2011	2012	2013	2014	2015
Euro area (19 countries)	108	108	107	107	107	106
Slovakia	74	75	76	77	77	77
Poland	62	65	67	67	68	69
Czech Republic	83	83	83	84	86	87
Hungary	64	66	65	67	68	68

Source: own calculations based on: (Eurostat 2016).

The above comparison points to two important phenomena. First of all, the Visegrad countries still lag behind the majority of the EU. Moreover, Poland and Slovakia are among the Union's least developed members.

The second conclusion, however, is more encouraging: their economic growth has been noticeably faster than in the case of the Czech Republic and Hungary. Nonetheless, their GDP per capita in PPS remains far below the EU average (see: Table 31).

For Berlin, the far lower salaries demanded by Polish and Slovak employees have become an important opportunity for improving the competitiveness of German businesses. By moving production to Poland and Slovakia, companies have cut substantial portions of their manufacturing expenses. At the same time, they were able to exert pressure on the German workforce to reduce labor costs (Popławski 2016). Furthermore, high efficiency of business operations located in the Visegrad region has helped many important sectors maintain competitiveness during the global crisis. Low salaries and good productivity meant that enterprises were able to use Poland and Slovakia as manufacturing locations in those cases where the production process could not have been moved to Asia (IMF 2013).

Very high volume of trade between Germany, Poland and Slovakia confirms the thesis that the latter two countries have become a part of German economic hinterland (Farkas, 2016b). Over the last 15 years, the role of foreign trade in German economy has grown significantly. Since the beginning of the global financial crisis, Visegrad countries have become important trading partners for Berlin (Wyżnikiewicz 2014), providing German exporters with manufacturing components and so contributing to the improvement in trading competitiveness of the German economy (Popławski 2016).

From Poland and Slovakia's perspective, trade relations with Germany are even more important (Handl & Paterson 2013). As far back as 2000, Polish export to Germany was worth almost €12 billion, which accounted for nearly 35% of all Polish exports globally. Import was slightly larger in absolute terms (approximately €13 billion), but constituted a somewhat smaller (24%) share of total imports (Małachowski 2002). When one compares these numbers with data for the first nine months of 2016, it turns out that Poland's dependency on trade with Germany decreased, albeit not by much. Export was worth €39 billion and corresponded to 27.4% of total exports, while import costs were at €31 billion and accounted for 23.6% of all imports. Nonetheless, Germany remains Poland's most important trade partner.

An identical pattern can be observed in the case of Slovak-German trade relations. In 2015, Slovak companies exported to Germany goods worth over €15 billion, which constituted 22.4% of all exports that year. The import from Germany was far less substantial at just over €10 billion, but, with the share of 15.7%, it still positions Berlin as a vital partner for Bratislava.

The structure of Polish-German and Slovak-German trade is fairly similar. Dominant sectors encompass primarily industry. More specifically: machinery, vehicles and chemicals (Elekdag & Muir 2013). Interestingly, both German exports and imports include large volumes of vehicles, semi-finished goods, finished products and chemicals. One specific feature in German imports from Poland is their somewhat greater diversity: a large percentage of Polish export to Germany is composed of foodstuffs (Sporek 2015).

Poland and Slovakia—economic relations in the multilateral European context

As part of the (so far) largest EU enlargement, Poland and Slovakia acceded to the Union on 1st of May 2004. The new members from Central Europe were followed in 2007 by Bulgaria and Romania and in 2013 by Croatia. All the above-mentioned countries share not only relative geographical proximity, but also economic profiles. Joining the EU has thus become their chance for Europeanizing their economic cooperation—a task that, given the challenges that the global and European economy has faced over the last decade, seems more urgent than ever. Today, Poland and Slovakia, together with the rest of the Union, face a number of issues which, while not exclusively economic in their character, can significantly affect Europe's economic landscape over the coming years. These include: tackling the effects of the global financial crisis and the difficulties of the Euro-zone; managing the migration crisis and instability in Ukraine and the Middle East; handling Brexit; overcoming the overall economic slowdown and macroeconomic disparities undermining the competitiveness of the EU as a whole, as well as addressing deficiencies in transport, digital and energy infrastructure.

Since the nature and scope of the afore-mentioned problems far exceed the potential of both Poland and Slovakia, solving them calls for a broader cooperation at the European level. Aware of that fact, the governments in Bratislava and Warsaw have tried to play an active role in reaching a Europe-wide agreement in regard to the measures that should be taken to address each issue. Their bilateral cooperation was most visible and successful when it came to shaping and absorbing European funds and covering EU policies. So far, the two governments have been able to agree on and articulate a consistent position in negotiations over multiannual financial frameworks for the 2007-2013 and 2014-2020 periods. Their primary focus was on drafting and pursuing common positions with regard to the Cohesion Policy. Such close cooperation resulted in cohesion funds being widely accessible to the new MS.

Both Poland and Slovakia belong to the biggest beneficiaries of the 2007-2013 and 2014-2020 financial agreements. They have obtained very substantial amounts of funding within the framework of the Cohesion Policy and Common Agricultural Policy (CAP). Between 2014 and 2020, Slovakia will receive almost €20 billion, of which €14 billion will come from the former and almost €5 billion from the latter. Poland's share in the 2007-2013 framework was as high as €95 billion: €68 billion through the Cohesion Policy and €27 billion through CAP. Between 2014 and 2020 its allocation of EU funding will be even larger: €105.8 billion (€72.8 billion from the Cohesion Policy and €28.5 billion from CAP). These numbers put Warsaw as the biggest beneficiary of the EU's 2014-2020 budget. It should be emphasized that both Poland's and Slovakia's allocations in the 2014-2020 framework were higher than in the 2007-2013 perspective (Marušiak 2013).

Slovak-Polish support for the development of the internal market

Further development of the internal market has constituted another important field for Polish-Slovak cooperation. The market itself is, unquestionably, the most successful aspect of European integration. While it brings tangible benefits to citizens and companies in all MS, Poland and Slovakia are among the biggest beneficiaries of the opportunities it offers. Unfortunately, in recent years it has come under intense pressure which today manifests itself in protectionist tendencies. Responding to this challenge and mirroring the efforts of European institutions,

Poland and Slovakia have worked together to ensure that the four fundamental freedoms (i.e. free movement of goods, services, people and capital) are still respected. Both Bratislava and Warsaw consider the unrestricted movement of workforce as a fundamental right that comes with the status of an EU citizen and an undisputable value to be protected by the Union. They have also cooperated on the implementation of the Strategy of the Internal Market in Goods and Services, which envisions steps to be taken with regard to the services sector, small and medium enterprises, start-ups and the single market in goods. Both countries strongly support the elimination of geo-blocking, the creation of a friendly environment for start-ups, as well as the introduction of services passports. Given the various excessive restrictions and conditions for providing services that remain in practice in the EU, Polish-Slovak cooperation in this respect is of utmost importance. Further liberalization of the freedom to provide services and their unrestricted movement within the EU are especially important for the small and medium-sized enterprises from the two countries. Therefore, their governments strongly support service providers' ability to travel to other MS and operate in Western European markets.

Moreover, Bratislava and Warsaw have made substantial joint efforts towards the goal of developing energy infrastructure and fostering the single European energy market. Poland's and Slovakia's strategic positions depend on the extent to which they can free themselves of dependence on Russian energy sources. One key step in that direction is the construction of the missing parts of the North-South gas interconnector, currently prioritized by the EU as a crucial transit corridor. When completed, the Polish-Slovak section of the interconnector will significantly improve energy security of the two countries by diversifying options for transferring gas within the region (European Commission 2011). The 158-kilometer interconnector will link the two countries through a gas pipeline from the compressor station in Veľké Kapušany in Slovakia to the compressor station in Strachocina, Poland. It will have a capacity of 4.7 billion cubic meters per year in the Poland-Slovakia direction and 5.7 billion cubic meters per year in the Slovakia-Poland direction (Law-Now 2016). Its opening is scheduled for 2021. Another undertaking of regional importance and implications is the construction of an LNG terminal in Świnoujście (Poland). Slovakia fully supports Warsaw's plans in this regard.

Both countries have made efforts to promote the completion of the single EU energy market as a key element of the Union's climate and energy policy. At the same time, they have underlined the sovereign right of every country to freely choose the most suitable energy mix. Representatives of the two governments have repeatedly stressed that each state should retain primary responsibility for areas such as nuclear power generation or the use of conventional and unconventional energy sources, including renewables (Visegrad Group 2014c). Such statements have been accompanied by plans to turn nuclear power into an energy source on par with renewable sources. Moreover, Poland tries to promote the development of certain technologies, such as hydrocarbons, that could also be utilized in a sustainable manner. The ultimate goal behind these efforts is to guarantee a level playing field for all technologies available on the energy market, while fully respecting the principle of technological neutrality and allowing MS to choose most appropriate measures of safeguarding the security of electricity supply (Visegrad Group 2016c).

Finally, Polish-Slovak cooperation has encompassed actions aimed at supporting the development of the Digital Single Market (DSM). As envisioned by the EU, such market would include much more than just common digital infrastructure. Governments in Bratislava and Warsaw consider modern technologies as holding great potential for boosting economic growth and job creation. They believe that building an economy based on digital technologies is a challenge of vital importance. In their eyes, formulating the DSM strategy is a way to enhance competitiveness of such technological solutions globally. The Strategy should include plans for deepening regional cooperation, with the goal of broadening societies' digital knowledge and activity through training and education. Given the scale and complexity of these tasks, the implementation of DSM calls for the use of public resources, but also for involving non-governmental organizations, researchers, businesses and social partners engaged in efforts to develop digital competences (Visegrad Group 2016c).

Cooperation for the development of transport infrastructure

Transport infrastructure in both Poland and Slovakia, particularly their eastern parts, still exhibits serious deficiencies. Cross-border links remain a problem all across Central Europe. This fundamentally hinders the economic development of the entire region and is a great burden on its competitiveness. Realizing that one possible method of addressing the issue more effectively is by lifting it to the European level, Bratislava and Warsaw cooperated on convincing European institutions of the strategic importance of several infrastructural investments. As a result, the Commission has agreed to finance two major road developments—the Baltic-Adriatic Core Network Corridor and Via Carpathia—from EU programs. The former constitutes one of the most important trans-European road and railway links and is included in the "TEN-T—Connecting Europe" program. The concept of core network corridors was introduced to facilitate a coordinated implementation of crucial infrastructural connections (including cross-border connections), remove potential bottlenecks in transport networks, as well as promote modal integration and interoperability. The Baltic-Adriatic Corridor is a trans-European road and railway trail that, when finished, will stretch over 2400 km to connect the Baltic and Adriatic seas. The Corridor's route crosses industrial areas in Southern Poland and continues through Bratislava, Vienna, the Eastern Alpine region and Northern Italy. It will comprise important railway projects such as the Semmering base tunnel and Koralm railway in Austria, as well as cross-border sections between Poland, the Czech Republic and Slovakia (European Commission 2016).

The latter investment—Via Carpathia—has so far not been included in the TEN-T program. Nevertheless, its importance has also been recognized, as it aims to connect the North Sea-Baltic Corridor with the Orient/East Med Corridor, both of which are parts of TEN-T. Via Carpathia will be an international road trail leading from Lithuania, through eastern Poland, Slovakia, Hungary, Romania and Bulgaria to Greece. It will reach both the Black Sea and the Aegean Sea. It is to be completed by 2030. The Polish section will be 630 km long and will go from Budzisk on the Lithuanian-Polish border, through Białystok, Lublin and Rzeszów to Barwinek on the Polish-Slovak border. The Slovak section,

127 km long, will go through Kosice and finish in Milhorst on the Slovak-Hungarian border. This transport corridor project will be crucial for the development of Poland and Slovakia's eastern regions.

Missed opportunities in Slovak-Polish cooperation

Although Poland and Slovakia were able to successfully cooperate on several occasions, they have not taken the opportunity to closely coordinate their sectoral policies. The most striking example of this failure is the adoption of the Euro. Upon signing their accession treaties in 2003, all new MS took on the obligation to introduce the common currency. However, so far only Slovenia, Slovakia, Estonia, Latvia and Lithuania have joined the Euro-zone (Li 2016). In the case of Poland, the process was delayed by its inability to meet the Maastricht criteria. Subsequent outbreak of the crisis in the Euro-zone and the resulting economic uncertainty weakened the Euro's position and appeal. Polish entrepreneurs and citizens have become more hesitant toward the concept of the common currency, fearing that its introduction would hurt the economy and lead to higher consumer prices without providing the counterbalance in the shape of faster growth. At the same time, Polish currency's depreciation against foreign currencies has been highly beneficial for exporters who have come to appreciate this side effect of the global financial crisis. At this point in time, Polish business sector is afraid that the Euro-zone has been transformed from a monetary union to a "transfer and debt" alliance. Entrepreneurs feel the need to carefully weigh potential costs and benefits of a possible future move to adopt the Euro. As a result, joining the Euro-zone is not being seriously debated at the moment.

While adopting the Euro has provided possibly the most high-profile case of shortcomings in the cooperation between Bratislava and Warsaw, even more important is their failure to coordinate the entire area of economic and competition policies, as well as labor- and tax-related legislation (Takáč & Sobják & Kaszab & Trejbal 2013). In fairness, it should be noted that the parties guilty of this negligence include all new EU MS. Since all post-communist countries share a similar economic profile, whereby development and innovation are driven by FDI and foreign-owned multinational corporations, joint formulation of strategies for attracting investments and fostering business activity seems to be a natural common interest for the entire Central Europe. Such strategies, had they been worked out, should have included coordination of tax systems and labor markets. Cooperation in this area has held significant potential for boosting the economies of many Central European states (Sobják 2012).

Seemingly oblivious to the above conclusion, the new EU members have instead engaged in fierce bidding wars over foreign direct investments (Medve-Bálint 2014). This competition began almost immediately after their democratic transition, when foreign capital started to flow quickly towards the region (Walsch 2014). The countries in question offered skilled and cheap labor, tax exemptions and investment grants for foreign-owned multinational businesses. Ever since the end of the 1990s, Slovakia has been the leader in using state aid to enhance FDI, particularly in the automotive industry. Allowances and preferential treatment granted to Kia and Jaguar Land Rover are good examples of that generosity.

The path selected by Central European countries has several far-reaching consequences. Firstly, salaries are still considerably lower than in Western and Southern Europe. Secondly, despite having been in the EU for over a decade, the new MS have remained junior partners to the key European actors, with relatively little influence on the Union's affairs. Hence, the shortcomings in cooperation have cost the region a chance for faster convergence with Western European economies and living standards (Medve-Bálint 2014).

Final remarks on economic relations between Slovakia and Poland

In terms of economic profile, Poland and Slovakia share a number of similarities that partly result from, but go well beyond, their common history and geographical proximity. They have long-standing industrial traditions and industrial production accounts for a substantial portion of their GDPs. Upon undergoing the transformation from command to free market economy, both countries constructed their economic models to gradually converge with the uniform market rules set by the European

Union. Their development has been based around attracting FDI, particularly in the manufacturing and financial sectors. As their domestic supply of raw materials is relatively low, they are greatly dependent on imported energy sources. In recent years, their growth has been driven to a substantial extent also by exports. The fact of joining the EU has provided the two governments with the chance to intensify their economic cooperation on both bilateral and multilateral bases.

The first part of the above analysis, focused on direct bilateral relations, details the spectacular growth of trade between Poland and Slovakia. For obvious demographic reasons, Poland's potential as a market for Slovak businesses is far greater than Slovakia's value for Polish companies. While Poland is the third-biggest recipient of Slovak exports, Slovakia ranks 11th among the importers of Polish goods. Nonetheless, the sheer numbers describing the development of trade are unquestionably impressive. Between 2004 and 2015, Polish export to Slovakia has increased in value from over €1 billion to almost €5 billion (by exactly 432%). Over the same period, the import of Slovak products has risen from €1.17 billion to €3.22 billion—an increase of 274%.

This truly exciting boom in bilateral trade would not be possible without mutual foreign direct investments between Slovakia and Poland. During the first decade of their EU membership, Slovak investments in Poland more than doubled, going from 134 million PLN in 2005 to 272 million PLN in 2014. Polish FDI in Slovakia have recorded the biggest jump in the post-crisis era. In 2010, their total value amounted to €178 million. In 2015, they reached €306 million.

The second part of the analysis was focused on strong economic ties between Slovakia, Poland and Germany. At the sub-regional level, Polish and Slovak economic reality has been shaped to a significant degree by their solid bond with Berlin and the fact they were integrated into German industrial export production and supply chain. Investments made to that end by German businesses accelerated Poland and Slovakia's economic growth and enhanced their international competitiveness.

The final part of the analysis covered the multilateral context of economic cooperation. After the two countries joined the EU in 2004, their ties were strengthened through the process of modernization which was largely funded from the Union's Cohesion Policy and CAP.

Thanks to concerted efforts in the process of negotiating long-term financial frameworks, both Poland and Slovakia managed to obtain hefty national allocations, with Warsaw becoming the biggest net beneficiary of the EU budget for the 2014-2020 period. At the same time, in the post-crisis era the two governments have managed to maintain a solid discipline of public finances and good levels of public investments.

Given the vital impact of European integration on their economies, further development of the European internal market has remained an important field for Poland and Slovakia to cooperate on. Hence, Bratislava and Warsaw have worked together to remove the existing barriers, particularly in the sector of services, and to ensure the continued observance of the four key freedoms that the single market is based upon.

While some joint efforts made at the European level have certainly had their desired impact, there is no question that the two countries did not fully utilize the potential of their cooperation. They failed to agree on a common path towards the Euro-zone, which resulted in Poland retaining its national currency to this day. Perhaps even more importantly, Poland, Slovakia and other states of the region have not developed any common strategies for attracting FDI and multinational businesses. Their competition over foreign investments has instead led to bidding wars and possibly slowed Central Europe's pursuit of Western levels of economic development.

The future of Polish-Slovak cooperation depends on the scale of their participation in the fourth industrial revolution and further European integration. In the coming decade, to avoid the middle-income trap, states will have to successfully navigate the challenge of shaping and absorbing the latest technologies. Moreover, the European Union is currently under great pressure that might lead to the implementation of the two-speed Europe concept. Should different parts of the Union integrate at different levels and pace (depending on their political situation), Slovakia, being the member of the Euro-zone, may well be included into the "core" of the integration process. By delaying the decision to adopt the common currency, Poland risks being marginalized and put on the fringes of further integration. The realization of this negative scenario would surely (at least to some extent) impact the commonality of interest between Poland and Slovakia and hamper their economic cooperation in the future.

Igor Kosír

Chapter five
Polish-Slovak cooperation in other fields of neighborhood relations

Introduction

Parallel to the development of bilateral political, economic and security relations, the analyzed period (i.e. between 2004 and 2016) saw a significant progress in several other areas of cooperation, achieved in the larger framework of the European integration. This chapter scrutinizes to what extent national interests, resulting from societal preferences formulated in the two states, have shaped their attitudes and positions with regard to both bi- and multilateral cooperation in areas such as science, culture, as well as preservation of heritage and folklore. When considering this issue, one should remember that the importance of education and science has increased greatly in the current era of globalization, making these fields key factors of nations' competitiveness. The World Economic Forum (WEF) acknowledged this trend in its Global Competitiveness Index framework. The chapter also includes the analysis of bilateral regional cross-border cooperation, as well as multilateral cooperation within the broader formula of Euroregions. This heterogeneous area is influenced as much by Poland and Slovakia's bilateral relations as by their membership in international organizations—primarily, in the process of European integration[22].

---

[22] The European Economic Area, based on the Oporto Agreement of May 2nd, 1992, (EEA) represents a higher-order integration of the EU and the European Free Trade Area (EFTA), minus Switzerland. Three EFTA states—Norway, Iceland and Lichtenstein—are integrated with the EU's free trade area and common market. The Union for the Mediterranean (UfM) is a unique model of integration, comprising 14 partners from North Africa and the Middle East, including Turkey, Israel and Mauretania. Currently, after Syria suspended its membership in 2011, the UfM has 42 members. The UfM represents an attempt (so far, not particularly successful) at flexible, exogenous integration with the EU's free trade area. It was created on July 13th, 2008, at the Paris Summit for the Mediterranean, attended by 42 delegations (including Libya as an observer), as a step to reinforce the Euro-Mediterranean Partnership (Euromed) set up in

The increasing interdependence and processes such as economic integration and globalization mean that interactions between the internal and external environment of every state are inevitable. Hence, none of these spheres (internal and external) can be considered as isolated from the other. In addition, the mainstream (i.e. European) model of continental integration is facing several substantial challenges—for example, devising and implementing a post-Brexit strategy. The quality and exact shape of bilateral cooperation among the future EU27 will significantly affect the process of European integration.

The subject of this chapter requires considering the impact European integration has had on Polish-Slovak relations since both countries joined the Union in 2004. It also calls for a close look at how effective the regional Central European forum—i.e. the Visegrad Group—has been in pursuing its members' individual and collective interests. This is because Poland and Slovakia's success in integrating with the EU owes a lot to their efforts at the local and regional level.[23]

Dynamics of the relations in the bilateral context

This chapter examines bilateral relations between Poland and Slovakia with regard to areas such as education, science, culture and comprehensive cross-border cooperation. First, it presents main evolutionary trends observed in the two countries in the above-mentioned fields. Then, it proceeds to a detailed analysis of strategic steps that influenced both actors throughout the period from 2004 to 2016.

Such an approach makes it possible to identify similarities and differences in Poland's and Slovakia's attitudes toward various domestic developments and the two key levels (local and regional) of bilateral cooperation. It also allows the author to draw certain conclusions as to areas that hold substantial potential for future cooperation. Subsequently, the chapter goes on to present formal agreements related to bilateral cooperation in the areas of science, education, culture and

---

1995. Until now, its biggest successes are leading to Malta and Cyprus' full membership in the EU, as well as establishing a free trade regime (a customs union) with Turkey.

[23] In this context, the terms "local" and "regional" are used from the perspective of a single state, rather than from the global perspective.

cross-border zones, as well as meetings between the representatives of both states. All the above-mentioned elements influenced the decisions on cooperative projects that have been launched since Poland and Slovakia acceded to the Union in May 2004. As one will be able to note, EU membership has been crucial to these developments.

Brief assessment of the legal framework for bilateral relations in the sectors of education, science, culture and regional cooperation

The key bilateral agreements setting up the legal background for cooperation were negotiated and signed in the period before Poland and Slovakia joined the EU. This was achieved thanks to a positive approach and efforts on the part of both governments, as well as numerous domestic institutions. These documents, very important for shaping cooperation during the challenging period of democratic transition, were drafted and signed at the governmental or sectoral level. They included:

1) The Agreement between the Government of the Slovak Republic and the Government of the Republic of Poland on Cross-Border Cooperation, signed in Warsaw on 18th August 1994. The document, registered in the Slovak legal system as low no. 44/1995, was drafted after an initial period of hesitation and uncertainty in the early 1990s. It introduced a very motivating framework for the development of cross-border relations.

2) The Agreement between the Government of the Slovak Republic and the Government of the Republic of Poland on Cultural, Educational and Scientific Cooperation, signed in Bratislava on 23rd March 2000. While originally designed to be in effect for five years (beginning in 2001), it allows for automatic extension for further five-year periods—an option that both governments have been exercising up to the present day.

3) The Agreement on Cooperation between the Ministry of Education of the Slovak Republic and the State Committee for Sport and Tourism of the Republic of Poland, signed in Zakopane on 19th February 1996.

4) The Program of Cooperation between the Ministry of Education of the Slovak Republic and the Ministry of National Education and Sport of the Republic of Poland for the years 2003-2006, signed in Warsaw on 20th December 2002. Originally val-

id until 2006, it has later been repeatedly prolonged for one-year periods.

The above-stated agreements have served to build the basis for accelerating, widening and deepening Polish-Slovak cooperation in several areas. The two countries decided to support the activities of the Polish-Slovak Commission for Humanities. They also identified state universities that would participate in academic exchange programs. It was agreed that the universities of Warsaw and Łódź, along with the Jagiellonian University in Kraków, would host lecturers of the Slovak language and literature, while Polish language and literature scholars would be regularly sent to the Comenius University in Bratislava, Prešov University and Matej Bel University in Banská Bystrica. Moreover, the legal arrangements allowed further institutionalization of cooperation. Bodies such as the Slovak-Polish Intergovernmental Commission for Trans-border Cooperation and the Culture Working Group assisted in the development of bilateral relations.

Overview of Polish-Slovak relations in the areas of education, science, culture and cross-border cooperation

It has to be emphasized that Slovakia is a relatively minor partner for Poland. This was evident both before and throughout the period analyzed here. Moreover, in some respects, such as attracting foreign investments, the two countries are direct competitors. Historically, the factor limiting their ability to draw foreign investors has been an insufficient infrastructure—a predicament that strongly affects their mountainous border areas. Nonetheless, despite a certain degree of rivalry, Poland and Slovakia have launched several very interesting joint projects and their cooperation has seen some success. A couple of initiatives, although terminated at some point, provided opportunities for both partners to learn about and develop a better understanding of one another.

Education and science

The education sector in both countries used the framework provided by bilateral agreements to develop cooperation both quantitatively and qualitatively. As a result, the last quarter of a century has seen the emergence of a large network of contacts among Polish and Slovak universities, affecting research and teaching staff, as well as students. Thanks to the EU's student exchange scheme (currently functioning under the Erasmus+ program), Poles and Slovaks have had a chance to meet and learn about each other. The academic exchange has not been narrowed down exclusively to top universities in Warsaw, Kraków, Bratislava and Košice—it has also encompassed numerous other institutions, many of which were created after 1989. In one case, a Polish scholar, Tadeusz Zasępa, was even appointed as the chancellor of a newly created Catholic University in Ružomberok (his tenure lasted from 2008 to 2014).

Table 32: An increase in the number of universities in Poland and Slovakia, 1990-2012.

Academic year	Poland		Slovakia	
	Number of state universities	Number of private universities	Number of state universities	Number of private universities
1990/1991	106	6	13	0
2011/2012	103	350	23	13

Source: Nestorová-Dická 2013: 199.

Table 33. An increase in the numbers of university students in Poland and Slovakia, 1990-2012.

Academic year	Poland		Slovakia	
	Students at state universities (in thousands)	Students at private universities (in thousands)	Students at state universities (in thousands)	Students at private universities (in thousands)
1990/1991	404	-	64	-
2011/2012	1 218	518	173	39

Source: Nestorová-Dická 2013: 199.

The very dynamic growth in the number of universities, evident in both Poland and Slovakia, has created certain issues with regard to capacity and teaching quality. Demographics have also had an increasing impact on this sphere, with numbers of students actually decreasing over the last couple of years. Despite these difficulties, the EU research and development policy has ensured a substantial potential for common initiatives. The best academic institutions in Poland and Slovakia have, on their part, proven fairly creative and willing to work together, providing a model for other bodies. Cooperation between national academies of science, headquartered in Warsaw and Bratislava respectively, has also shown a positive development trend. As for the influence of Europeanization, its impact on Polish and Slovak universities is reflected in several developments: first and foremost, in the progress of the Bologna process, but also in the way academic institutions in both countries have participated in the formation of the European Higher Education Area, as well as their membership in the European University Association (EUA).

The following section presents several cases of Polish-Slovak bilateral cooperation that have emerged after the two countries joined the European Union. Given the long-standing tradition of Polish-Czecho-Slovak cooperation, some of these initiatives were, in reality, trilateral, benefiting from an active role of Czech partners. The aim here is not to describe all the projects, processes and events in detail—rather, it is to highlight the turning points that shaped the framework for further cooperation. In other words, to point out specific issues common to both countries and identify to what extent European integration has influenced bilateral cooperation.

An important contribution to academic cooperation came in the shape of "The New Educational Review"—a journal founded jointly by the faculties of pedagogy at three Central European universities: the University of Silesia in Katowice (Poland), Matej Bel University in Banská Bystrica (Slovakia) and the University of Ostrava (Czechia). The editorial board, formally seated at the Faculty of Psychology and Pedagogy in Katowice, is composed of deans and deputy deans from each of the three faculties. The significance of this publication stems partly from the fact that it is the only multinational academic journal in Central Europe. The Review constitutes a continuation of the initiative started by Professor Bogdan Suchodolski, who headed the international editorial board of an annual paper entitled "Paideia", published by the Committee for Educational Sciences of the Polish Academy of Sciences from 1972 until 1994 in three languages: English, French and Russian. The concept of the New Educational Review is very ambitious—it aspires to being an international forum for the exchange of thoughts on post-modern educational, social and cultural realities—not only in Central Europe, but globally. The board's intention is to publish articles sent from all over the world. Upon receiving papers, the editors appoint consultants who act as the first reviewers. Each article needs to receive at least two independent peer-reviews. The New Educational Review is indexed in the EBSCO database, Education Research Complete, Education Source, ERIH PLUS, Google Scholar, Index Copernicus, Open Academic Journals Index, Scopus as well as Ulrichsweb. It is published by the Adam Marszałek Publishing House in the Polish city of Toruń.

Another notable example is the Polish-Slovak-Czech Optical Conference—a biannual event with almost 40 years of tradition, the Conference is a forum for reporting the latest research advances and stimulating the exchange of expertise among academic and industrial communities in the three countries. The 19th Conference was hosted by the Institute of Physics at Wrocław University of Science and Technology (Poland). The speakers covered a wide variety of fields in the research on optics. The 20th edition, dedicated to wave and quantum aspects of optics, was held in Jasná (Slovakia), in September 2016. A number of institutions, including the University of Žilina, the International Laser Center Bratislava and the Slovak Electrotechnical Society, were involved in organizing it.

A similar event is the Polish-Slovak-Czech Symposium on Mining and Environmental Geophysics. This highly specialized subject is relevant for all three partners, since mining continues to be an important sector of their economies (particularly in Poland and Czechia). The Symposium, similarly to the Conference discussed above, is hosted on a rotational basis. In 2007, it took place in Janov nad Nisou (Czechia). The subsequent year, the edition—this time focused on geophysics in mining and environmental protection—was held in Piechowice (in the Sudety Mountains, southern Poland). In 2009, the honor of hosting the event went to the town of Staré Splavy (Czechia). The 34th Symposium in 2010 was organized jointly by the Faculty of Earth Sciences of the University of Silesia and the Institute of Geophysics of the Polish Academy of Sciences. The following year, the event came back to Slovakia, with the Faculty of Mining, Ecology, Process Control and Geotechnologies of the Technical University in Košice (Slovakia's leading university with regard to the involvement in the EU's 7th Framework Programme) acting as the host. In 2015, the Symposium took place in Kežmarské

Žľaby (Slovakia). With its substantial traditions, the Symposium has been an example of continued cooperation among educational institutions of Central Europe.

The exchange of academic staff is an area characterized by increasing intensity. It includes several outstanding cases of long-term, extremely fruitful joint efforts on the part of Polish and Slovak scholars. One such example is that of Professor Andrzej Jerzy Sadlej, a world-renowned Polish expert on quantum chemistry. In 2006, the Scientific Council of the Comenius University in Bratislava awarded Professor Sadlej its Gold Medal of Merit in recognition of his 30-year long cooperation with Slovak colleagues (including a number of young scholars and doctoral candidates). Sadlej's contribution to the development of quantum chemistry has been widely acknowledged not only in Slovakia, but also all over Europe, in the USA and other OECD member states (Naša univerzita 2006). Conversely, several Slovak scholars—e.g. Professor Pavel Fobel and his wife, Professor Daniela Fobelová (both experts on ethics) of Matej Bel University in Banská Bystrica—have enjoyed a tremendous reputation in the Polish academic community. In 2012, the University of Silesia in Katowice awarded them both a prestigious honorary title of doctor *honoris causa* for their cooperation with the Polish staff working at the University's Institute of Philosophy. The work of Professors Fobel and Fobelová helped shape the University's curricula, contributing essential knowledge in the field of ethics and societal organization (Šuša 2012:4).

One more area that needs mentioning is the ongoing work on the issue of mutual recognition of undertaken studies and obtained degrees. The bilateral agreement on the recognition of academic titles, dating back to 2005, was amended on 16th March 2016, as confirmed by the signatures of Polish Deputy Prime Minister Jarosław Gowin and the Slovak Ambassador Dušan Krištofík. According to the new version of the agreement, the Slovak title of "docent" (similar to associate professor) is now considered as equivalent to the Polish procedure of "habilitation" (which is an intermediate step between a PhD and a full professorial title) only after scientific achievements of a given Slovak scholar are verified and recognized by relevant Polish academic bodies. The Head of the International Cooperation Department in the Polish Ministry of Science and Higher Education, Juliusz Szymczak-Gałkowski, explained that the Ministry became aware of the need for such changes based on feedback received from the academic community. Polish institutions of higher education have repeatedly argued that the Polish title of "doktor habilitowany" (abbreviated "dr hab.") and the Slovak title of "docent" were, on principle, not equivalent. In response to their suggestions, the amended agreement introduced a new procedure—so-called "nostrification"—to remedy the problem. On the occasion of resolving this particular issue, J. Szymczak-Gałkowski stated that he was generally in favor of internationalizing the education sector, also with regard to Polish-Slovak relations. The Ministry he represented was very satisfied that increasing numbers of people were seeking and acquiring education abroad (PAP 2016b). However, in the case of Poland and Slovakia, the phenomenon seems asymmetrical: over the last two decades Polish scholars seeking to obtain academic titles at Slovak universities far outnumbered their Slovak colleagues looking to pursue scholarly work in Poland.

Cultural cooperation

Due to geographical proximity and frequent contacts between the citizens of both states, particularly those living in the border regions, cultural cooperation has progressed continuously over the years. Crucially, it has been undertaken in response to a genuine social need, allowing Poles and Slovaks to learn about and from each other. Presented below are several cases of fruitful cooperation that have contributed to the overall state of bilateral relations.

The first example worth mentioning is the activity of the Polish Institute in Bratislava and the Slovak Institute in Warsaw. Dedicated to promoting their homelands' culture, art and scientific achievements, both Institutes operate as organizational units in the respective ministries of foreign affairs. The establishment in Bratislava was first founded in 1950 under the name of New Poland. In 1982, it was replaced by the Polish Cultural and Information Center. Its current form and name were adopted in 1994. Today, The Polish Institute is one of the most active foreign cultural organizations in Slovakia: it arranges approximately 200 various events every year (also outside Bratislava). Until recently, it was headed by Andrzej Jagodziński—counselor at the Polish Embassy in Bratislava and a renowned interpreter of Slovak and Czech literature. Jagodziński's work, which also included tenures as the director of the Polish Institute in Prague and the executive director of the IVF, contributed enormously to the process of building mutual understanding and appreciation between the two national cultures. His current counterpart in Warsaw is Milan Novotný (Slovenský inštitút 2016), who also cooperates with the Slovak Embassy and Consulate General in the effort to promote culture, art and science emanating from his homeland. Both Institutes organize conferences, exhibitions, evenings with poetry, academic seminars, book presentations, as well as meetings with writers, linguists and interpreters of Polish and Slovak literature.

The fact that cooperation in the areas of culture and science is sometimes managed by the same bodies indicates this sphere of bilateral relations is fairly well-developed. To illustrate this point, one could evoke the example of the Center of Polish Language and Culture—an organizational unit established in 2012 at the Department of Slavic Languages, Faculty of Arts, Matej Bel University in Banská Bystrica. Matej Bel University is one of three Slovak universities that regularly participate in Polish-Slovak cooperation by providing courses on Polish language, history and culture (Katedra slovanských jazykov 2012). The Center's activities mirror those of the Polish Institute in Bratislava (conferences, concerts, meetings with Polish authors, book presentations etc.), but also extend to forms such as seminars and research on Polish Slovak intercultural dialogue. The Center issues its own journal, entitled "Język Polski i Kultura" (Eng. Polish Language and Culture). It cooperates with the National Scientific Library in Banská Bystrica, as well as numerous Polish and Slovak institutions, including other universities.

One other example seems worth mentioning. From 27th November 2014 to 1st February 2015, Slovakia's second-largest city, Košice[24], hosted an exhibition of paintings by several Polish artists: Marcin Maciejowski, Monika Niwelińska, Agnieszka Piksa, Wilhelm Sasnal and Jakub Woynarowski, all of whom live and work in Kraków (Podhorská 2014). The event commemorated Kraków's role in shaping positive

---

[24] In 2013, Košice, alongside Marseille, acted as the European Capital of Culture. In preparation to this role, eight investment projects were implemented, the largest of which (costing €24 million) envisioned transforming a former military complex into a space for cultural events (Podhorská 2014).

relations between the two countries—specifically, the activities of the Jagiellonian University which back in the 1930s began teaching the Slovak language and became the strongest center of Polish-Slovak cooperation. The exhibition also referred to minor political concepts from that period, according to which religious and cultural similarities might enable creating a union between Poland and Slovakia.[25] While none of these ideas ever got close to being implemented, the event itself was a good attempt at celebrating the efforts of Poles and Slovaks who had strived to create a broader space for cooperation among Central European countries.

The region near the Polish-Slovak border is well-known for various colorful events celebrating the local folklore. The largest and most recognizable of them is the Beskidy Culture Week, organized by the Regional Center of Culture in Bielsko-Biała (EU Grants Map 2016). Each year, nearly 100 bands perform in five Polish towns: Wisła, Szczyrk, Oświęcim, Żywiec and Maków Podhalański. The Week has regular fans who attend it every year to applaud the musicians, visit art fairs and taste traditional dishes. On the other side of the border, the Slovak town of Skalité hosts an annual festival of Czech, Slovak and Polish highland cultures. The village of Malatiná (also in Slovakia) holds an international festival of shepherd cultures, while a Polish village of Wieprz (near Żywiec) invites tourists to listen to folk storytellers and musicians playing rare instruments. Żywiec itself hosts a winter festival, called Gody Żywieckie, where folk bands cultivate Christmas and New Year customs and traditions. Every January, the festival gathers carol singers and folk dancers, also allowing visitors to try traditional Christmas dishes. While the Beskidy Culture Week and Gody Żywieckie are the two most popular events promoting local culture, those interested in the subject could

---

[25] The notion of closer political cooperation between Poland and Slovakia was examined and promoted in Karol Sidor's book, "Cesta do Poľska" (Eng. "Journey to Poland", published in 1927). Similar ideas were explored in a two-volume publication entitled "Slovensko a Slováci" (Eng. "Slovakia and Slovaks"), edited by Władysław Semkowicz and issued by the Jagiellonian University in Kraków in 1937-38. A Polish member of parliament, Feliks Gwiżdż (leader of the Sanacja party), born in the border region of Podhale, exhibited strong pro-Slovak leanings. He considered the inhabitants of the highlands as an integrating factor that could facilitate a Polish-Slovak union (Podhorská 2014). Another concept, this time of a Polish-Czech-Slovak (con)federation was developed during World War II. It was supported by the Polish government-in-exile and, to a lesser extent, also by Great Britain and the USA (Levy 2007: 200).

find something interesting almost every month throughout the year. Between 2004 and 2006, the Interreg Poland-Slovakia program funded a very interesting project entitled Cyber Folklore. The initiative envisioned promoting the cultural heritage of Polish-Slovak borderlands by means of modern technologies. One of its results is a website (www.etnofoto.net) that serves as a compendium of folk bands and artists and presents an impressive gallery of photos taken during various festivals. It also includes a tourist guide (called "A trail of tradition") with extensive information about a number of Polish and Slovak museums, as well as a calendar of cultural events to be used by fans of folklore or those planning to spend their free time in the regions near the border. Apart from directly promoting regional traditions, the project has facilitated communication between the organizers of various events, allowing them to better coordinate their efforts.

Cross-border cooperation
While the regions near the Polish-Slovak border are not among the most-developed areas one can find in the two countries, they do hold a substantial potential as tourism destinations. Gradually established local and regional partnerships have faced difficulties stemming from overall underdevelopment. In Poland and Slovakia alike, the persistent disparity between the richer, western parts and the less affluent east is clearly visible in various statistics. For instance, the five regions along Poland's eastern and northern border exhibit the lowest growth rates and provide the smallest contribution to the country's GDP (OECD 2008a).

In response to the challenges signaled above, Polish and Slovak regional authorities governing the mountainous areas near the border decided to form the Tatra Euroregion, currently registered in the Association of European Border Regions (AEBR 1997). According to a definition adopted by the Council of Europe in the early 1970s, cross-border regions are "characterized by homogenous features and functional interdependencies" (Council of Europe 1972: 29). As the Council stated over 20 years later, a "transfrontier region is a potential region, inherent in geography, history, ecology, ethnic groups, economic possibilities and so on, but disrupted by the sovereignty of the governments ruling on each side of the frontier" (Council of Europe 1995: 10). The founding congress for the Tatra Euroregion, formed by one Polish and one Slovak association, was held on 26th August 1994 in Nowy Targ (Poland). In 1996, after two years of legal groundwork, the new entity became a member of AEBR. In 2013, the two associations established a new European Grouping of Territorial Cooperation (EGTC) under the name of "TATRY s r.o."[26]. A common Polish-Slovak legal entity, the Grouping is a result of sustained cooperation and improving relations between the two partners. It utilizes their experience from numerous joint projects and events. The Polish-Slovak Economic Forum, organized annually by the Euroregion, contributes to a further development of trade and economic relations. It covers such aspects as tourism, sport, regional development, cooperation among businesses, scientific activities and strengthening the links between towns and villages of the involved regions. Cross-border cooperation also revolves around the Natura 2000 network and its joint program for protected areas, fauna and flora species. In February 2015, the European Commission (EC) approved the Interreg V-A Poland-Slovakia 2014-2020 program, which may prove very helpful in supporting future initiatives of the Tatra Euroregion.

Having become an independent country in 1993, Slovakia needed to build its image in the international community. This, of course, is necessarily a long-term effort that requires good planning and diligence. However, occurrences such as notable sporting achievements or successful organization of large sporting events affect a country's reputation more directly and immediately. Sports diplomacy has the capacity to transcend cultural differences, bringing nations and countries together, if only briefly. These considerations were probably the main reasons why Slovakia launched bids to organize the 2002 and 2006

---

[26] The *acquis communautaire* defines EGTCs as legal entities set up to facilitate cross-border, transnational and inter-regional cooperation within the EU. The structure allow local, regional and, sometimes, national authorities from different MS to set up legal entities with the aim of delivering joint services. MS have to agree to the participation of any of their domestic bodies. In 2013, the original law, Regulation (EC) No 1082/2006, was amended by Regulation (EU) No 1302/2013 to facilitate the process of forming the Groupings. The "s r.o." in the name of the entity is the Slovak abbreviation denoting a limited liability company.

Winter Olympic Games (Slovenský olympijský výbor 2013)[27]. Having seen both bids unsuccessful, the Slovak Olympic Committee decided to work with its Polish counterpart in order to prepare a common candidacy for the 2022 Games, with Kraków acting as the formal host city, and the towns of Zakopane (Poland) and Jasná (Slovakia) as venues for most competitions. The intention to present the joint candidacy was announced by President Lech Kaczyński on 6th March 2010 (Gazeta Wyborcza 2010), while the bid itself was formally confirmed in November 2013 (Butler 2013). However, the bid was later withdrawn after Kraków's residents had voted overwhelmingly against hosting the Games in a local referendum. The turnout, although relatively low at approximately 36 per cent, was enough to make the result valid (Šebela 2014). Almost 70 per cent of voters opposed the bid, arguing that the financial burden of organizing the Olympic Games would prove disastrous to the municipal budget. Their fears were based on financial data from the previous host cities: the 2010 Winter Games in Vancouver cost $6,4 billion, while London's 2012 Summer Games required $14 billion. In the case of Sochi, where infrastructure had to be constructed essentially from ground up, the total bill reached as much as $51 billion (Abend 2014). Speaking after the referendum, the president of the Polish Ski Federation, Apoloniusz Tajner, stated he was surprised with the result and expressed his regret, claiming that the Games could have been an excellent opportunity to develop winter sports and the infrastructure of the region (Polska The Times 2014). Slovak partners—representatives of towns, districts and sport federations that would have been involved in the organization—utilized the prematurely ended bid not only for conceptual work, but also to build a network of contacts with their Polish counterparts, to be used for the purpose of future cooperation.

---

[27] The Games were to be hosted by the city of Poprad, located near the High Tatra mountains. A centre of winter sports, primarily skiing and ice hockey, Poprad has an international airport. The bid to host the Winter Olympic Games was launched in the hope of attracting international interest in in the region, with the ultimate goal of boosting the tourism sector (Danková, 2016).

Summary of development trends in the bilateral Polish-Slovak cooperation

Polish-Slovak relations have been shaped by a variety of factors, including the European integration process, domestic developments at the national and regional level, as well as common elements of history. The phenomenon of Europeanization created a framework that has now been supporting the progress of bilateral relations for over a decade. While the asymmetry of positions is still evident, with Slovakia being only a minor partner for its larger neighbor, the development of cooperation is undeniable—as proven by an increasing number and quality of joint projects and initiatives. As more and more entities on both sides of the border get involved in various common undertakings, the cooperation is entering a new dimension.

Of course, several issues remain unresolved and, in general, Polish-Slovak relations hold much more potential for tangible results than their current state would suggest—this refers to both national-level cooperation and regional cross-border initiatives. The latter (regional) component calls for opening new external "access channels" that would connect the borderlands with areas of higher demographic potential (e.g. Warsaw and Budapest) and nearby regions by shortening travel time. Such development could turn the mountainous borderlands into a destination potentially able to compete with the Austrian Alps. In practice, this would require: 1) first and foremost, completing the system of road connections between Warsaw, Kraków, Ružemberok, Banská Bystrica and Budapest (S7, R3, R1 routes); 2) improving the road infrastructure connecting Czechia and Slovakia; 3) developing large-scale infrastructure necessary to attract tourists to the eastern parts of the Polish-Slovak borderlands (including roads, primarily the sections of A4 and D1 motorways leading to the Ukrainian border, as well as the S19 and R4 motorways connecting Rzeszów, Košice and Miskolc (Więckowski & Michniak & Bednarek-Szczepańska 2012).

One final remark on the development of Polish-Slovak relations must draw readers' attention to the fact that while numerous initiatives were undertaken on a bilateral basis, they have been shaped to a significant extent by the multilateral framework of European integration and the work of numerous intergovernmental bodies such as the Council of

Europe, the European University Association, the Association of European Border Regions and the European Association of Development Agencies.

Although the bond between Warsaw and Bratislava is far from inadequate, it cannot be said it is free of issues. Several challenges hinder further improvements, both at the level of central governments and in the cooperation between local and regional authorities of the border areas. When contrasted with the relatively well-developed cultural cooperation, the above-mentioned example of infrastructural shortcomings hints at how much could be achieved if all respective ministries of the two governments could coordinate their efforts as well as it has been done in the sectors of culture and science (Algayerová 2010).

Dynamics of the relations in the multilateral context

The aim of this part of the chapter is to examine Polish-Slovak cooperation within the multilateral framework of European integration and international organizations. Effective multilateralism which governs the work of numerous regional (both in the narrower and wider sense) bodies, constitutes the basis for foreign policies pursued by the two states in a number of areas, including economy, energy security, environment, social development, culture, education and science.

Importance of the European integration processes for the Slovak-Polish-Slovak neighborhood relations development

Poland and Slovakia's strategic position within the international community evolved as they completed the process of democratic transition and became integrated with various inter- and supranational structures. By the end of 2000, both were members of the Council of Europe and the OECD, with Poland also having a full membership in NATO (Slovakia was admitted to NATO later, in 2004). On 1st of May 2004, after a 12-year long period of negotiations and pre-accession procedures[28], Poland and Slovakia joined the EU. Integrating with the Union

---

[28] Both countries' integration began in December 1991, with the signing of bilateral association agreements with the EU. After Slovakia became an independent country

required them to adapt their national economies and implement the *acquis communautaire* into their legal systems.

Table 34. Poland and Slovakia's integration with the EU and other international organizations.

International organization	Poland	Slovakia
UNESCO	6th November 1946	9th February 1993
Council of Europe	26th November 1991	30th June 1993
OECD	22nd November 1996	14th December 2000
NATO	12th March 1999	29th March 2004
EU Association Agreement signing	16th December 1991	4th October 1993[29]
Negotiations on full membership to EU	1998, after the December 1997 Luxembourg summit	2000, after the December 1999 Helsinki summit
EU as full member	1st May 2004	1st May 2004
EU EMU[30]	-	1st January 2009

Source: Adapted by author on the basis of official websites of the above-named organizations.

In the early 1990s, Poland had an important advantage over Slovakia as regards the integration process. Having been the first former Soviet bloc state to undertake fundamental economic and political reforms, it was perceived as the ideological leader of the "new Europe". It was also the first country to shift from USSR-dominated structures (the Warsaw Pact and the Council for Mutual Economic Assistance) towards Euro-Atlantic structures. Later on, its efforts to maintain the principle of solidarity among EU MS and to negotiate a revision of US visa policy were fully compatible with the interests of other Visegrad Group members. The beginning of the 21st century saw a slight decline in Poland's position within the EU, as Warsaw found itself in disagreement with Germany and France as to several vital political issues. Nonetheless, it

---

on 1st January 1993, the new Slovak government signed a new association agreement later that year.
[29] This date refers to the EU-Slovak agreement, not the original one negotiated and signed by the Czechoslovak government.
[30] The EMU represents the highest stage of economic integration. The term has been used in Europe since the 1980s. Some scholars (notably Béla Balassa) referred to it as an „economic union" and argued for one extra, even more advanced, level of integration („complete economic integration"—a term introduced in 1961). However, the latter concept is not used in the contemporary theoretical debate.

has remained an important partner for other European states, particularly its neighbors.

Upon acceding to the EU on 1st May 2004, Poland and Slovakia implemented the *acquis communautaire*, including chapters 17 (science and research), 18 (education and training), 20 (culture and audio-visual policy) and 21 (regional policy and coordination of structural instruments) (European Commission 2003b: 37-38, 40-41).[31] The new reality of full EU membership prompted Central European states to consider what role the Visegrad Group might have within larger European structures. Some argued that the Group should continue its work as a regional body and seek to solidify its position in the fashion of the Benelux traditions.[32] There was also a proposal of creating a V4-Benelux forum. However, other opinions, emanating particularly from Czechia and Hungary, saw the V4 as a body that had already fulfilled its historical role by facilitating its members' progress on the way towards the Union. Ultimately, it was decided that the V4 cooperation would be continued as a regional initiative. Shortly after celebrating their accession to the EU, representatives of the four states met in the town of Kroměříž to sign a new document on the future of the Visegrad Group. The Kroměříž Declaration, signed on 12th of May, identified numerous common interests and envisioned further development of cooperation in a number of areas (Visegrad Group 2004b).

---

[31] Accession negotiations were split into 29 basic areas (plus 2 additional ones) identified by the EU (Report on the results... 2004). Four of these corresponded to the four basic principles of economic integration adopted in the process of building the single market: the free movement of goods, services, people and capital.

[32] The Benelux countries have operated as a customs union since 1948, and an economic union since 1960. Their tri-lateral cooperation provided a model for the creation of the European Economic Community customs union.

Table 35. Key areas of future Visegrad cooperation identified in 2004.

Co-operation within the V4 area	Co-operation of V4 countries within the European Union
Culture	Consultations and cooperation on current issues of common interest
Education	Active contribution to the development of the second column of the Maastricht EU structure—the EU CFSP, including the "Wider Europe—New Neighbourhood" policy[33] and the EU strategy towards Western Balkans[34]
Science	
Youth exchange	
Continuation of the strengthening of the civic dimension of the Visegrad cooperation within the International Visegrad Fund and its structures	Creating new possibilities and forms of economic cooperation within the European Economic Area (between EU and the three countries of the European Free Trade Association—EFTA)
Cross-border cooperation	Consultations, cooperation and exchange of experience in the area of justice and domestic affairs (the third column of the Maastricht EU structure); Schengen cooperation, including protection and management of the EU external borders, visa policy
Schengen co-operation	
Infrastructure	Consultations on national preparations for joining the EMU, the highest level of Europe's economic integration
Environment	Active participation in the development of the ESDP[35], as a contribution to the strengthening of relations between the European Union and NATO and developing the dialogue between the two organizations
Exchange of views on possible cooperation in the field of labor and social policy	
Exchange of experiences on foreign development assistance policy	
Disaster management	
Fight against terrorism, organized crime and illegal migration	
Defense and arms industries	

Source: Visegrad Group 2004b.

---

[33] In 2003-2004 the concept was renamed as the European Neighbourhood Policy.
[34] The region of Western Balkans became one of the top priorities of the Slovak foreign policy.
[35] Currently known as Common Security and Defence Policy under CFSP.

As the table above indicates, the areas pointed out as priorities of further V4 cooperation included culture, education, science, cross-border cooperation, development of infrastructure in the borderland areas, youth exchange and the continuation of the civic dimension through the IVF. The Fund has proven to be an invaluable tool for strengthening the ties between the four countries, as it provides resources to support cultural and scientific cooperation, including a network of personal contacts and communities willing to share their experiences, also with partners outside the V4.

EU membership and the continuation of regional cooperation within the Visegrad Group were the two key factors that affected the development of bilateral Polish-Slovak relations. Both countries and societies were introduced to a heterogeneous, interlinked structure of various integration frameworks, some of which were related to the activities of the Visegrad Group, the CEI[36], as well as a number of international organizations, including the Council of Europe, OECD, UNESCO and the European Association of Development Agencies. They have also participated in the implementation of the EU Lisbon Strategy for Growth and Employment and have contributed to the functioning of the European Free Trade Association (EFTA). They have also taken part in developing the comprehensive framework of a European regional policy.

Poland and Slovakia's accession to the EU came at the time when the Union's general integration framework was outlined in the Lisbon Strategy for Growth and Employment, designed for the period of 2001-2010. The Strategy, reflecting several global trends, was aimed at achieving better competitiveness in the context of an increasingly globalized economic environment. In February 2005, the newly appointed President of the EC, José Manuel Barroso[37], initiated a number of stra-

---

[36] Initially, the forum, then known as Quadragonale, involved four states: Austria (then an EFTA member), Italy, Hungary and Yugoslavia. Czechoslovakia and Poland joined in 1990 and 1991, respectively. The name of Central European Initiative was adopted in 1992, after several other countries of the region joined. The CEI constitutes a regional intergovernmental platform for supporting European integration. It combines multilateral diplomacy and joint project management efforts.

[37] During his two terms of office as the President of the Commission (2004-2009 and 2009-2014), Barroso, who had previously served as the Prime Minister of Portugal, became a personal symbol of European integration.

tegic projects meant to support the work towards meeting the goals specified in the Strategy.[38]

The enlarged EU faced the challenge of undergoing systemic changes that would allow it to adapt not only to its new, larger geographical scope, but also to some more general economic and social issues. Some of these issues were outlined in a report presented in 2004 to the EC by the High Level Group chaired by a Dutch MP, Wim Kok. Kok's team came to the conclusion that "to increase its living standards, it [the EU] needs to accelerate employment and productivity growth via a wide range of reform policies" (European Communities 2004: 6). The reforms suggested in the report encompassed a wide range of areas and problems: increasing the role and quality of research and development activities, broader use of information and communication technologies, better legislation, completing the formation of the single market, improving the environment for businesses, education, as well as eco-innovations (Ibidem: 6). The team recommended that each member state ought to prepare its own reform program so as to account for country-specific issues and concerns, while the EU should monitor the progress and act to ensure some degree of compatibility and synergy of efforts. Addressing the problems outlined in the Group's report would be particularly challenging to the newest EU MS that had barely completed their already difficult transition to European standards of economic and social development.

Another example of how the EU framework shaped conditions and circumstances for Polish-Slovak relations after 2004 came in the form of the EHEA project. Initiated as part of the Bologna process, the effort to create EHEA represented the Union's attempt at devising a common system for providing and recognizing education, but also at adapting national education systems to the challenges of the current era. As a whole, the Bologna process constitutes a rather unique approach to reforming higher education and building regional convergence. At its heart is a partnership between national governments—while it is a voluntary inter-governmental initiative (not a supranational one), all

---

[38] One of these projects, presented in October 2006 by EU Commissioner for Trade, Peter Mandelson, envisioned a strategy for external trade and investments that was meant to turn the EU into a leader in global trade.

EU MS, along with the EC, are involved. Decisions on reforms are made jointly, but the task of implementing them is the exclusive prerogative of individual national governments. The process was initiated by the EU's four representatives in the G8 (France, Germany, Great Britain and Italy), who shared the conviction that national segmentation of the higher education sector in Europe was an outdated, harmful concept. 2010 saw a milestone in the Bologna process: at the Vienna-Budapest Ministerial Conference, the EHEA was launched as the next stage and continuation of the initiative.

Ministers responsible for higher education meet once every two or three years to assess progress and set out new goals. Since 2009, the Bologna Policy Forum has been organized as an event accompanying the ministerial conferences. The Bologna Follow-up Group (BFUG)—a body responsible for guiding the process—gathers twice or three times a year to decide on rules and methods to be employed, set up working groups and engage parties from outside the BFUG. Both Poland and Slovakia have been active participants of the Bologna framework and have contributed to numerous events. Governments in Warsaw and Bratislava work closely with the EUA and the OECD. The latter organization is very actively involved in analyzing the education sector and preparing recommendations for further reforms (OECD 2016). Its work resulted in a number of proposals, especially for vocational education institutions.[39]

As for culture, the role of the Visegrad Group remained highly visible. The meeting of ministers of culture of the V4, held in November 2004 in Sárospatak, was a milestone for the continuation of Polish-Slovak cooperation in the era of EU membership. It was preceded by working sessions of expert groups that prepared various projects, proposals and documents to be decided on. Conclusions from the meeting touched on several issues and initiatives, including the International Visegrad Prize, joint exhibitions, the Slovak project of the Visegrad Library and the Polish concept for an event celebrating musical traditions of the Visegrad countries, as well as problems related to sharing muse-

---

[39] For instance, it was recommended that work-based learning becomes a mandatory element of all vocational programs. A number of measures for ensuring the quality of internships and apprenticeships was also suggested (OECD 2009).

um collections. Moreover, the ministers took the opportunity to discuss possibilities that would be opened up by the EU's culture-oriented programs for the 2007-2013 financial perspective. Throughout the following decade, the area of culture saw some of the most intense joint efforts undertaken both in the quadrilateral V4 format and on the bilateral basis.

Table 36. Selected joint Visegrad group (V4) declarations related to educational, scientific, cultural as well as cross-border cooperation.

Document	Place / Date	Highlights
Towards Union of Trust and Action—Joint V4 Prime Ministers' Statement (just after the British referendum result: not to remain in EU)	Brussels, 28th June 2016	The countries of the V4 *deeply regret that the United Kingdom has chosen not to remain a member of the European Union*, but stated they respected that sovereign decision. They expressed their firm belief that the European Union of 27 MS would continue and that, instead of endless theoretical debates on "more Europe" or "less Europe", *we need to focus on "better Europe"*. The Union should focus on a *practical restart of convergence*. Therefore, all involved governments ought to make sure the Union uses the key instruments to this end: cohesion, boosting investment, supporting innovation, completing the digital and energy single market, promoting free trade and free movement, and strengthening a resilient labor market bringing sustainable jobs. The countries of the V4 thus believe that working on these objectives will deliver *a Union of trust and action* only if all 27 MS are at the table in their diversity and provide their unique inputs. Only through such inclusive approach will the EU be faster in its decision-making and stronger, both internally and externally, *to be able to better react to challenges before us*. Only this way will it once again become attractive to its citizens. Only this way will it provide a tangible proof that a *united Europe remains the best option*.
Memorandum of Understanding for Regional Cooperation in the Areas of Innovation and Startups	Prague, 12th October 2015	The MS of the Visegrad Group—Czechia, Hungary, Poland and Slovakia—were aiming *to position themselves as innovative economies* with a vibrant start-up ecosystem. While governments of the V4 countries have launched individual programs to support global expansion of *local start-ups and fast-growing innovative small and middle sized enterprises* (SMEs) and strengthened their national innovation ecosystems, limited activities have been carried out in coordination and cooperation across

			the Visegrad region. For the purpose of increasing such cooperation, the Slovak Republic (as the former Presidency of the V4) established the *"V4 Innovation Task Force"* initiative in November 2014. Among its priorities were: discussing *efficient methods of attracting investors to the Visegrad region*; exchange of information on grants and international programs that can be utilized for *financing the activities of the Task Force*, as well as organizing *common networking and awareness raising events*.
MoU Concerning the Roadmap for Determining the Future Development of Transport Networks (Adopted by the V4 Prime Ministers)		Budapest, 24th June 2014	V4 countries agreed that further steps have to be taken to coordinate the future development of the *transport networks, including the North–South connections of the Visegrad Region*, and a solid common approach needs to be worked out before the negotiations on the financial period beyond 2020 begin. In the framework of this common approach, the V4 countries undertook to establish a *joint list of transport infrastructure projects of high importance* to all four Visegrad Group MS, with the intention to present it together during the negotiations on the next EU financial perspective beyond 2020, as well as during the revision of the TEN-T network (*trans-European transport network*). In order to attain these goals, the Ministries responsible for transport and the High Level Working Group on transport connections presented a *plan to elaborate a short-, medium- and long-term program*.
Communiqué from the 23rd Meeting of V4 Ministers Responsible for Culture		Cracow, 14th June 2013	The V4 ministers responsible for culture discussed the topics given below: the progress of the *implementation of cultural programs* since the 22nd meeting of V4 ministers responsible for culture in Prague 2012; *Ongoing Coloquium of Library Information Employees* from the V4 countries; Information on the *Working Group for Cultural Heritage* in the V4 countries and the second edition of the *Heritage Forum of Central Europe* in Cracow in 2013; *Cooperation in the field of performing arts* in the V4 countries; seminars on *evaluation of the use of EU funds in the area of culture*. New project proposals: *System of Post-Napoleonic Fortresses of the Habsburg Empire*; working meeting on the implementation of the Convention on the Protection and Promotion of the Diversity of Cultural Expressions; *Visegrad Initiative for Audiovisual Cooperation*; support for further research and development in *digitization, digital restoration and preservation* to enhance existing methods and processes in these areas. The ministers also debated on the idea of signing the *Declaration on Juris-*

		dictional Immunities of State Owned Cultural Properties. The ministers welcomed the projects and activities directed toward the priorities of the Polish V4 Presidency, particularly the organization of the V4 expert conference "*Building cultural capacity for digitization and enabling access to cultural heritage*", held in Warsaw in 2013.
Joint Statement from the 5th Meeting of the Committees on Public Administration and Regional Policy of the Parliaments of the Visegrad Group Countries and Croatia	Warsaw, 28-29th January 2013	V4 representatives called on their governments to use, to the greatest extent possible, *various instruments supporting territorial development*, arguing that such instruments were going to increase the involvement and accountability of regional and local authorities as well as local communities in programming and funds management; V4 representatives believed that future cohesion policy programs should present a *strategy for achieving specific goals with respect to the development of a specific region or thematic area*; the 2014-2020 programming period should see much more emphasis on the results of the financed activities rather than focus on the pace of absorption; V4 representatives wished to emphasize that they found it equally important to support innovation, research and development, which enable their states *to modernize their economic structures*, as well as basic transportation, energy and environmental infrastructure, which is still underdeveloped in those countries and which is a necessity in a modern, innovative state; V4 representatives appreciated the previous efforts on the part of the governments of the Visegrad Group states and their efficiency in pursuing national interests; They expressed hope that such cooperation would be continued during the negotiations over the 2014-2020 Multiannual Financial Framework and the cohesion policy legislative package. V4 Parliaments' representatives were in favor of strengthening cooperation between Central European states in *exchanging good practices and knowledge on computerization of public administration*, in the belief that the process was indispensable for the implementation of the Digital Agenda for Europe.
Joint Declaration of the Visegrad Group and Slovenia on the Negotiation Process of the Commission's Proposals for the Cohesion Policy 2014–2020 Regulatory Package	Katowice, 12th October 2012	The V4 and Slovenia expressed the opinion that in order to ensure a clear and coherent regulatory framework for the Common Strategic Framework (CSF) funds, provisions should also refer to specific cases of implementation—for instance, projects implemented under national programs and *involving regions of various categories*, or those utilizing phasing and bridging, which needs transparent transitional provisions. The V4 and Slovenia also emphasized that *capital regions were important*

		catalysts of the Europe 2020 objectives and engines of economic growth adding that these regions were often stricken *by internal disparities*, with their relatively high development level resulting from the statistical effect of the capital. The Visegrad Group and Slovenia, therefore, stressed that addressing the issue of *capital regions with customized solutions* was indispensable for facilitating the progress towards the Europe 2020 goals and for enhancing *competitiveness both at regional and national level*.
Joint Statement of V4 Culture Ministers	Prague, 1st June 2012	The V4 ministers responsible for culture discussed the following topics: the *Coloquium of Library Information Employees* from the V4 countries; information on the *Working Group for Cultural Heritage* in the V4 countries and its new proposals; the follow-up of the V4 seminar on the *use of EU structural funds and programs for culture*. The ministers welcomed the project and activities that followed the priorities of the Czech V4 Presidency, particularly the organization of the V4 conference on the *incorporation of culture into future Cohesion Policy*, held in Mikulov in 2011.
Meeting of the Ministers for Education of the Visegrad Group	Olomouc, 15th November 2011	The V4 ministers responsible for education discussed reforms to be adopted in the area of the tertiary education. All V4 countries wished to improve the *quality and transparency of the tertiary education* through reforms and systemic changes enhancing public confidence in tertiary education and universities. These changes should *improve the results of the universities in international comparisons*. The participants agreed on several common steps: setting quality standards and *professionalization of accrediting agencies*; introduction of a transparent system of information access; establishment of a working group of V4 ministries tasked with developing proposals for the modernization of the tertiary education area, including evaluation.
Joint Statement of the Visegrad Group Culture Ministers	Mikulov, 6-7th October 2011	The ministers expressed their agreement on the importance of *improving the inclusion of culture in the future EU cohesion policy* as well as in the planning of all relevant financial instruments. Furthermore, they unanimously stressed that culture contributed to the goals of the Europe 2020 strategy. They also agreed on the *social and economic importance of culture* in the development of the European Union.

Polish-Slovak cooperation in other fields of neighborhood relations 217

Experts' report on Progress in Approved and Implemented Visegrad Group Programs and Projects, and on New Proposals presented at the 19th Meeting of the Ministers for Culture of the Visegrad Group	Warsaw, 29th May 2009	The ministers acknowledged the success of the Visegrad Anthology project (publication of a contemporary literature anthology of the V4 countries, first suggested in 2006) as a symbol of close cooperation in the area of culture. They also discussed the progress and results of a number of other initiatives related to literature, digitization of and access to literary resources (including academic publications), as well as protection of cultural heritage. Finally, the ministers supported the "Visegrad Days" festival and encouraged all V4 countries to host the event on a regular basis.
Communiqué from the Visegrad Group Ministers of Culture	Warsaw, 29 May 2009	The V4 ministers responsible for culture expressed their acknowledgment of the 2nd *Colloquium of Library Information Employees* from the V4 countries, which had taken place in Brno in 2008, and voiced their support for organizing the 3rd Colloquium in Poland in 2010. They expressed their appreciation for the activities of the Working Group on Cultural Heritage as well as the implementation of the Visegrad Anthology project as a symbol of a close V4 cultural cooperation.
Communiqué from the 18th Meeting of the Ministers of Culture of the Visegrad Group Countries	Olomouc, Czechia, 19–20 June 2008	The ministers welcomed the continuation of the Visegrad Anthology project and appreciated the efforts made by the V4 editors and experts involved in it. They discussed *new possible directions of the Visegrad Literary Anthology project*. The ministers recommended awarding the Visegrad Library project a grant from the International Visegrad Fund. They welcomed and supported the follow-up of the *Colloquium of Library Experts* from the V4 countries. They appreciated the preparation of the second meeting that was to take place in the Moravian Library in Brno in July 2008. The ministers agreed on further activities of the Visegrad Working Group analyzing *the effects of economic and social transformation on cultural heritage* in the Visegrad Group MS and welcomed the report (entitled "Culture in the light of Transformation—the experience of the Czech Republic and the Republic of Poland") produced as a result of a bilateral meeting held in the Moravian Gallery in Brno in May 2008.
Conclusions from the Meeting of Ministers responsible for regional development of the Visegrad Group countries, Bulgaria and Romania	Prague, 3–4 June 2008	The V4 ministers responsible for regional development assessed positively *the role of Cohesion Policy for the EU economic growth as well as for the balanced and sustainable development of all European regions, leading to regional cohesion* and to the strengthening of competitiveness. They underlined the strategic nature of the Cohesion Policy and its high added value at all levels. The ministers

		strongly emphasized that its implementation brought sound effects in the economic and social fields at regional, national and European levels. They recognized *the importance of spatial planning in strengthening territorial cohesion* and declared their commitment to prepare a common document on spatial development of the Visegrad group countries.
Communiqué of the 17th Meeting of the Ministers of Culture of the Visegrad Group Countries	Bratislava, 11–12 October 2007	The V4 Ministers of Culture welcomed the joint project of the *Visegrad Anthology* and appreciated the effort of the editors and experts involved in publishing the works of 13 contemporary authors from the four countries. The Visegrad Anthology was officially presented at a press conference in Bratislava. They recommended that the *joint project of the Visegrad Library* be awarded a grant from the IVF and considered the possibility of providing financial support from budgets of respective ministries. The Ministers welcomed and supported the continuation of the *Colloquium of Library-Information employees* from the V4 countries to be held in Czechia in 2008. They also welcomed national presentations of the Visegrad Anthology during the *Bibliotéka Book Fair* in November 2007 in Bratislava, April 2008 in Prague, May 2008 in Warsaw; April and September 2008 in Budapest. The Ministers agreed on further development of the Visegrad working group tasked with analyzing the implications of the *economic and social transformation for the cultural heritage* in the Visegrad Group countries and welcomed *Polish initiative to organize the expert meeting and seminar* in the field of heritage preservation in 2008. In view of the Communication from the Commission on the *European agenda for culture in a globalizing world*, the Ministers agreed to support three strategic priorities: the *promotion of cultural diversity and intercultural dialogue*, the promotion of *culture as a catalyst of creativity* and the *cultural cooperation with third countries*. The V4 Ministers of Culture welcomed experts' participation in the conference "*Memory reclaimed*" organized by the International Cultural Center in Cracow in June 2007. Finally, they acknowledged the programs and achievements of the International Visegrad Fund.
Communiqué of the 16th Meeting of the Ministers for Culture of the Visegrad Group Countries	Budapest, 11–12 January 2007	In view of the preparations for the *Year of Intercultural Dialogue*, ministers agreed to support V4 cooperation within the EU framework. Having in mind the November 2006 meeting of the EU Education, Youth and Culture Council and the motto "*Money spent for culture is not a subsidy but an investment in the society*", the V4 ministers dis-

			cussed several *aspects of the economy of culture*, using a study being prepared for the Commission as a basis for debate. The Slovak proposal aimed at promoting Common Digital Broadcasting was welcomed. Warsaw's initiative of creating and setting up a working group within the V4 forum *to examine the effects of economic and social transformation on cultural heritage* in the Visegrad countries was accepted. The ministers welcomed Wrocław's candidature for the organization of the EXPO 2012 World Exhibition as an opportunity to promote the whole Central European region, notably in the context of that EXPO's subject—"*The culture of leisure in world economies*"—and its growing importance. They agreed on *strengthening of the V4 cooperation in the field of culture*, particularly in the EU Working Groups.
Communiqué on the 15th Meeting of the Ministers of Culture of the Visegrad Group Countries	Krakow, September 3–5, 2006		The parties acknowledged the *positive role of culture in international cooperation*. They made a commitment to draft joint programs in the spirit of intercultural dialogue by 2008. Ministers accepted the report on the first *Colloquium of Library Experts*. They discussed the possibility of continuing the initiative, possibly with the role of host granted on a rotational basis. Another project to be prolonged was the *International Visegrad Library*. With regard to the upcoming meeting of the EU Education and Culture Council, the Ministers discussed issues related to the ratification of the UNESCO Convention on the Protection and Promotion of the Diversity of Cultural Expression. They were also presented with Poland's initiative to create a working group to *examine the effects of the changed status of cultural heritage caused by the process of economic and social transformations* in the Visegrad countries.
Declaration of the V4 ministers responsible for regional development	Sliač (Slovakia), December 2, 2005		The V4 Ministers responsible for regional development acknowledged the need for the smoothest possible progress as well as successful conclusion of negotiations on the next programming period (2007–2013), that would ensure the equal approach toward both old and new EU MS. The main goal of the negotiations was to develop the regulatory framework for the EU Cohesion Policy that would *address specificities of both old and new EU MS*. In this context, they welcomed the European Commission's initiative to strengthen its commitment to the integrated urban renewal and to underline the *role of the cities in the cohesion policy* and the urban contribution to growth and jobs in the regions. They repeatedly stressed the importance of one of the main urban problems of the

Communiqué on the 14th Meeting of the Ministers of Culture and Cultural Heritage of the Visegrad Group Countries	Karlovy Vary, Czechia December 8–9, 2005	new MS—the *post-war panel housing estates*. The V4 Ministers of Culture appreciated the cooperation of the V4 countries, Austria and Slovenia in the discussion on the draft of the new European Commission programs—*Culture 2007* (2007–2013) and *Media 2007*. The Hungarian Minister reported on the Conference "*Inclusive Europe*", held earlier in Budapest. The Ministers stated they shared the view of those intellectuals who called for allocating more resources to the *Culture 2007* program. It was also mentioned that the *European Year of Intercultural Dialogue* provided an opportunity for the V4 countries to undertake joint initiatives. To develop concepts for possible projects, a meeting of expert groups was arranged. The Ministers exchanged their plans for the next programming perspective (2007-2013) and agreed on the importance of coordinating and sharing experience on the use of EU structural funds for culture.
Communiqué on the 13th Meeting of the Ministers of Culture of the Visegrad Group Countries, Banská Bystrica (April 28–29, 2005)	Banská Bystrica, Slovakia (April 28–29, 2005)	The V4 Ministers of Culture agreed to launch a joint comparative study on *economic and social impact of the cultural industry development in the Visegrad Group countries*. Slovakia was commissioned to host the first expert meeting in Bratislava in September 2005. The V4 Ministers appreciated Poland's efforts at implementing the project of creating a common collection of classical music recordings. The other countries declared they would grant relevant bodies access to their national archives, and would promote the initiative in the media. Poland also introduced another project that would result in creating TV-recorded profiles of renowned writers from the V4 countries. The Ministers awarded the Visegrad Prize to Mr. Laszlo Szigeti, in recognition of his contribution to the deepening of cultural cooperation among nations of Central Europe.
Communiqué on the 12th meeting of the Ministers of Culture of the Visegrad Group Countries (10–11 November 2004)	Sarospatak, Hungary, November 10–11, 2004	The V4 Ministers of Culture agreed on the final text of the *Statutes of the International Visegrad Prize* and decided on the first nominations. They encouraged the finalization of the Slovak project on the *Visegrad Library* and the Polish project, *Music of the Visegrad Countries*. To this end, they agreed to provide funding for one meeting of experts per each project.
Meeting of representatives of Ministries of Education in format V4+Slovenia	Warsaw July 21, 2004	The representatives of the V4 and Slovenia's Ministries of Education discussed the *future cooperation of the education sectors* of Visegrad Group countries in the light of their newly acquired status of full EU members.

Source: Adapted by author on the basis of Visegrad Group Official Statements and Communiqués, (Visegrad Group 2004a; Visegrad Group 2005).

Activities of the Visegrad Group reveal the primacy of societal actors, whose interests in the areas discussed here provide the basis for the formulation of national policies. States, operating under constrains imposed by conflicting values, pursue these interests according to a rational and risk-averse logic by organizing the exchange of resources and undertaking collective actions. Culture has proven to be the area of most intense cooperation among the V4, providing a blueprint for desirable progress in other sectors of bilateral and cross-border activities, including transport and education.

One final episode worth mentioning in the overview of Polish-Slovak relations in the multilateral context is the cultural program of the Slovak Presidency in the EU Council (July–December 2016). It was prepared to be presented not only in Europe, but in all countries around the world where Slovakia has its diplomatic missions. The program comprised projects in the fields of music, dance, theatre, film and design. Events were coordinated primarily by the Ministry of Culture and its subordinate organizations, with the assistance of the Ministry of Foreign and European Affairs, as well as diplomatic missions. Some of the events were to be hosted by local and regional authorities, non-governmental organizations and educational institutions. Apart from promoting Slovak culture, the program was aimed at increasing the public's awareness of Slovakia's Presidency and the EU as a whole. One example of a successful event held as part of the program was an exhibition presenting the town of Bardejov—a UNESCO World Heritage site. The exhibition, organized by the Šariš Museum and Bardejov's municipal authorities, visited nine Polish cities, starting with Kraków, where it was hosted by the Archaeological Museum.

Poland and Slovakia's role in multilateral regional cooperation within the framework of Euroregions[40]

The legal and organizational framework provided by the system of Euroregions constitutes foundations for cross-border cooperation[41]

---

[40] For the purpose of this assessment we will understand trilateral, quadrilateral and other plurilateral cooperation as multilateral one.

[41] „Cross-border cooperation" must be distinguished from „trans-national cooperation" and „inter-regional cooperation". For definitions and key characteristics see: (AEBR 1997: 2-3).

(CBC) among European states. CBC involves direct cooperation between local and regional authorities from two or more neighboring countries. As it may encompass all areas of life, its subject matter is potentially vast and ranges from strictly local problems to issues covered by the international law. CBC may involve bottom-up initiatives, strategies for regional development, as well as the use of EU-wide projects and programs. To ensure the synergy effect of CBC, its various forms are supported by institutions such as the Council of Europe, the European University Association (EUA), the Association of European Border Regions (AEBR) and the European Association of Development Agencies (EURADA), among others. Several sectors, including education, science and culture, have been shown as having a potential to accelerate CBC and increase the visibility of its results.

Apart from a single bilateral Euroregion "Tatry" (Euroregión Tatry 2016), Polish and Slovak authorities are involved in two other Euroregions: the trilateral Czech-Polish-Slovak "Beskidy" Euroregion and the multilateral Carpathian Euroregion (CER). The latter one, encompassing the Carpathian Mountains range stretching across several Central European states, is one of 17 large-scale CBC undertakings in Europe. It was formed in 1993 in Debrecen (Hungary) by the representatives of regional administrations from Hungary, Poland, Slovakia[42] and Ukraine. In 2002, the founding members accepted the request from several Romanian regions to join the initiative, bringing the total number of administrative units involved to 19. CER covers the area of 145 153 km² and is inhabited by over 15 million people.

The "Beskidy" Euroregion was formed by three associations—based in Frýdek-Místek (Czechia), Bielsko-Biała (Poland) and Žilina (Slovakia) respectively—in June 2000. Its total area of 3 900 km² is inhabited by over 780 000 people (Euroregión Beskydy 2016).[43]

Euroregions constitute a tool of the EU Regional Policy, which targets all regions and cities across the Union and is designed to support the provision of jobs, improve business competitiveness, overall eco-

---

[42] Participation of the East Slovakian regional administrations was initially based on a status of associated membership.

[43] The website of the Polish member of the Euroregion (http://www.euroregion-beskidy.pl/euroregion-beskidy-2/o-euroregionie/) provides somewhat different data: 6 343 km² and the population of 1 385 036 people.

nomic growth and sustainable development at the regional level. In less-developed areas, Euroregions are also an important instrument of the Cohesion Policy—the Union's main tool for addressing economic and social disparities among European regions and countries. The budget allocated for the Cohesion Policy in the 2014-2020 financial framework amounts to over €350 billion—over a third of the EU's total budget for that period. As for cooperation between regional authorities in Poland and Slovakia, the funding is available under the Interreg V-A program (Interreg Pol'sko-Slovensko 2015).

Final summary of Polish-Slovak cooperation in the areas of education, science, culture and cross-border cooperation

Relations between Poland and Slovakia, be it those strictly bilateral or those occurring in the multilateral context, have been—and will likely continue to be—affected by the disparities in their basic characteristics: size of the territory and population, access to natural resources and overall economic potential. This asymmetry is one of the main features of the dialogue between Warsaw and Bratislava. The factor that in many instances brings them close and allows them to agree on common positions and policy directions is the shared history. When Poland and Slovakia regained genuine independence after the dissolution of the Soviet Bloc, misfortunes experienced over the last two centuries prompted them to cooperate toward the goal of "returning to Europe". The strategic decision to resort to regional cooperation resulted first in the Central European Initiative and, shortly afterwards, the emergence of the Visegrad Group. The latter, in particular, has proven to be a very effective forum for coordinating efforts aimed at joining the process of European integration and, after Poland and Slovakia acceded to the EU, of preserving and strengthening bonds existing among the countries of Central Europe.

The process of entering the mainstream of European integration was unquestionably challenging—particularly for Slovakia, which embarked on it as a newly independent state. This was reflected in a certain hesitation with which Bratislava initially approached the formulation of its internal and foreign policies. Both states' integration with (and, later on, presence in) EU structures has been shaped by the so-called Europeanization—a multidimensional phenomenon affecting both official policies and informal internal discourse, not only at the national, but also at the regional and local level. Research conducted up to date revealed the presence of various aspects of Europeanization (up-, down- and cross-loading) in both Polish and Slovak politics.

As part of their "socialization" within the European community of states, Poland and Slovakia have gradually learned about what influence they can exert on the formulation of EU norms, rules and policies—be it as individual governments, or when acting as a group of states that adopts a common standpoint on a given issue. For various EU bodies, the Visegrad Group has become a recognized and legitimate platform for representing the interests of its members.

The 12 years that have so far elapsed since Poland and Slovakia joined the Union saw some notable successes for both countries in terms of their presence and relevance in EU structures. For Poland, the first significant appointment came within the first months of its EU membership—in November 2004 professor Danuta Hübner was nominated as the Commissioner for Regional Policy. Warsaw consequently presented itself as a pro-European government and the leader among Central European countries. Its resolve on this matter resulted in a very substantial sign of recognition, when in 2014 the then-Prime Minister Donald Tusk was elected to the seat of the President of the European Council—the highest post yet awarded to any representative of the new MS. For Slovakia, the two biggest appointments came in 2009 and 2010. In 2010, Miroslav Lajčák, former Minister of Foreign and European Affairs, was chosen as the Managing Director for Russia, Eastern Neighborhood and Western Balkans in the newly created European External Action Service. Lajčák held the post until 2012. A couple of months before his appointment, Maroš Šefčovič was nominated as the Commissioner for Interinstitutional Relations and Administration. In 2014, when Jean-Claude Juncker replaced Jose Manuel Barroso as the President of the Commission, Šefčovič was promoted to the post of the EC's Vice-President, responsible for a strategically important and difficult sector—the Energy Union.

With its 25 year-long history, the Visegrad Group represents a valuable cooperation forum—it is the first major documented example of an effective, sustained multilateral cooperation among the states of Central Europe. Its existence virtually guarantees the absence of substantial tensions in the region for the foreseeable future.[44] In practice, the Group's *modus operandi* leads to three possible outcomes when it comes to dealing with specific issues:

- all V4 countries adopt a common position from the outset with no need for substantial negotiations;
- their initial positions differ slightly, and a compromise is reached by means of negotiations;
- their initial positions differ too much to allow a compromise and, consequently, they act individually (Strážay 2015).

The Visegrad Group provides a platform through which Czechia, Hungary, Poland and Slovakia are able to coordinate their policies in all areas in which they identify common interests. The Group's institutions (e.g. the presidency and various advisory bodies) and procedures (e.g. working group meetings or summits), although devoid of a highly structured formal basis, constitute important pillars of cooperation. The V4 format has resulted in successful cooperation in a wide variety of areas (economy, science, culture, education, cross-border cooperation) and at various levels, from central governments to civic initiatives.

As for future developments, the governments in Warsaw and Bratislava share a very similar vision of the desirable course of European integration, advocating the continuation of close cooperation, but objecting any version of continental federalism. Their similar geopolitical situation—i.e. being located on the borders of the Schengen area, having Ukraine as a neighbor, with Russia and Western Balkans in their vicinity—has led them to adopt postures and positions (revealed by their recent political statements) that guarantee compatible reactions to current challenges, risks and threats.

The analysis presented in this chapter leads to several important conclusions. First of all, education, science and culture have proven to

---

[44] V4 has served an important role in regulating the situation among the V4 itself. For instance, it helped to stabilize and improve Slovak-Hungarian relations which, back in the early 1990s, had been rather tense. The Visegrad forum also helped Bratislava to forge more equitable (and, hence, satisfying) relations with Prague.

be the fields of effective bilateral and multilateral cooperation. In the context of the contemporary international environment, further effort in these areas, coupled with increased spending, can become an important accelerator of overall cooperation. Secondly, areas that hold the greatest potential for future cooperation include, first and foremost, subjects covered by specific integration bodies and specialized organizations. Thirdly, functional, legal and organizational frameworks adopted by these organizations require MS to develop individual approaches to implementing reforms and cooperative efforts in a given area. Hence, the system calls for active participation of not only national, but also regional and local authorities—a mechanism exhibited very well in Polish-Slovak cross-border cooperation.

Areas of agreement and disagreement between the governments in Warsaw and Bratislava are shaped not only by national interests, as identified by parliaments and ministries. They are also affected by events that resonate all across Europe and influence the general process of continental integration—the global economic crisis, fiscal difficulties experienced by some countries in the Mediterranean area, the migration crisis and Brexit. Their status as EU MS has forced both governments to recognize and acknowledge each other's interests to an even greater degree than before. At the same time, it has influenced their ability (and willingness) to react to emerging international developments, be it individually or in concert with their European partners. As a result, it has spurred their further cooperation within the Visegrad Group, as both Poland and Slovakia see the V4 as a platform that strengthens their common voice in the EU. For Poland, the Group is also an instrument that can be used for pursuing the position of a regional leader.

It may be argued that both governments (as well as their particular ministries, agencies and other institutions responsible for policies related to education, science, culture and regional cooperation) should be more consistent in the implementation of joint declarations adopted at the level of international organizations or by the Visegrad Group. It is also important that such statements and decisions are given a bilateral framework that would allow governments to seek domestic political support and work together on utilizing instruments available at the supranational level. Only this way will the two countries be able to consistently find an agreement on (and support) the development of cooperation in specific areas.

While cooperation in fields such as education, science, culture and cross-border initiatives frequently occurs on a bilateral basis, Poland and Slovakia's membership in integrational organizations such as the EU, the Council of Europe, EURADA, AEBR and UNESCO provides a multilateral framework that serves to direct and support efforts in a given area. The positive impact of European integration on Polish-Slovak relations remains unquestionable.

As for an overall effectiveness of cooperation between Warsaw and Bratislava, its assessment is necessarily mixed. While much work has already been done at both national and regional level, at this point in time the potential hidden in Polish-Slovak bilateral cooperation is far from being fully exploited. This is particularly true with regard to issues such as developing tourism, promoting culture and improving political governance. In other fields, particularly education, successes achieved thus far can be used to reinforce trust and willingness to broaden and deepen the scope of cooperation.

The methodology adopted for the purpose of research presented here has led to the identification of several spheres where Poland and Slovakia share vital interests: the establishment of the EHEA and cooperation within EUA (with the goal of developing a knowledge-based society); development of tourism; promotion of contemporary culture and preservation of cultural heritage. Of these, culture seems to hold the most substantial potential for future development of cooperation. As for possible obstacles, one clear issue is the insufficient infrastructure that hinders communication between mountainous border regions—overcoming it is particularly important if economic prospects (also related to tourism) of these somewhat generally underdeveloped regions are to be boosted.

In the effort to further forge amicable and durable relations with its northern neighbor, Slovakia is keen to intensify the political dialogue, particularly in those areas that directly affect the citizens of both countries. This calls for consultation forums and a more intense communication. Aspects such as regional economic development and cross-border infrastructure may prove especially important in the coming decades. This is why substantial emphasis should also be put on the issues of regional cohesion and close cooperation among the V4 countries. As both governments have already invested much in building the V4 brand, it would be a grave mistake not to use the potential it offers. This, of course, applies not only to Polish-Slovak cooperation, but to all four members of the Group. The V4's importance as a forum for coordinating policies and developing common approaches has gradually increased. This has been especially true for sectors such as education, science and culture. As cooperation between Poland and Slovakia has systematically deepened, it has reached a stage when it may well become an important stabilizing factor not only for the Visegrad Group, but also the entire region as a vital unit within the evolving European Union.

Summary and conclusions

In the preceding pages we have attempted to analyze the development of Polish-Slovak relations from 2004 until 2016. While each author focused on a different aspect of bilateral relations, all of them shared the conviction that bilateral relations between Warsaw and Bratislava have been strongly affected by the process of European integration and the phenomenon of international interdependence. This refers to interactions that occurred within the framework of not only the EU, but also other groupings, such as the Visegrad Group, NATO, the UN and several others. Following this line of argument, authors assumed at the early stage of the research that external influences had as much impact on Polish-Slovak relations as motivations and direct contacts between the two governments in question. The importance of international interdependence has been considered at four complementary levels: local, subregional, regional (European) and global.

Research questions presented in the introduction to this volume served as the linchpin for each of the four chapters devoted to particular areas of Polish-Slovak relations. Keeping in mind the character of issues discussed in each chapter, authors made an effort to answer the questions in a detailed and comprehensive manner. The first question concerned the **state of Polish-Slovak relations** over the relevant time period, also with regard to their dynamics in both the bi- and the multilateral dimension. One of the first and most basic conclusions was that the goals of Polish and Slovak foreign policies were, in general, not divergent. In most situations, they were either nearly identical or at least complementary. As a result, the two parties were able to preserve an atmosphere conducive to the development of constructive political dialogue. However, neither government considered its ties with the other to be of strategic value when formulating concepts of foreign policy. Consequently, Warsaw and Bratislava afforded the task of building mutual rapport only a limited attention, especially when compared to their efforts at cooperation with other neighbors. Instead, they focused on the multilateral context provided by the Visegrad Group, the EU and, in a broader perspective, NATO. When one moves further and examines activities undertaken by both countries at the European level (and within a wider international system), it becomes apparent that Poland has defined its role differently to Slovakia. In Polish domestic socio-political discourse, issues of international politics have traditionally held a prominent spot and attracted a lot of interest among the general public. Moreover, Warsaw harbored ambitions to co-create the EU's political processes. Meanwhile, Slovak decision-makers believed that the issues of so-called hard politics were secondary to the needs of the domestic society—a stance that explains why policies adopted in Bratislava were highly economized. Such circumstances created a peculiar ground for Polish-Slovak cooperation, whereby self-perceptions exhibited by each partner could be seen as complementary to those of the other. At the same time, they generated a certain complication for the functioning of long-lasting strategic political alliances.

The second aim adopted by the authors was to identify **crucial areas** in bilateral relations—i.e. to find out where interests expressed by the two governments were similar and where they were divergent. The analysis of primary and secondary sources (including official state documents and statistical data) allowed the research team to reveal the following areas of common interests: energy security, cross-border cooperation, policy coordination at the European level, the migration crisis and the instability of the EU's neighboring countries (particularly Ukraine). The drive to infuse Polish-Slovak relations with more dynamism and solid content came primarily from trans-border initiatives aimed at developing infrastructure, fostering socio-economic growth and protecting the environment. Many of these projects were implemented with the support of EU funds (for instance Interreg), while others were devised within the framework of Euroregions. At the same time, functioning inside the European system—with its institutions, regulations, politics and peculiar sociology—forced Warsaw and Bratislava to change previous patterns and mechanisms of shaping bilateral relations. One example of this phenomenon is the way Visegrad Group evolved in terms of the approach to cooperation and its content. Moreover, after acceding to the Union in 2004, both countries gained new instruments, communication channels and mechanisms (e.g. interactions within European institutions and participation in EU programs) that could be used to mold bilateral relations. The areas defined as key to Polish-Slovak relations in the context of EU membership included the CFSP (especially the ENP and the energy policy) and efforts towards energy security in the national, sub-regional and European dimensions. As Poland and Slovakia identified their shared interests at the level of the international system, their interdependence in the broad European and global context seemed ever-increasing. This trend was further strengthened by the process of Europeanization which implied the necessity of taking into consideration the positions and actions of other relevant actors of the system, as well as its external environment.

There is no doubt that multilateral cooperation dominated relations between Warsaw and Bratislava. It generally had a positive impact on both partners' effectiveness in pursuing individual and common goals, be it in the bilateral context or through activities undertaken as EU members. It may be argued that the areas holding biggest potential for further development (e.g. migration, energy security, common projects related to the defense industry or enhancing military capabilities, cross-border cooperation and regional policy) encompass primarily issues covered by international organizations. However, even though they are the subject of multilateral cooperation, they still require individual approaches on the part of the MS when it comes to implementing specific concepts. It should also be remembered that they are often shaped in reaction to events that affect entire organizations—vide the example of proposals to strengthen NATO's military presence in Central in Eastern Europe, the ideas to tackle the migration crisis or the approach to handling the so-called Brexit.

The next question addressed by the authors considered the most important factors that shaped Polish-Slovak relations. This first and most obvious of those is their status as neighbors, along with the baggage of historic, cultural and social experience that such status necessarily entails. Geopolitical and geoeconomic determinants were also at play. The second element to be considered is their membership in the European Union. The third one involves the stimuli and expectations emanating from outside the European system, particularly from the United States and the Russian Federation. Given that the majority of Polish-Slovak cooperation occurs within the multilateral format (the Visegrad Group, the Union, NATO etc.), it is hardly surprising that the international environment frequently affects Polish-Slovak relations to a significant extent. One example of this influence is the fact that their membership in various international organizations presented the two governments with the need to coordinate certain policies (e.g. security, economic, regional). The prevalent role of the multilateral format also virtually guarantees the absence of serious tensions between Warsaw and Bratislava (also in a broader Central European perspective).

When formulating **general conclusions**, the authors have noticed that Polish-Slovak relations in every analyzed realm are characterized by a significant asymmetry. As was emphasized on several occasions throughout this volume, when examining bilateral cooperation between the two states, one needs to keep in mind the difference in quantifiable aspects such as territory, economic and demographic potential, the composition of armed forces or access to natural resources. A quick glance at these numbers reveals how far apart Poland and Slovakia are in terms of their political and economic positions in Europe. However, one also needs to remember that their similar geopolitical situation—being located on the borders of the Schengen area, having Ukraine as a neighbor, with Russia and Western Balkans in their vicinity—has led Poland and Slovakia to adopt postures and positions (revealed by their recent political statements) that guarantee compatible reactions to current challenges, risks and threats. Such situation has created an atmosphere of international interdependence in a multidimensional environment of the European system.

Another remark that deserves a place in these concluding pages of the book refers to the impact of Poland and Slovakia's integration with the EU and NATO. As the two countries pressed on to become fully-fledged members of Euro-Atlantic structures, their geopolitical situation and broadly similar policy goals spurred the creation of the Visegrad Group—a forum that both Warsaw and Bratislava have since considered as a platform for developing common positions, making their voice heard in Europe and (particularly for Poland) pursuing their national interests more effectively. The EU accession procedure, which both states underwent simultaneously, preserved and strengthened the bonds between all V4 partners. The process of entering the mainstream of European integration was unquestionably challenging. As members of the Union, Poland and Slovakia have been subjected to the so-called Europeanization—a multidimensional phenomenon affecting both official policies and informal internal discourse, not only at the national, but also at the regional and local level. Research conducted so far has allowed scholars to distinguish the impact of various aspects of Europeanization (up-, down- and cross-loading) on Polish and Slovak politics. Furthermore, while undergoing their socialization in the European community, the two countries have gradually learned about what influence they can exert on the formulation of EU norms, rules and policies—be it as individual governments, or when acting as a group of states that adopts a common standpoint on a given issue. For instance, the Visegrad Group has been recognized by many EU bodies as a legitimate platform that the V4 partners use to represent their regional interests.

A final conclusion stemming from the research conducted for the purpose of creating this volume refers to the approach that Warsaw and Bratislava adopted to shaping their mutual relations. It seems that both governments have increasingly made efforts to take account of **interests expressed by their domestic social groups** when formulating their foreign policies. Hence, regular bilateral relations were mostly focused on issues such as the development of transport infrastructure and cross-border cooperation in the area of tourism. In effect, the two states have gradually worked out the way to obtain pragmatic benefits from their joint efforts. If political alliances were formed, they were temporary and usually concerned the dynamics of European integration, e.g. negotiations over the EU's long-term budgets and climate policies. Since these issues remained essentially **unpoliticized** (i.e. they were not the subject of domestic political rivalries), Polish-Slovak bilateral relations were largely immune to the shifts in the political climate in Warsaw or Bratislava. Moreover, as both partners were aware of the disproportion in Poland's and Slovakia's political and economic potential, this discrepancy, that might have otherwise hampered cooperation, has also been a relatively neutral element. The analysis presented in this book suggests that the areas where bi- and multilateral relations were most dynamic were: mutual investments, trade, education, science and culture. As for an overall effectiveness of cooperation between Warsaw and Bratislava, its assessment is necessarily mixed. While much work has already been done at both the national and the regional level, at this point in time the potential hidden in Polish-Slovak bilateral cooperation is far from being fully exploited. This is particularly true with regard to issues such as developing tourism, promoting culture and improving political governance. In other fields (particularly education), successes achieved thus far can be used to reinforce trust and willingness to broaden and deepen the scope of cooperation between the two neighbors.

Combined references

Documents, official statements and data

Ambasada RP w Bratysławie (2015). „Relacje polsko-słowackie były, są i będą znakomite", 08.03.2015, available online at http://www.bratyslawa.m sz.gov.pl/pl/aktualnosci/0_relacje_polsko_slowackie_byly__sa_i_beda_ znakomite_, (access: 20.07.2016).

Centrum Badania Opinii Społecznej CBOS(2014). „Poczucie zagrożenia i zainteresowanie sytuacją na Ukrainie", Komunikat z Badań 164/2014, available online at http://www.cbos.pl/SPISKOM.POL/2014/K_164 _14.PDF, (access: 10.05.2016).

Centrum Badań Opinii Społecznej CBOS (2015a). „Stosunek do innych narodów", Komunikat z Badań 14/2015, available online at http://www.cbos.pl/SPISKOM.POL/2015/K_014_15.PDF, (access: 20.09.2016).

Centrum Badań Opinii Społecznej CBOS (2015b). „O stosunkach z sąsiednimi krajami—relacje polityczne a nastawienie do nacji", Komunikat z Badań 30/2015, available online at http://www.cbos.pl/SPISK OM.POL/2015/K_030_15.PDF, (access: 22.08.2016).

Council of Europe (1972). "1. Europäisches Symposium der Grenzregionen. Die Zusammenarbeit europäischer Grenzgebiete. Basisbericht, ausgearbeitet von V. Frhr. von Malchus", Strasbourg.

Council of Europe (1995). *Manuel de coopération transfrontaliére à l'usage des collectivités locales et régionales en Europe*. Strasbourg.

European Commission (2003a). "European Neighbourhood Policy — Strategy Paper", Communication from the Commission, COM(2004) 373 final Brussels, 12.5.2004, available online at http://eur-lex.europa.eu/leg al-content/EN/TXT/PDF/?uri=CELEX:52004DC0373&from=PL, (access: 21.09.2016).

European Commission (2003b). "Report on the results of the negotiations on the accession of Cyprus, Malta, Hungary, Poland, the Slovak Republic, Latvia, Estonia, Lithuania, the Czech Republic and Slovenia to the European Union", available at https://ec.europa.eu/neighbourhood-enla rgement/sites/near/files/archives/pdf/enlargement_process/future_ prospects/negotiations/eu10_bulgaria_romania/negotiations_report_ to_ep_en.pdf, (access 17.09.2009).

European Commission (2011). "Action Plan for North-South Energy Interconnections in Central-Eastern Europe", available online at https://ec.eu ropa.eu/energy/sites/ener/files/documents/2011_north_south_east_ action_plan_0.pdf, (access: 21.09.2016).

European Commission (2016). "Infrastructure TEN-T—Connecting Europe", available online at: http://ec.europa.eu/transport/themes/infrastruct ure/ten-t-guidelines/corridors_en, (access: 04.02.2017).

European Communities (2004). "Facing the challenge: The Lisbon strategy for growth and employment", Report from the High Level Group chaired by Wim Kok, Brussels: European Communities, available online at https://ec.europa.eu/research/evaluations/pdf/archive/fp6-evidence-base/evaluation_studies_and_reports/evaluation_studies_and_report s_2004/the_lisbon_strategy_for_growth_and_employment_report_from_the_high_level_group.pdf, (access: 11 March 2016).

European Council (2016). "Timeline—EU restrictive measures in response to the crisis in Ukraine", available online at http://www.consilium.europa.eu/en/policies/sanctions/ukraine-crisis/history-ukraine-crisis/, (access: 10.12.2016).

European Union (2009). "Consolidated versions of the Treaty on European Union and the Treaty on the Functioning of the European Union", C 326/01, available online at http://eur-lex.europa.eu/legal-content/en/TXT/?uri=CELEX:12012E/TXT, (access: 05.05.2016).

European Union (2010). "EU internal security strategy", available online at http://eur-lex.europa.eu/legal-content/EN/TXT/HTML/?uri=URISERV:jl0050&from=GA, (access: 05.05.2016).

Eurostat (2016.) „Economy and finance", available online at http://ec.europa.eu/eurostat/web/national-accounts/data/main-tables, (access: 15.12.2016).

Główny Urząd Statystyczny (2004). "Statistical Yearbook of the Republic of Poland", Warsaw: GUS.

Główny Urząd Statystyczny (2005). "Statistical Yearbook of the Republic of Poland", available online on: http://stat.gov.pl/en/topics/statistical-yearbooks/statistical-yearbooks/statistical-yearbook-of-the-republic-of-poland-2012,2,7.html, (access: 15.12.16).

Główny Urząd Statystyczny (2006). "Statistical Yearbook of the Republic of Poland", http://stat.gov.pl/en/topics/statistical-yearbooks/statistical-yearbooks/statistical-yearbook-of-the-republic-of-poland-2012,2,7.html, (access: 15.12.16).

Główny Urząd Statystyczny (2007a). "Economic Activity of Entities with Foreign Capital in 2007", available online at http://stat.gov.pl/obszary-tematyczne/podmioty-gospodarcze-wyniki-finansowe/przedsiebiorstwa-niefinansowe/dzialalnosc-gospodarcza-podmiotow-z-kapitalem-zagranicznym-w-2015-r-,4,11.html, (access: 15.12.2016).

Główny Urząd Statystyczny (2007b). "Statistical Yearbook of the Republic of Poland", available online on: http://stat.gov.pl/en/topics/statistical-yearbooks/statistical-yearbooks/statistical-yearbook-of-the-republic-of-poland-2006,2,1.html, (access: 15.12.16).

Główny Urząd Statystyczny (2008a). "Economic Activity of Entities with Foreign Capital in 2008", available online at http://stat.gov.pl/obszary-tematyczne/podmioty-gospodarcze-wyniki-finansowe/przedsiebiorstwa-niefinansowe/dzialalnosc-gospodarcza-podmiotow-z-kapitalem-zagranicznym-w-2015-r-,4,11.html, (access: 15.12.2016)

Główny Urząd Statystyczny (2008b). "Statistical Yearbook of the Republic of Poland", available online on: http://stat.gov.pl/en/topics/statistical-y

earbooks/statistical-yearbooks/statistical-yearbook-of-the-republic-of-poland-2008,2,3.html, (access: 15.12.16).
Główny Urząd Statystyczny (2009a). "Economic Activity of Entities with Foreign Capital in 2009", available online at http://stat.gov.pl/obszary-tematyczne/podmioty-gospodarcze-wyniki-finansowe/przedsiebiorst wa-niefinansowe/dzialalnosc-gospodarcza-podmiotow-z-kapitalem-z agranicznym-w-2015-r-,4,11.html, (access: 15.12.2016).
Główny Urząd Statystyczny (2009b). "Statistical Yearbook of the Republic of Poland", available online on: http://stat.gov.pl/en/topics/statistical-yearbooks/statistical-yearbooks/statistical-yearbook-of-the-republic-of-poland-2008,2,3.html, (access: 15.12.16).
Główny Urząd Statystyczny (2010a). "Economic Activity of Entities with Foreign Capital in 2010", available online at http://stat.gov.pl/obszary-te matyczne/podmioty-gospodarcze-wyniki-finansowe/przedsiebiorstw a-niefinansowe/dzialalnosc-gospodarcza-podmiotow-z-kapitalem-zag ranicznym-w-2015-r-,4,11.html, (access: 15.12.2016).
Główny Urząd Statystyczny (2010b). "Statistical Yearbook of the Republic of Poland", available online on: http://stat.gov.pl/en/topics/statistical-y earbooks/statistical-yearbooks/statistical-yearbook-of-the-republic-o f-poland-2008,2,3.html, (access: 15.12.16).
Główny Urząd Statystyczny (2011a). "Economic Activity of Entities with Foreign Capital in 2011", available online at http://stat.gov.pl/obszary-te matyczne/podmioty-gospodarcze-wyniki-finansowe/przedsiebiorstw a-niefinansowe/dzialalnosc-gospodarcza-podmiotow-z-kapitalem-zag ranicznym-w-2015-r-,4,11.html, (access: 15.12.2016)
Główny Urząd Statystyczny (2011b). "Statistical Yearbook of the Republic of Poland", available online on: http://stat.gov.pl/cps/rde/xbcr/gus/sy_ statitical_yearbook_of_the_rep_of_poland_2011.pdf, (access: 15.12.16).
Główny Urząd Statystyczny (2012a). "Economic Activity of Entities with Foreign Capital in 2012", available online at http://stat.gov.pl/obszary-te matyczne/podmioty-gospodarcze-wyniki-finansowe/przedsiebiorstw a-niefinansowe/dzialalnosc-gospodarcza-podmiotow-z-kapitalem-zag ranicznym-w-2015-r-,4,11.html, (access: 15.12.2016)
Główny Urząd Statystyczny (2012b). "Statistical Yearbook of the Republic of Poland", available online on: http://stat.gov.pl/en/topics/statistical-y earbooks/statistical-yearbooks/statistical-yearbook-of-the-republic-o f-poland-2012,2,7.html, (access: 15.12.16).
Główny Urząd Statystyczny (2013a). "Economic Activity of Entities with Foreign Capital in 2013", available online at http://stat.gov.pl/obszary-te matyczne/podmioty-gospodarcze-wyniki-finansowe/przedsiebiorstw a-niefinansowe/dzialalnosc-gospodarcza-podmiotow-z-kapitalem-zag ranicznym-w-2015-r-,4,11.html, (access: 15.12.2016)
Główny Urząd Statystyczny (2013b). "Statistical Yearbook of the Republic of Poland", available online on: http://stat.gov.pl/en/topics/statistical-yearbooks/statistical-yearbooks/statistical-yearbook-of-the-republic-of-poland-2013,2,8.html, (access: 15.12.16).

Główny Urząd Statystyczny (2014a). "Economic Activity of Entities with Foreign Capital in 2014", available online at http://stat.gov.pl/obszary-te matyczne/podmioty-gospodarcze-wyniki-finansowe/przedsiebiorstw a-niefinansowe/dzialalnosc-gospodarcza-podmiotow-z-kapitalem-zag ranicznym-w-2015-r-,4,11.html, (access: 15.12.2016)

Główny Urząd Statystyczny (2014b). "Statistical Yearbook of Foreign Trade Statistics of Poland", available online at http://stat.gov.pl/obszary-te matyczne/roczniki-statystyczne/roczniki-statystyczne/rocznik-statys tyczny-handlu-zagranicznego-2014,9,8.html, (access: 15.12.16).

Główny Urząd Statystyczny (2014c). "Statistical Yearbook of the Republic of Poland", available online on: http://stat.gov.pl/obszary-tematyczne/r oczniki-statystyczne/roczniki-statystyczne/rocznik-statystyczny-han dlu-zagranicznego-2016,9,10.html, (access: 15.12.16).

Główny Urząd Statystyczny (2015a). "Statistical Yearbook of the Republic of Poland", available online at http://stat.gov.pl/obszary-tematyczne/ro czniki-statystyczne/roczniki-statystyczne/rocznik-statystyczny-rzecz ypospolitej-polskiej-2015,2,10.html, (access: 15.12.16).

Główny Urząd Statystyczny (2015b). "Statistical Yearbook of the Republic of Poland", available online on: http://stat.gov.pl/obszary-tematyczne/ roczniki-statystyczne/roczniki-statystyczne/rocznik-statystyczny-rze czypospolitej-polskiej-2015,2,10.html, (access: 15.12.16).

Główny Urząd Statystyczny (2016a). "Statistical Yearbook of the Republic of Poland", available online at http://stat.gov.pl/obszary-tematyczne/ro czniki-statystyczne/roczniki-statystyczne/rocznik-statystyczny-handl u-zagranicznego,

Główny Urząd Statystyczny (2016b). "Statistical Yearbook of the Republic of Poland", available online on: http://stat.gov.pl/obszary-tematyczne /roczniki-statystyczne/roczniki-statystyczne/rocznik-statystyczny-handlu-zagranicznego-2016,9,10.html, (access: 31.12.16).

Government Office of the Slovak Republic (2013). "Národná rada Informácia o priebehu a výsledkoch spoločného rokovania predstaviteľov vlád Slovenskej republiky a Poľskej republiky", Poprad, 27. marca 2013. available online at http://www.rokovania.sk/File.aspx/Index/Mater-Dokum-154321, (access: 09.05.2016).

Government Office of the Slovak Republic (2016a). "Manifesto of the Government of the Slovak Republic 2016—2020", available online at http://www.vlada.gov.sk/manifesto-of-the-government/, (access: 20.09.2016).

Government Office of the Slovak Republic (2016b). "Biela kniha o obrane Slovenskej republiky", available online at http://www.rokovania.sk/File.a spx/ViewDocumentHtml/Mater-Dokum-201890?prefixFile=m_, (access: 30.08.2016).

Government Office of the Republic of Poland (2013). "Polsko-słowackie konsultacje międzyrządowe", 27.03.2013, available online at https://www.premier.gov.pl/wydarzenia/aktualnosci/rozpoczely-sie -polsko-slowackie-konsultacje-miedzyrzadowe.html, (access: 20.09.2016).

Government Office of the Republic of Poland (2014a). "6 wizyt, 12 spotkań. Premier Tusk promuje polską koncepcję unii energetycznej w Europie", 21.05.2014, available online at https://www.premier.g ov.pl/wydarzenia/aktualnosci/6-wizyt-12-spotkan-premier-tusk-pro muje-polska-koncepcje-unii-energetycznej-w.html, (access: 20.09.2016).

Government Office of the Republic of Poland (2014b). "Deklaracja Bratysławska szefów rządów państw Grupy Wyszehradzkiej w sprawie pogłębienia współpracy obronnej w ramach GW", 09.12.2014, available online at https://www.premier.gov.pl/deklaracja-bratyslawska-szefow-rzadow -panstw-grupy-wyszehradzkiej-w-sprawie-poglebienia-wspolpracy.ht ml, (access: 20.09.2016).

Interreg Poľsko-Slovensko (2015). "Program cezhraničnej spolupráce Interreg V-A Poľsko-Slovensko", available online at: https://sk.plsk.eu/-/test, (access:22.04.2016).

Interview (2016). Personal interview with the Expert at the Ministry of Defense of the Slovak Republic, (notes are available in the author's archive).

Ministry of Defence of the Slovak Republic (2007). "Minister Kašický na návšteve Poľska", available online at http://www.ustreps.sk/minister-kas icky-na-navsteve-polska/?day=2015-12-01&_od=2016-01-08&_do=2 016-01-08, (access: 02.05.2016).

Ministry of Defence of the Slovak Republic (2008). "Poľský minister obrany na návšteve Slovenska", available online at http://www.ustreps.sk/pol sky-minister-obrany-na-navsteve-slovenska/, (access: 02.05.2016).

Ministry of Defence of the Slovak Republic (2012). „M.Glváč: S Poľskom nechceme zostať len pri deklaráciách, očakávame konkrétne výsledky", available online at http://www.ustreps.sk/26139/mglvac-s -polskom-nechceme-zostat-len-pri-deklaraciach-ocakavame-konkretn e-vysledky/, (access: 01.05.2016).

Ministry of Defence of the Slovak Republic (2013). "Biela kniha o obrane Slovenskej republiky", available online at http://www.rokovania.sk/File. aspx/ViewDocumentHtml/Mater-Dokum-155890?prefixFile=m_, (access: 11.05.2016).

Ministry of Defence of the Slovak Republic (2014a). "Slovenské tanky sú opäť v akcii", available online at http://www.ustreps.sk/slovenske-tanky-su-opat-v-akcii/, (access: 02.05.2016).

Ministry of Defence of the Slovak Republic (2014b). "M. Glváč: Spolupráca s Poľskom v oblasti obrany naberá ďalšie dimenzie", available online at http://www.ustreps.sk/31565-sk/m-glvac-spolupraca-s-polskom-v-o blasti-obrany-nabera-dalsie-dimenzie/, (access: 02.05.2016).

Ministry of Defence of the Slovak Republic (2016). "M. Glváč: Vítame iniciatívu NATO prijať opatrenia na riešenie migračnej krízy", available online at http://www.mosr.sk/36607-sk/m-glvac-vitame-iniciativu-nato-prijat -opatrenia-na-riesenie-migracnej-krizy/, (access: 02.05.2016).

Ministry of Foreign and European Affairs of the Slovak Republic (2005). „Správa o plnení úloh zahraničnej politiky SR v roku 2005", available online at https://www.mzv.sk/documents/10182/1635498/Aktu%C

3%A1lny+ro%C4%8Dn%C3%BD+komponent+2005.pdf, (access: 01.05. 2016).
Ministry of Foreign and European Affairs of the Slovak Republic (2006). „Správa o plnení úloh zahraničnej politiky SR v roku 2006", available online at https://www.mzv.sk/documents/10182/1635498/2006. pdf, (access: 01.05.2016).
Ministry of Foreign and European Affairs of the Slovak Republic (2009). "Report on the Foreign Policy Activities of the Slovak Republic in 2009", available online at http://www.foreign.gov.sk/documents/30297/25 68657/100415+2009+Report+on+the+Foreign+Policy+Activities+of+ the+Slovak+Republic+2009, (access: 20.09.2016).
Ministry of Foreign and European Affairs of the Slovak Republic (2010a). "Orientation of the foreign policy of the Slovak Republic in 2010", available online at https://www.mzv.sk/documents/30297/124861/Zame ranie_2010_fin_EN.pdf, (access: 20.09.2016).
Ministry of Foreign and European Affairs of the Slovak Republic (2010b). "Slovak Foreign Policy Report 2010", available online at http://www.fore ign.gov.sk/documents/30297/2568657/110401+2011+Slovak+Forei gn+Policy+Report+2010, (access: 20.09.2016).
Ministry of Foreign and European Affairs of the Slovak Republic (2010c). *Správa o plnení úloh zahraničnej politiky Slovenskej republiky v roku 2010.* available online at https://www.mzv.sk/documents/10182/ 621946/Vyhodnotenie_2010.pdf, (access: 01.05..2016).
Ministry of Foreign and European Affairs of the Slovak Republic (2011a). "Slovak Foreign Policy Guidelines 2011", available online at http://ww w.foreign.gov.sk/documents/30297/2568657/110331+Slovak+Forei gn+Policy+Guidelines+2011, (access: 20.10.2016).
Ministry of Foreign and European Affairs of the Slovak Republic (2011b). "Report on the Fulfilment of Foreign Policy Tasks of the Slovak Republic in 2011", available online at http://www.foreign.gov.sk/documents/ 30297/2568657/120509+Report+on+the+Fulfilment+of+Foreign+Po licy+Tasks+of+the+Slovak+Republic+in+2011, (access: 20.10.2016).
Ministry of Foreign Affairs of the Slovak Republic (2012a). "Slovakia will contribute to the European Endowment for Democracy", Aktivity ministra, 21.8.2012, available online at https://www.mzv.sk/web/en/ news/current_issues/-/asset_publisher/lrJ2tDuQdEKp/content/slova kia-will-contribute-to-the-european-endowment-for-democracy/101 82, (access: 21.09.2016).
Ministry of Foreign and European Affairs of the Slovak Republic (2012b). "Správa o plnení úloh zahraničnej politiky Slovenskej republiky v roku 2012", available online at https://www.mzv.sk/documents/10182/ 1635498/130228_sprava_o_plneni_uloh_ZP_2012.pdf, (access: 02.05.2016).
Ministry of Foreign Affairs of the Slovak Republic (2013). "The European Endowment for Democracy ready to start its activities soon", 11.01.2013, available online at https://www.mzv.sk/web/en/news/current_issue s/-/asset_publisher/lrJ2tDuQdEKp/content/the-european-endowmen

t-for-democracy-ready-to-start-its-activities-soon/10182, (access: 23.09.2016).
Ministry of Foreign Affairs of the Slovak Republic (2014a) "Report on Fulfilling Slovakia's Objectives and Responsibilities in Foreign and European Policy in 2013", available online at http://www.foreign.gov.sk/docum ents/30297/2568657/140718_Report_2013_EN_final.pdf, (access: 23.09.2016).
Ministry of Foreign Affairs of the Slovak Republic (2014b). "Direction of Slovak Foreign and European Policy in 2014", available online at http://www.foreign.gov.sk/documents/30297/2568657/140214+2014+Directio n+of+Slovak+Foreign+and+European+Policy+2014.pdf (access: 23.09.2016).
Ministry of Foreign Affairs of the Slovak Republic (2015a). "Slovak Foreign and European Policy Agenda in 2015", available online at http://www.fo reign.gov.sk/documents/30297/2568657/150108_SK_Foreign_Policy _Agendadoc.pdf (access: 23.09.2016).
Ministry of Foreign Affairs of the Slovak Republic (2015b). "Foreign and European Policy in 2014 Annual Report of the Ministry of Foreign and European Affairs of the Slovak Republic", available online at https://w ww.mzv.sk/documents/30297/124856/150416_vyrocna_sprava_MZ VaEZ_SR_2014_EN.pdf (access: 23.10.2016).
Ministry of Foreign and European Affairs of the Slovak Republic (2015c). "Zameranie zahraničnej a európskej politiky Slovenskej republiky na rok 2015", available online at https://www.mzv.sk/App/wcm/media.nsf/ vw_ByID/ID_16A59B91DCF4DF52C1257DB2005968D3_SK/$File/za meranie2015.pdf, (access: 11.02.2015).
Ministry of Foreign and European Affairs of the Slovak Republic (2015d). „Návrh zamerania činnosti Veľvyslanectva Slovenskej republiky v Poľskej republik", internal documents available in the author's archive.
Ministry of Foreign and European Affairs of the Slovak Republic (2015e). "Slovenská republika a Organizácia Spojených národov", available online at http://www.mzv.sk/zahranicna_politika/slovensko_v_osn-sr_v_osn, (access: 05.05.2016).
Ministry of Foreign and European Affairs of the Slovak Republic (2015f). "Slovensko v OBSE", available online at http://www.mzv.sk/zahranicna_p olitika/slovensko_v_obse, (access: 05.05.2016).
Ministry of Foreign and European Affairs of the Slovak Republic (2015g). "Spoločná zahraničná a bezpečnostná politika", available online at https://www.mzv.sk/zahranicna_politika/europske_zalezitosti-spoloc na_zahranicna_a_bezpecnostna_politika_szbp, (access: 05.05.2016).
Ministry of Foreign and European Affairs of the Slovak Republic (2015h). "Informácia o realizácii programu predsedníctva SR vo V4 a vyhodnotenie hlavných aktivít vyšehradskej spolupráce v období od 1.7.2014 do 30.6.2015" available online at https://www.mzv.sk/documents/1018 2/12475/151019_ODV4_material.pdf/07d45dae-e54a-43bb-96bc-46 002d16628b, (access: 08.052016).

Ministerstwo Spraw Zagranicznych Rzeczypospolitej Polskiej (2004). "Informacja rządu na temat polskiej polityki zagranicznej w 2004 roku przedstawiana na posiedzeniu Sejmu w dniu 21 stycznia 2004 roku przez ministra spraw zagranicznych RP Włodzimierza Cimoszewicza", available online at http://www.msz.gov.pl/pl/polityka_zagraniczna/p riorytety_polityki_zagr_2012_2016/expose2/expose_2004/, (access: 23.09.2016).

Ministerstwo Spraw Zagranicznych Rzeczypospolitej Polskiej (2005). "Informacja rządu na temat polskiej polityki zagranicznej przedstawiana na posiedzeniu Sejmu w dniu 21 stycznia 2005 roku przez ministra spraw zagranicznych RP prof. Adama Daniela Rotfelda", available online at http://www.msz.gov.pl/resource/47f55 1c9-fa2e-4e93-9436-5be43b389755:JCR, (access: 22.09.2016).

Ministerstwo Spraw Zagranicznych Rzeczypospolitej Polskiej (2006). "Informacja rządu na temat polskiej polityki zagranicznej w 2006 roku przedstawiana na posiedzeniu Sejmu w dniu 15 lutego 2006 roku przez ministra spraw zagranicznych RP Stefana Mellera", available online at http://www.msz.gov.pl/resource/47f551c9-fa2e-4e93-943 6-5be43b389755:JCR (access: 12.12.2014).

Ministerstwo Spraw Zagranicznych Rzeczypospolitej Polskiej (2007). "Informacja rządu na temat polskiej polityki zagranicznej w 2007 roku przedstawiana na posiedzeniu Sejmu w dniu 11 maja 2007 roku przez ministra spraw zagranicznych RP Annę Fotygę", available online at http://www.msz.gov.pl/resource/a0e6bf27-f0b3-4864-83ad-18a425211525:JCR, (access: 12.12.2014).

Ministerstwo Spraw Zagranicznych Rzeczypospolitej Polskiej (2008). "Informacja ministra spraw zagranicznych Radosława Sikorskiego na temat polityki zagranicznej RP w roku 2008, przedstawiana na posiedzeniu Sejmu w dniu 7 maja 2008 roku", available online at http://orka2.sejm.gov.pl/Debata6.nsf/main/20C429OE, (dostęp: 11.012.2014).

Ministerstwo Spraw Zagranicznych Rzeczypospolitej Polskiej (2009). "Informacja Ministra Spraw Zagranicznych o zadaniach polskiej polityki zagranicznej w 2009 roku, przedstawiana na posiedzeniu Sejmu w dniu 13 maja 2009 roku", http://orka2.sejm.gov.pl/Deb ata6.nsf/main/72FD280E, (access: 23.09.2016).

Ministerstwo Spraw Zagranicznych Rzeczypospolitej Polskiej (2010). "Informacja ministra spraw zagranicznych Radosława Sikorskiego o założeniach polskiej polityki zagranicznej w 2010 roku, przedstawiana na posiedzeniu Sejmu w dniu 8 kwietnia 2010 roku", available online at http://orka2.sejm.gov.pl/Debata6.nsf/main/583 C4C86, (access: 23.09.2016).

Ministerstwo Spraw Zagranicznych Rzeczypospolitej Polskiej (2011). "Informacja ministra spraw zagranicznych Radosława Sikorskiego o założeniach polskiej polityki zagranicznej w 2011 roku, przedstawiana na posiedzeniu Sejmu w dniu 16 marca 2011 roku",

available online at http://orka2.sejm.gov.pl/Debata6.nsf/main/42A5 B0D0, (access: 23.09.2016).
Ministerstwo Spraw Zagranicznych Rzeczypospolitej Polskiej (2012a). "Priorytety Polskiej Polityki Zagranicznej 2012-2016", Warszawa, marzec, available online at https://www.msz.gov.pl/resource/aa1c4a ec-a52f-45a7-96e5-06658e73bb4e:JCR, (access: 20.07.2016).
Ministerstwo Spraw Zagranicznych Rzeczypospolitej Polskiej (2012b). "Informacja ministra spraw zagranicznych Radosława Sikorskiego o założeniach polskiej polityki zagranicznej w 2012 roku, przedstawiana na posiedzeniu Sejmu w dniu 29 marca 2012 roku", available online at https://www.msz.gov.pl/pl/p/msz_pl/polityka_zag raniczna/priorytety_polityki_zagr_2012_2016/expose2/expose_2012 /, (access: 23.09.2016).
Ministerstwo Spraw Zagranicznych Rzeczypospolitej Polskiej (2013). "Informacja ministra spraw zagranicznych Radosława Sikorskiego o założeniach polskiej polityki zagranicznej w 2013 roku, przedstawiana na posiedzeniu Sejmu w dniu 20 marca 2013 roku", available online at https://www.msz.gov.pl/pl/p/msz_pl/polityka_zag raniczna/priorytety_polityki_zagr_2012_2016/expose2/expose_2013 /, (access: 23.09.2016).
Ministerstwo Spraw Zagranicznych Rzeczypospolitej Polskiej (2014). "Informacja ministra spraw zagranicznych o zadaniach polskiej polityki zagranicznej w 2014 roku, przedstawiana na posiedzeniu Sejmu w dniu 08 maja 2014 roku", available online at https://www.msz.gov.pl/pl/p/msz_pl/polityka_zagraniczna/priorytet y_polityki_zagr_2012_2016/expose2/expose_2014/, (access: 23.09.2016).
Ministerstwo Spraw Zagranicznych Rzeczypospolitej Polskiej (2015). "Informację Ministra Spraw Zagranicznych o zadaniach polskiej polityki zagranicznej w 2015 roku. przedstawiana na posiedzeniu Sejmu w dniu 23 kwietnia 2015 roku", available online at https://www.msz.gov.pl/pl/p/msz_pl/polityka_zagraniczna/priorytet y_polityki_zagr_2012_2016/expose2/expose_2015/, (access: 23.09.2016).
Ministerstwo Spraw Zagranicznych Rzeczypospolitej Polskiej (2016). "Joint Statement of the Heads of Governments of the V4 Countries", Bratislava, 16 September 2016, available online https://www.msz.gov.pl/res ource/4e985f7f-8a2d-416b-8b3f-52e7f704c414:JCR, (access: 23.12.2016).
Ministry of Foreign Affairs Republic of Poland (2016a). "Organisation for Security and Co-operation in Europe", available online at http://www.ms z.gov.pl/en/foreign_policy/security_policy/osce/, (access: 05.05.2016).
Ministry of Foreign Affairs Republic of Poland (2016b). *Eastern Partnership*, available online at http://www.msz.gov.pl/en/foreign_policy/eastern _partnership/, (access: 05.05.2016).

Ministry of National Defence Republic of Poland (2009). "Strategia obronności Rzeczypospolitej Polskiej 2009", available online at http://www.bbn.g ov.pl/portal/pl/475/2826/Strategia_Obronnosci_Rzeczypospolitej_Po lskiej.html (access: 10.01.2013).
Ministerstwo Ochrony Środowiska (2014). „Grupa Wyszehradzka o klimacie", available online at http://klimada.mos.gov.pl/blog/2014/02/12/gru pa-wyszehradzka-o-klimacie/ (access: 23.10.2016).
National Bank of Poland (2016). "Polish Direct Investments", Warsaw: NBP, available online at http://www.nbp.pl/home.aspx?f=/publikacje/pib/ pib.html, (access: 31.12.2016).
National Council of the Slovak Republic (2005a). "Bezpečnostná stratégia Slovenskej republiky z roku 2005", available online at http://www.mod.go v.sk/data/files/833.pdf, (access: 11.05.2016).
National Council of the Slovak Republic (2005b). "Obranná stratégia Slovenskej republiky z roku 2005", available online at http://www.mod.gov.sk/ data/files/832.pdf, (access: 11.05.2016).
National Security Bureau (2007). "National Security Strategy of the Republic of Poland. 2007", available online at https://www.files.ethz.ch/isn/1567 96/Poland-2007-eng.pdf, (access: 10.05.2016).
National Security Bureau (2013). „Biała Księga bezpieczeństwa narodowego Rzeczypospolitej Polskiej 2013", available online at https://www.bb n.gov.pl/ftp/dok/01/Biala_Ksiega_inter_mm.pdf, (access: 01.05.2016).
National Security Bureau (2014). *National Security Strategy of the Republic of Poland 2014.* available online at https://www.bbn.gov.pl/ftp/dok/ NSS_RP.pdf, (access: 11.05 2016).
North Atlantic Treaty Organization NATO (2010). "Active Engagement, Modern Defence. Strategic Concept 2010 for the Defence and Security of the Members of the North Atlantic Treaty Organization Adopted by Heads of State and Government" at the NATO Summit in Lisbon 19-20 November 2010, available online at http://www.nato.int/nato_static_ fl2014/assets/pdf/pdf_publications/20120214_strategic-concept-201 0-eng.pdf, (access: 05.05.2016).
Premier RP (2016). "Premierzy III Rzeczypospolitej", available online at https://www.premier.gov.pl./ludzie.html, (access: 20.07.2016).
Ośrodek Badania Opinii Publicznej TNS OBOP (2004). „Sąsiedzi", komunikat z badań 078/04, available online at http://tnsglobal.pl/archiv_files/ 078-04.pdf, (access: 20.07.2016).
Sejm RP (2016). „Internatowy System Aktów Prawnych", available online at http://isip.sejm.gov.pl/KeyWordServlet?viewName=thasS&passName =S%C5%82owacja&isNext=true, (access: 20.07.2016).
Slovenský inštitút (2016). "Slovenský inštitút vo Varšave", available online at https://www.mzv.sk/web/sivarsava/o_nas, (access:22.03.2016).
The German Marshall Fund of the United States (GMF) (2012). "Transatlantic Trends: Public Opinion and NATO", 16.05.2012, available online at http://www.gmfus.org/commentary/transatlantic-trends-public-opin ion-and-nato, (access: 20.07.2016).

Úrad vlády Slovenskej republiky (2016). "Členovia vlády", available online at http://www.vlada.gov.sk/clenovia-vlady, (access: 11.05.2016).
Visegrad Group (1999). "Contents of Visegrad Cooperation 1999", available online at http://www.visegradgroup.eu/cooperation/contents-of-visegrad-110412, (access: 11.05.2016).
Visegrad Group (2001). "Presidents of the V4 States (19 January 2001)". available online at http://www.visegradgroup.eu/2001/presidents-of-the-v4, (access: 11 May 2016).
Visegrad Group (2004a). "Communiqué on the 12th meeting of the Ministers of Culture of the Visegrad Group Countries", 10–11 November 2004, available online at http://www.visegradgroup.eu/2004/communique-on-the-12th, (access: 18.03.2016).
Visegrad Group (2004b). "Guidelines on the Future Areas of Visegrad Cooperation", available at: http://www.visegradgroup.eu/cooperation/guidelines-on-the-future-110412, (access: 11.03.2016).
Visegrad Group (2005). "Fields of Cooperation between the Visegrad Group Countries and the Benelux. List of Decisions for the Meeting in Bratislava on the 15–16th of February 2005", available online at http://www.visegradgroup.eu/2005/fields-of-cooperation, (access: 12.03.2016).
Visegrad Group (2007). "Joint Communiqué of the Ministers of Defence of the Visegrad Group Countries", available online at http://www.visegradgroup.eu/2007/joint-communique-of-the, (access: 11.05.2016).
Visegrad Group (2011). "The Bratislava Declaration of the Prime Ministers of the Czech Republic, the Republic of Hungary, the Republic of Poland and the Slovak Republic on the occasion of the 20th anniversary of the Visegrad Group", available online at http://www.visegradgroup.eu/2011/the-bratislava, (access: 11.05.2016).
Visegrad Group (2012a). "Declaration of Prime Ministers of the Czech Republic, the Republic of Hungary, the Republic of Poland and the Slovak Republic on cooperation of the Visegrad Group countries after their accession to the European Union", 12 May 2004 Kroměříž, available online at http://www.visegradgroup.eu/2004/declaration-of-prime, (access: 22.09.2016).
Visegrad Group (2012b). "Guidelines on the Future Areas of Visegrad Cooperation", 12 May 2004 Kroměříž, available online at http://www.visegradgroup.eu/cooperation/guidelines-on-the-future-110412, (access: 22.09.2016).
Visegrad Group (2014a). "Joint Statement of the Visegrad Group and Ukraine", available online at http://www.visegradgroup.eu/calendar/2014/joint-statement-of-the-141217, (access: 11.05.2016).
Visegrad Group (2014b). "Long-Term Vision of the Visegrad Countries on Deepening their Defence Cooperation", available online at http://www.visegradgroup.eu/calendar/2014-03-14-ltv, (access: 11.05.2016).

Visegrad Group (2014c). "Slovak Presidency Program 2014–2015", available online at: http://www.visegradgroup.eu/documents/presidency-pro grams/20142015-slovak, (access: 23.01.2017).
Visegrad Group (2015). "Joint Communiqué of the Visegrad Group Ministers of Defence", available at: http://www.visegradgroup.eu/calendar/2015 /joint-communique-of-the, (access: 08.05.2016).
Visegrad Group (2016a). "Calendar of selected events", available online at http://www.visegradgroup.eu/calendar, (access: 22.09.2016).
Visegrad Group (2016b). "Statement of V4 Interior Ministers on the Establishment of the Migration Crisis Response Mechanism", Warsaw, November 21, available online at https://www.msz.gov.pl/resource/4e985f7 f-8a2d-416b-8b3f-52e7f704c414:JCR, (access: 22.01.2017).
Visegrad Group (2016c). "Polish Presidency Program 2015-2016", available online at http://www.visegradgroup.eu/documents/presidency-pro grams/program-of-the-polish, (access: 22.01.2017).

Reports, Analyses

Association of European Border Regions AEBR (1997). "*The EU Initiative INTERREG and future developments*" December 1997, available online at http://www.aebr.eu/files/publications/interreg_97.en.pdf, (access: 10.08.2016).
Atkinson, Sarah & Vyas, Lily (2013). "Financial Instruments—A Stock-taking Exercise: TA Survey Analysis. Final Report", Brussels: Mazars LLP / European Investment Bank, available online at http://www.eib.org /attachments/documents/jessica_stocktaking_survey_analysis_en-pdf .pdf ,(access: 05.05.2016).
Atradius N.V. (2016). "Industry match-ups Wales vs Slovakia", *Industry Match-up Reports*, June 6th 2016, available online at https://group.atrad ius.com/publications/industry-match-ups-wales-slovakia-2016.html, (access: 5.05.2016).
Bodnárová, Barbora (2013). "Visegrad four Battle Group 2016: Run up to Visegrad four NATO Response Force 2020?", *Policy Paper*, Centre for European and North Atlantic Affairs, available online at http://cenaa.org /wp-content/uploads/2014/05/Barbora-Bodnarova-PP-No.-9-2013-Vol.-2.pdf, (access 11.05.2016).
Brudzińska Kinga (2012). „Początki Europejskiego Funduszu na rzecz Demokracji", *Biuletyn PISM*, 104 (969), Polski Instutut Spraw Międzynarodowych, available online at https://www.pism.pl/files/ ?id_plik=12481,
Elekdag, Selim & Muir, Dirk (2013). "Trade Linkages, Balance Sheets, and Spillovers: The Germany-Central European Supply Chain". *IMF Working Paper* WP/13/210, International Monetary Fund, available online at https://www.imf.org/external/pubs/ft/wp/2013/wp13210.pdf, (access: 22.09.2016).

Estrin, Saul & Uvalic, Millica (2013). "FDI Into Transition Economies: Are The Balkans Different?", *LEQS Paper* 64/2013, London: European Institute London School of Economics available online at http://www.lse.ac.uk/europeanInstitute/LEQS%20Discussion%20Paper%20Series/LEQSPaper64.pdf, (access: 13.01.2017r.).

Gotkowska, Justyna & Osica, Olaf, (eds.) (2012). "Closing the gap?: military co-operation from The Baltic Sea to The Black Sea", *OSW Raport*, Warsaw: Centre for Eastern Studies, December 2012, available online at http://www.osw.waw.pl/sites/default/files/closing_the_gap_net_0.pdf, (access: 04.05.2016).

Gromadzki, Grzegorz (2015). "Perception of the Russia-Ukraine conflict in Germany and in Poland—an evaluation". Warsaw: Heinrich-Böll-Stiftung, available online at https://pl.boell.org/en/2015/09/08/perception-russia-ukraine-conflict-germany-and-poland-evaluation, (access: 10.05.2016).

Grodzki, Radosław (2015). „Grupa Wyszehradzka i kryzys uchodźczy: solidarnie przeciw solidarności europejskiej?", *Biuletyn Instytutu Zachodniego Seria Specjalna—'Uchodźcy w Europie*, 203/2015, available online at http://www.iz.poznan.pl/plik,pobierz,93,16b1dedc4c06f692c1c2f5a9f493258f/1271-Wyszegrad-uchodzcy.pdf, (access: 10.12.2016).

Guagliano, Claudia & Riela, Stefano (2005). "Do special economic areas matter in attracting FDI? Evidence from Poland, Hungary and Czech Republic", Milano: ISLA Istituto di Studi Latino-Americani e dei Paesi in transizione, available online at ftp://ftp.unibocconi.it/pub/RePEc/slp/papers/islawp21.pdf, (access: 10.05.2016).

Górka-Winter, Beata (2013). "Poland", Center for European and North Atlantic Affairs, available online at http://cenaa.org/analysis/wp-content/uploads/2013/10/Chapter-6-Poland.pdf, (access: 11.05.2016).

International Monetary Fund (IMF) (2009). "Balance of payments and international investment position manual", *Sixth Edition (BPM6)*, available online at http://www.imf.org/external/pubs/ft/bop/2007/pdf/bpm6.pdf, (access: 22.01.2017).

International Monetary Fund IMF (2013). "IMF Multi-Country Report, German-Central European Supply Chain-Cluster Report", *IMF Country Report*,13/263, August 2013 available online at http://www.imf.org/external/pubs/ft/scr/2013/cr13263.pdf, (access: 22.01.2017).

International Monetary Fund (2014). "Central, Eastern, and Southeastern Europe", *Regional Economic Issues*, April 2014, available online at https://www.imf.org/external/pubs/ft/reo/2014/eur/eng/pdf/ereo0414.pdf, (access: 22.06.2016).

Kaczmarski Marcin (2011). „The fragile 'reset'. The balance and the prospects for changes in Russian", *Policy Brief. Punkt Widzenia*, Warsaw: Centre for Eastern Studies, April 2011, available online at http://www.osw.waw.pl/sites/default/files/policy_briefs_24.pdf, (access: 23.09.2016).

Majer, Marian (2013). "Slovakia", Center for European and North Atlantic Affairs, available online at http://cenaa.org/analysis/wp-content/upl oads/2013/10/Chapter-7-Slovakia.pdf, (access 11.05.2016).

Majer, Marián et al. (2015). "From Bullets to Supersonics: V4 in the Brink of Industrial Cooperation", *DAV4 III Expert Group Report*, Central European Policy Institute, Bratislava available online at http://www.cepo licy.org/sites/cepolicy.org/files/attachments/dav_4_full_report_2015_ web_0.pdf, (access: 08.05.2016).

Majer, Marián & Schneider, Jiří & Šuplata, Milan (2016). "Crisis in Ukraine and the V4's Defence and Military Adoption", The Centre for Euro-Atlantic Integration and Democracy (CEID), available online at http://www.ce id.hu/ukraine-crisis-and-the-v4s-defence-and-military-adaption/ (access: 11.05.2016).

Marušiak, Juraj (2005). "Hlavné politické a ekonomické determinanty slovensko-pol'ských bilaterálnych vzťahov", *Analýzy*, available online at http://euractiv.sk/analyzy/uncategorized/hlavne-politicke-a-ekonom icke-determinanty-slovensko-polskyc/, (access: 11 March 2016).

Mix, Derek E. (2016). "Poland and Its Relations with the United States", *CRS Report Prepared for Members and Committees of Congress*, Washington D.C., 7 March, available online at https://fas.org/sgp/crs/row/R4421 2.pdf (access: 08.05.2016).

Mottaleb, Khondoker A. (2007). "Determinants of Foreign Direct Investment and Its Impact on Economic Growth in Developing Countries" MPRA Paper no. 9457, available online at https://mpra.ub.uni-muenchen.de /9457/1/, (access: 22.01.2017).

Naď, Jaroslav & Šuplata, Milan & Majer, Marián (2016). "DAV4 five years later: Success or a missed opportunity?",The GLOBSEC Policy Institute, available online at http://www.cepolicy.org/publications/dav4-five-years-later-success-or-missed-opportunity, (access: 08.05.2016).

O'Donnell, Clara M. (2012). "Poland's U-turn on European defence: A missed opportunity?", *Policy Brief*, Centre for European Reform, available online at http://www.cer.org.uk/sites/default/files/publications/att achments/pdf/2012/pb_poland_9march12-4791.pdf, (access: 11.05.2016).

Ondrejcsák, Róbert (2014). "Slovak National Security Strategy is Outdated and Needs a Change", *Policy Papers* 3(9), Center for European and North Atlantic Affairs, available online at: http://cenaa.org/en/wp-conte nt/uploads/2014/10/Strategy-PP1.pdf, (access: 11.05.2016).

Organisation for Economic Cooperation and Development OECD (2002), "Foreign Direct Investment For Development. Maximising benefits, minimising costs", *Report*, available online at https://www.oecd.org/inv estment/investmentfordevelopment/1959815.pdf, (access: 14.01.2017).

Organisation for Economic Cooperation and Development OECD (2008a). "Regional Development in Poland", *Policy Brief*, November 2008. Paris: OECD.

Organisation for Economic Cooperation and Development OECD (2008b), "OECD Benchmark Definition of Foreign Direct Investment", Firth edition, available online at https://www.oecd.org/daf/inv/investment statisticsandanalysis/40193734.pdf, (access: 14.01.2017).

Popławski, Konrad (2016). "The role of Central Europe in the German economy", *OSW Report*, Centre for Eastern Studies—Warsaw, September 2016, available online at https://www.osw.waw.pl/sites/default/fi les/report_role-ce_2.pdf, (access: 14.01.2017).

Stehrer, Robert and Stöllinger, Roman (2015). "The Central European Manufacturing Core: What is Driving Regional Production Sharing?", *FIW-Research Reports*, 15(2), available online at http://www.fiw.ac.at/filea dmin/Documents/Publikationen/Studien_2014/02_Stoellinger_FIW% 20Research%20Report_The%20Central%20European%20Manufactu ring%20Core%20What%20is%20Driving%20Regional%20Productio n%20Sharing.pdf, (access: 29.02.2016).

Strážay, Tomáš (2015). "Exploring possibilities of deepening the internal cohesion of the V4: Polish and Slovak perspectives", *Visegrad Experts Project*, available online at http://www.sfpa.sk/wp-content/uploads/20 15/09/Internal-Cohesion-of-the-V4_SK-and-PL-perspectives.pdf, (access: 12.01.2017).

Šuplata, Milan, et al. (2012). "DAV II Export Group Report on Visegrad Defence Collaboration. From Battlegroup to Permanent Structure", Central European Policy Institute, available online at https://www.pism.pl/file s/?id_plik=15827, (access: 12.01.2017).

Šuplata, Milan (2013a). "The Visegrad Battlegroup: Building new capabilities for the region", The GLOBSEC Policy Institute, 17.04.2013, available online at http://www.cepolicy.org/publications/visegrad-battlegro up-building-new-capabilities-region, (access: 11.05.2016).

Šuplata, Milan, et. al. (2013b). "From battlegroup to permanent structures", The GLOBSEC Policy Institute, available online at 18.11.2013, http://ww w.cepolicy.org/publications/dav4-ii-report-battlegroup-permanent-st ructures, (access: 11.05.2016).

Takáč, Kristián & Kaszab, Róbert, & Sobják, Anita & Trejbal, Václav (2013). "Once in a lifetime: opportunities for Visegrad in EU energy infrastructure plans", *Policy Brief*, GLOBSEC Policy Institute, 15.04.2013, available online at http://www.cepolicy.org/publications/once-lifetime-op portunities-visegrad-eu-energy-infrastructure-plans, (access: 12.01.2017).

Tarasovič, Vladimír (2013). "Reformy ozbrojených síl Slovenskej republiky nielen ako podmienka integrácie do NATO", Center for European and North Atlantic Affairs, available online at http://cenaa.org/analy sis/reformy-ozbrojenych-sil-slovenskej-republiky-nielen-ako-podmienka-integracie-do-nato/, (access: 11.05.2016).

Toporowski, Patryk (2015). "A Post-Crisis Eurozone: Still an Attractive Offer for Central Europe", *PISM Policy Paper* 22(124), available online at http://www.pism.pl/Publications/PISM-Policy-Paper-no-124, (access: 12.01.2017).

Wyżnikiewicz, Bohdan (2014). „Współpraca gospodarcza Polska—Niemcy", Instytut Badań nad Gospodarką Rynkową & Fundacja Konrada Adenauera w Polsce, Warszawa, available online at http://ahk.pl/file admin/ahk_polen/OA/Polska-Niemcy_2014-www.pdf, (access: 14.01.2017).

Valášek, Tomáš, et al. (2012). "Towards a Deeper Visegrad Defence Partnership", *DAV4 Full Report*, Central European Policy Institute, available online at http://www.cepolicy.org/publications/dav4-full-report-tow ards-deeper-visegrad-defence-partnership (access: 11.05.2016).

Books, journal articles

Acocella, Nicola & Di Bartolomeo, Giovanni & Hallett, Andrew H. (2016). "Macroeconomic Paradigms and Economic Policy", Cambridge: Cambridge University Press.

Alecu de Flers, Nicole & Müller, Patrick (2012). „Dimensions and mechanism of the Europeanization of member state foreign policy: state of the art and new research avenues", *Journal of European Integration* 34(1): 19-35.

Algayerová, Oľga (2010). "Establishment of Public Diplomacy in Slovakia. An Effective New Approach", La Valetta: University of Malta, available online at: https://www.diplomacy.edu/sites/default/files/30112010 145436%20Algayerova%20%28Library%29.pdf, (access: 11.06.2016).

Ali, Fathi & Fiess, Norbert & MacDonald, Ronald (2010), "Do Institutions Matter For Foreign Direct Investment", *Open Economic Review* 21(2): 201–219.

Allen E., Roy (2009). "Financial crises and Recession in the Global Economy", 3rd edition, Cheltenham UK: Edward Elgar Publishing Ltd.

Anyanwu, John C. (2012). "Why Does Foreign Direct Investment Go Where It Goes?: New Evidence From African Countries", *Annals of Economics and Finance* 13(2): 425-462.

Asmus, Ronald D. (2002). "Dvere do NATO", Bratislava: Kaligram.

Asongu, Simplice & Kodila-Tedika, Oasis (2015). "Conditional Determinants of FDI in Fast Emerging Economies: An Instrumental Quantile Regression Approach", *African Governance and Development Institute Working Paper* 15/003.

Bajda, Piotr (2010). „Polityka zagraniczna Słowacji", in Pałka, Elżbieta (ed.) *Współczesna Słowacja. Sytuacja wewnętrzna i pozycja międzynarodowa*, Wrocław: Oficyna Wydawnicza Arboretum: 255–278.

Banat, Małgorzata & Pałłasz, Urszula (2006). "Poland in the European Union", *Yearbook of Polish Foreign Policy*, 1: 42-66.

Banerjee, Biswajit & Jarmuzek, Mariusz (2010)."Economic Growth and Regional Disparities in the Slovak Republic", *Comparative Economic Studies* 52(3): 379-403.

Baláž, Peter & Margan, Forián & Ružeková, Viera & Zábojník Stanislav (2011). "Energetická bezpečnosť v období globalizácie a jej vplyv na konkurencieschopnosť EÚ", Bratislava: Sprint dva.
Berend, Ivan T. (2009). "From the Soviet Bloc to the European Union", Cambridge: Cambridge University Press.
Bieniek, Jakub (2012). "Bezpieczeństwo i obronność jako nowe dyscypliny naukowe", *Obronność—Zeszyty Naukowe Wydziału Zarządzania i Dowodzenia Akademii Obrony Narodowej*, 2012(2): 5-15.
Bilčík, Vladimír (2010). "Foreign Policy in Post-Communist EU Foreign Policy in Post-Communist EU", *International Issues & Slovak Foreign Policy Affairs* 19/4: 3-17.
Bojnec, Štefan & Fertő, Imre (2008). "European Enlargement and Agro-Food Trade" *Canadian Journal of Agricultural Economics* 56(4): 563–579.
Bolotov, Ilya (2015). "Performance in the Visegrád Group since the EU Accession: A Quantitative Analysis", *Central European Business Review* 4(4): 5–17.
Botrić, Valerija, Škuflić, Lorena (2006). "Main determinants of foreign direct investment in the South-east European countries", *Transition Studies Review*, 13(2), 359–377.
Bureš, Jan (2014). "Political Change in Czechoslovakia: The Fall of the Nondemocratic Regime in 1989 in the perspective of theory of Transition", *Revista de Stiinte Politice* 41: 115-125.
Busse, Matthias & Hefeker, Carsten (2007). "Political Risk, Institutions and Foreign Direct Investment", *European Journal of Political Economy* 23(2): 397-415.
Bútora, Martin & Kollár, Miroslav & Mesežnikov Grigorij (2011). "Slovakia 2010. Trends in Quality of Democracy" Bratislava: Inštitút pre verejné otázky.
Carstensen, Kai & Toubal, Farid (2004). "Foreign Direct Investment in Central and Eastern European Countries: A Dynamic Panel Analysis", *Journal of Comparative Economics*, 32 (1): 3–22.
Clausing, Kimberly & Dorobantu, Cosmina (2005). "Re-Entering Europe: Does European Union Candidacy Boost Foreign Direct Investment?", *Economics of Transition* 13(1): 77–103.
Cicha, Aleksandra (2012). „Różne modele prezydencji w Radzie Unii Europejskiej w świetle zmian instytucjonalnych wprowadzonych przez traktat lizboński. Przykład Republiki Czeskiej i Polski", *Studia i Analizy Europejskie* 2(10): 27-40.
Czaputowicz, Jacek (2008). „Teorie Stosunków Międzynarodowych. Krytyka i systematyzacja", Warszawa: Wydawnictwo Naukowe PWN.
Czyż, Anna (2014). „Grupa Wyszehradzka– 20 lat współpracy", *Athenaeum. Polskie Studia Politologiczne* 42: 7-23.
Ćwikliński, Henryk & Pawłowski, Grzegorz (2015). „Systemowe i polityczne uwarunkowania rozwoju gospodarki słowackiej", *Studia Ekonomiczne. Zeszyty Naukowe Uniwersytetu Ekonomicznego w Katowicach* 213: 113–129.

Dangerfield, Martin (2012). "Visegrad Group Co-operation and Russia", *Journal of Common Market Studies* 50(6): 958–974.
Dangerfield, Martin (2014). "V4: A new brand for Europe? Ten years of post-accesion regional cooperation in Central Europe", *Poznań University of Economics Review* 14(4): 71-90.
Danics, Štefan (2012). "Evropská bezpečnostní a obranná politika", *Socioekonomické a humanitní studie* 2(1): 5-12.
Dębicki, Marcin (2013). „Stosunek Polaków wobec Słowaków a inne aspekty wspólnego sąsiedztwa", in Kasperk, Andrzej (ed.) *Pogranicze—Sąsiedztwo—Stereotypy. Przypadek polsko-słowackich relacji. Grupy etniczne i etnograficzne na polskim Podkarpaciu*, Katowice-Cieszyn: Polska Akademia Nauk Oddział w Katowicach, Stowarzyszenie Rozwoju i Współpracy Regionalnej „Olza".
Dorożyński, Tomasz & Kuna-Marszałek, Anetta (2016). „Investment attractiveness of the region the Case of the Visegrad Group Countries ", *Comparative Economic Research* 19(1): 119-140.
Duffield, John S. (2012). "Alliances", in Williams, Paul D. (ed.), *Security Studies: An Introduction*. London: Routledge.
Duleba, Alexander (2011). "Twenty years of Slovak foreign policy: teething problems, successful integration and post-accession challenges", *International Issues & Slovak Foreign Policy Affairs* (21)3/4: 24-63.
Duleba, Alexander (2014). "Russian-Ukrainian crisis: what next for Eastern Partnership?", *International Issues & Slovak Foreign Policy Affairs* (23)3/4: 57-70.
Dunning, John H. (2000). "The Eclectic Paradigm as An Envelope for Economic and Business Theories of MNE Activity", *International Business Review* 9: 163–190.
Dunning, John H. (2003). "The Role of Foreign Direct Investment in Upgrading China's Competitiveness", *Journal of International Business and Economy* Fall 2003: 1-13.
Dunning, John H. (2004). "Determinants of Foreign Direct Investment: Globalization-Induced Changes and The Role of Policies" in: Bertil Tungodden & Nicholas Stern & Ivar Kolstad (eds.) *Toward Pro-Poor Policies. Aid, Institutions and Globalization*, Washington: World Bank.
Dunning, John H. (2006). "Towards A New Paradigm of Development: Implications for the determinants of international business", available at https://pdfs.semanticscholar.org/9eda/6e68a8df536d656393e37eb01fbe59072424.pdf, (access: 08.01.2017).
Dyduch, Joanna (2016). „Europeizacja polskiej polityki zagranicznej w perspektywie realizmu strukturalnego", Wrocław: Wydawnictwo Uniwersytetu Wrocławskiego.
Eising, Rainer (2007). "Intrest Groups and Social Movements", in Vink Maaten P. & Graziano Paolo (eds.). *Europeanization. New Research Agendas*, Basigtstoke / New York: Palgrave Macmillan.
Farkas, Beáta (2012). "The Impact of the Global Economic Crisis in the Old and New Cohesion Member States of the European Union", *Public Finance Quarterly* 57(1): 53-70.

Farkas, Beáta (2016a). "Economic and Political Relations between Germany and Visegrád Countries in Turbulent Times", Paper presented at ECPR General Conference, Charles University in Prague, Prague,7-10 September 2016, available at https://ecpr.eu/Filestore/PaperProposal /e7062017-80d6-45c3-a3f2-bf6008d6b9bb.pdf, (access: 08.01.2017).

Farkas Beáta (2016b). "Models of Capitalism in the European Union—Postcrisis Perspectives", Basingstoke: Palgrave Macmillan.

Fitzová Hana & Žídek Libor (2015). "Impact of trade on economic growth in the Czech and Slovak Republics", *Econmics & Sociology* 8(2): 36–50, available online at http://www.economics-sociology.eu/files/ES_8_2_Fitzo va.pdf, (access: 07.01.2017).

Gabrizová, Zuzana (2014). "The EU in Slovak political discourse—the neglected battlefield", *International Issues & Slovak Foreign Policy Affairs* 23(1/2): 55-70.

Gálová, Jana (2013). "Opportunities for Doing Business with Countries Neighbouring V4 : The Case of Ukraine", *Entrepreneurial Business and Economics Review* 1(1): 77–91.

Gašparovič, Ivan (2010). Slovak foreign policy in 2010 as seen by the President of the Slovak Republic", *Yearbook of Slovakia's Foreign Policy* 2010: 9-18.

Gawron-Tabora, Karolina (2015). "New Quality of Defense Cooperation within the Visegrad Group in 2010-2014", *Obrana a strategie* 15(1): 63-78.

Gerasymchuk, Sergiy (2014). "Visegrad group's solidarity in 2004–2014: tested by Ukrainian crisis", *International Issues & Slovak Foreign Policy Affairs* 23(1-2): 42-54.

Goda, Samuel (2015). "Slovakia and international crisis management", in Goda, Samuel (ed.), *In search for greater V4 engagement in international crisis management.* Bratislava: Slovak Foreign Policy Association.

Guay, Terrence R. (2016). "The business environment of Europe—Firms, Governments, and Institutions". Cambridge: Cambridge University Press.

Handl, Vladimir & Paterson, William E. (2013). "The continuing relevance of Germany's engine for CEE and the EU", *Communist and Post-Communist Studies* 46(3): 327–337.

Horváth, Gábor (2011)."Perceptions of ESDP/CSDP in the Visegrad countries: Current and future EU-NATO relations", in Törö, Csaba. (ed.). *Visegrad cooperation within NATO and CSDP.* Warsaw: The Polish Institute of International Affairs.

Hodor, Anna (2008). „Stanowisko państw członkowskich, organów Unii Europejskiej oraz stan europejskiej debaty publicznej wobec rozmieszczenia w Polsce i Republice czeskiej elementów tarczy antyrakietowej", in Gorośnicki, Michał & Gruszczak, Artur, *Wpływ tarczy antyrakietowej na pozycje międzynarodową Polski.* Kraków: KSSM Uniwersytet Jagielloński.

Ivančík, Radoslav (2012). "Alokačná a technická efektívnosť financovania obrany v Slovenskej republike", Liptovský Mikuláš: Akadémia ozbrojených síl gen. M. R. Štefánika.

Ivančík, Radoslav & Ušiak, Jaroslav (2013). "Analýza trendov výdavkov na obranu vo vybraných krajinách Severoatlantickej aliancie pod vplyvom globálnej hospodárskej a finančnej krízy", *Krízový manažment* 12(2): 29-36.

Ivanová, Eva & Masárová, Jana (2016). "Assessment of innovation performance of Slovak regions", *Journal of International Studies* 9(2): 207–218, available online at: http://www.jois.eu/files/JIS_Vol9_No2_Ivanova_M asarova.pdf (access: 22.01.2016).

Janicki, Hubert & Wunnava, Phanindra (2004). "Determinants of Foreign Direct Investment: Empirical Evidence from EU Accession Candidates" *Applied Economics* vol. 36(5): 505-509.

Juncos, Anna & Reynolds, Christopher (2007). "The Political and Security Committee: Governing in the Shadow", *European Foreign Affairs Review* 12(2): 127-147.

Kmec, Vladimír & Korba, Matúš & Ondrejcsák, Róbert (2005). "Transformácia NATO a bezpečnostná a obranná politika SR", Bratislava: Centrum bezpečnostných štúdií.

Kałan, Dariusz (2012). "The End of a "Beautiful Friendship?" U.S. Relations with the Visegrad Countries under Barack Obama (2009-2013)", *The Polish Quarterly of International Affairs* 4:83-100.

Kosárová, Dominika (2016). "Suverenita v kontexte zlyhávania štátu", *Bezpečnostné fórum 2016*. Banská Bystrica: Belianum.

Kosír, Igor (2010). "Medzinárodná ekonomická integrácia. Od autarkie ku globálnej ekonomickej integrácii". Banská Bystrica: Univerzita Mateja Bela.

Kosír, Igor (2013). „Global and continental environment of regional development in Poland", in Pająk, Kazimierz, Polcyn, Jan (eds.) *Determinanty rozwoju regionalnego w Polsce: Społeczeństwwo—Gospodarka—Środowisko*. Toruń: Wydawnictwo Adam Marszałek 2013.

Krokosová, Katarína (2013). „Genéza a budúcnosť Smart Defence", in *Národná a medzinárodná bezpečnosť 2013. 4. medzinárodná konferencia*. Liptovský Mikuláš: Akadémia ozbrojených síl generála Milana Rastislava Štefánika.

Kutěj, Libor (2015). "Nová polská bezpečnostní strategie", *Obrana a strategie* 15(1): 47-62.

Ladrech, Robert (2010). "Europeanisation and National Politics". Basingstoke: Palgrave Macmillan.

Lavigne, Marie (1999). "The Economics of Transition", 2nd edition, New York: St. Martin's Press.

Levy, Jonathan (2007). "The Intermarium: Wilson, Madison, & East Central European Federalism". Boca-Raton: Universal-Publishers.

Li, Jiang (2016). "Analysis of the Czech and Slovak different strategic choices towards the Eurozone", *Romanian Journal of European Affairs* 16(1): 72–87.

Lorenz, Wojciech (2015). "Development of Polish crisis management tools", in Goda, Samuel, (ed.), *In search for greater V4 engagement in interna-

tional crisis management. Bratislava: Slovak Foreign Policy Association.
Lubicz-Miszewski, Michał (2008). „Polacy i Słowacy—bliscy (?) sąsiedzi. Polacy w oczach Słowaków. Słowacy w oczach Polaków", in Baluk, Walenty & Winnicki, Zdzisław (eds.) *Badania wschodnie. Problematyka wewnętrzna i międzynarodowa*. Wrocław: Oficyna Wydawnicza Arboretum.
Lukáč, Pavol et al. (1999). "Vzťahy Slovenska so susednými štátmi, Nemeckom a Ruskom", in Mešežnikov, Grigorij.—Ivantyšyn, Michal (eds.), *Slovensko 1998–1999: súhrnná správa o stave spoločnosti*. Bratislava, Inštitút pre verejné otázky.
Lukášek, Libor (2010). "Visegrádská skupina a její vývoj v letech 1991-2004". Praha: Karolinum.
Małachowski, Witold (2002). „Niemcy jako strategiczny partner gospodarczy Polski". Warszawa: Wydawnictwo Szkoła Główna Handlowa—Kolegium Gospodarki Światowej.
Machnikowski, Ryszard M. (2015). "NATO and the Ukraine—Russian Armed Conflict" in Czulda, Robert & Madej, Marek (eds.), *Newcomers No More? Contemporary NATO and the Future of the Enlargement from the Perspective of "Post-Cold War" Members*. Warsaw: International Relations Research Institute.
Madej, Marek (2015). "Poland and NATO's Future—Let's Get Serious About the Basics", in Czulda, Robert & Madej, Marek (eds.), *Newcomers No More? Contemporary NATO and the Future of the Enlargement from the Perspective of "Post-Cold War" Members*. Warsaw: International Relations Research Institute.
Marczuk, Karina Paulina (2012). "Democratization of Security and Defence Policies of Poland (1990-2010)", *Revista de Stiinte Politice* 2012(36): 80-93.
Marušiak, Juraj (2006). "Slovak Presidency—Second Breath of Visegrad?", *Yearbook of Slovakia's Foreign Policy* 2006: 97-108.
Marušiak, Juraj (2013). „Slovakia", in *Bulletin on European and CIS Studies: EU Budget 2014-2010: Views from across Europe after 7-8 February 2013*. Moscow: Institute of Europe, Russia Academy of Science.
Marušiak, Juraj (2014). "National interests and the European integration. Contradictions or Complementarities? The case of Slovakia", in Materials of the international scientific and practical conference, Republic of Belarus—European Union: problems and perspectives of partnership, June 13-14 2013, Minsk: Institute of Philosophy NASB–: Law and Economy.
Marušiak, Juraj (2015). "Russia and the Visegrad Group—more than a foreign policy issue", *International Issues & Slovak Foreign Policy Affairs* 24(1/2): 28-46.
Mazalová, Veronika (2006). "Strategické dokumenty ČR a jejich reflexe v oblasti finančních zdrojů pro potřeby ozbrojených sil", *Obrana a strategie* 6(1): 61-70.

Medve-Bálint, Gergő (2014). "The role of the EU in shaping FDI flows to East Central Europe", *Journal of Common Market Studies* 52(1): 35-51.
Mihálik, Miroslav (2012). "Moskovský Fulcrum", *Obrana* 20(12): 47
Mitrache, Marius-Mircea (2011). "Poland, a Regional Power through the European Union. A New Direction of its Foreign Policy", *Studia Europaea* 56(4): 135-148.
Mišík Matúš (2012). "Crisis as Remedy? the 2009 Gas Crisis and Its Influence on the Increase of Energy Security within Visegrad Group Countries", *International Issues & Slovak Foreign Policy Affairs* 21(1/2): 56-72.
Missiroli, Antonino (2010). "The new EU 'Foreign Policy' system after Lisbon: a work in progress", *European Foreign Affairs Review* 15: 427–452.
Moravcsik, Andrew (1993). "Preferences and Power in the European Community: A Liberal Intergovermantalist Approach", *Journal of Common Market Studies* 31(4): 473-524.
Moravcsik, Andrew (1997). "Taking Preferences Seriously: A Liberal Theory of International Politics", *International Organization* 51(4): 513–553.
Moravcsik, Andrew (1998). "The Choice of Europe. Social purpose and state power from Messina to Maastricht". Ithaca, New York: Cornell University Press.
Moravcsik, Andrew (2008). "European integration: looking ahead" in *Great Decisions 2008*. The Foreign Policy Association.
Moravcsik, Andrew (2009). "Europe. The quite superpower". *French Politics* 7(3): 403-422.
Moravcsik, Andrew & Vachudova Milada Anna (2003). "National Interests, State Power, and EU Enlargement", *East European Politics and Societies* 17(1): 42–57.
Moumoutzis, Kyriakos (2011). "Still fashionable yet useless? Addressing problems with research on the Europeanization of foreign policy", *Journal of Common Market Studies* 49 (3): 607–629
Moumoutzis, Kyriakos & Zartaloudis, Sotirios (2016)."Europeanization Mechanisms and Process Tracing: A Templet for Research", *Journal of Common Market Studies* 54(2): 337–352.
Najšlová, Lucia (2011). "Slovakia in the East: Pragmatic Follower, Occasional Leader", *Perspectives* 19 (2): 101-122.
Najšlová, Lucia (2012). "Slovakia's Eastern Policy: A Blend of Pragmatism and Solidarity", in Tulmets, Elsa (ed.), *Identities and solidarity in foreign policy: East Central Europe and the Easter Neighborhood*, Prague: Institute of International Relations.
Nestorová-Dická, Janetta (2013). "Vysoké školstvo v krajinách Vyšehradskej štvorky v čase postsocialistickej transformácie", *Acta Geographica Universitatis Comenianae* 57(2): 195-211.
Nosko, Andrej & Ševce, Peter (2010). "The Evolution of Energy Security in the Slovak Republic", *Journal of Energy Security*, September 2010, available online at http://www.ensec.org/index.php?option=com_content&view=article&id=262:the-evolution-of-energy-security-in-the-slovak-republic&catid=110:energysecuritycontent&Itemid=366 (access: 22.09.2016).

Nowakowski, Zdzisław & Protasowicki, Igor (2008). "Polska w euroatlantyckiej przestrzeni bezpieczeństwa. miejsce polski w NATO i Unii Europejskiej", in Jemioło, Tadeusz & Rajchel, Kazimierz (eds.), *Bezpieczeństwo narodowe i zarządzanie kryzysowe w Polsce w XXI wieku—wyzwania i dylematy.* Warszawa: Wyższa Szkoła Informatyki, Zarządzania i Administracji.

Obadi, Saleh Mothana & Korcek, Matej (2016). „Energy Consumption and the Drivers of CO2 Emissions in the Central European Countries", *Ekonomický časopis* 64(4):331-352.

Ondrejcsák, Róbert (2005). "Bezpečnostná politika Poľska a Maďarska v roku 2004-2005", in Tarasovič, Vladimír & Ondrejcsák, Róbert & Lupták, Ľubomír (eds.), *Panoráma globálneho bezpečnostného prostredia 2004-2005.* Bratislava: Ministerstvo obrany SR.

Ondrejcsák, Róbert (2008). "Zahraničná a bezpečnostná politika v strednej Európe: deklarácie, stratégie a prax", in Lupták, Ľubomír & Ondrejcsák, Róbert & Valášek, Tomáš (eds.), *Panoráma globálneho bezpečnostného prostredia 2007-2008.* Bratislava: CENAA.

Owczarczuk, Magdalena (2013). "Government Incentives and FDI inflow into R&D—The Case of Visegrad Countries", *Entrepreneurial Business and Economics Review* 1(2): 73-86.

Ozbay, Fatih & Aras, Bulent (2008). "Polish-Russian Relations: History, Geography, Geopolitics", *East European Quarterly* 42(1): 27-42.

Pawlas, Iwona (2014). "The First Decade in the European Union: Poland—Strengths and Weaknesses of the Economy, Effects of Integration with the EU Structures", *Advances in Management & Applied Economics* 4(6): 39-49.

Paulech, Michal & Urbanovská, Jana (2014). "Visegrad Four EU Battlegroup: Meaning and Progress", *Obrana a strategie* 14(2): 49-60.

Pietrzak, Paweł (2012). "Armed Forces of the Republic of Poland in International Operations—Legal Grounds, Strategic Considerations, and Practical Implementation", in *Polish-Ukrainian Bulletin.* Warsaw: National Security Bureau.

Pollack, Mark A. (2005). "Theorizing the European Union: International Organization, Domestic Polity or Experiment in New Governance?", *Annual Review of Political Science* 8: 357-398.

Pomorska, Karolina (2011). "Poland: Learning the Brussels game", in Wong Reuben & Hill Christopher (eds.). *National and European Foreign Policies. Towards Europeanization.* London / New York: Routledge.

Rácz, András (2012). "The greatest common divisor: Russia's Role in Visegrad Foreign Policies", *The Polish Quarterly of International Affairs* 21(4): 32-51.

Radaelli, Claudio M. (2004). "Europeanisation: Solution or problem?", *European Integration online Papers (EIoP)* 8(16).

Rosputinský, Peter (2011). "Úvod do štúdia medzinárodných organizácií". Banská Bystrica: Univerzita Mateja Bela v Banskej Bystrici.

Ruszkowski Janusz (2003). „Wschodni wymiar Unii Europejskiej. Implikacje dla Polski", *Studia Europejskie* 2: 37-52.

Ruszkowski, Janusz (2013). „Struktura wielopoziomowego zarządzania w Unii Europejskiej", in Ruszkowski, Janusz & Wojnicz, Luiza (eds.). *Multi-Level Governance w Unii Europejskiej*, Szczecin– Warszawa: Instytut Politologii i Europeistyki Uniwersytetu Szczecińskiego & Instytut Europeistyki Uniwersytetu Warszawskiego.

Rytko, Anna (2014). "Competitiveness of Polish and Slovak agrifood products on the European market", *Zeszyty Naukowe Szkoły Głównej Gospodarstwa Wiejskiego w Warszawie. Polityki Europejskie, Finanse i Marketing* 12(61): 187–198.

Segeš, Vladimír (2015). *Vojenské dejiny Slovenska a Slovákov*. Praha: Ottovo nakladatelství.

Salamonová, Alena (2014). "Slovak V4 presidency priorities, goals and key achievements in energy", *International Issues & Slovak Foreign Policy Affairs* 23(3/4): 37-56.

Saurugger Sabine & Radaelli Claudio (2008). „The Europeanization of Public Policies: Instroduction", *Journal of Comparative Policy Analysis: Research and Practice* 10(3): 213-219.

Schimmelfennig, Frank & Sedelmeier Ulrich (2007). „Candidate Countries and Conditionality", in Vink Maaten P. & Graziano Paolo (eds.). *Europeanization. New Research Agendas*, Basigtstoke / New York: Palgrave Macmillan

Schimmelfennif, Frank (2009). „Europeanization beyond Europe", *Living Reviews in European Governance* 4(3).

Schimmelfennig, Frank (2015). "Liberal intergovernmentalism and the euro area crisis", *Journal of European Public Policy* 22(2): 177-195.

Smith, Michael E. (2004). "Toward a theory of EU foreign policy-making: multi-level governance, domestic politics, and national adaptation to Europe's common foreign and security policy", *Journal of European Public Policy* 11(4): 740-758.

Smith, Michael E. (2000). "Conforming to Europe: the domestic impact of EU foreign policy co-operation", *Journal of European Public Policy* 7(4): 613-631.

Sobják, Anita (2012). "Rethinking the Future of the Visegrad Group at a Time of Heated Debate on the Future of the EU", *Polish Quarterly of International Affairs* 21(4): 122-139.

Sporek, Tadeusz (2015). „Polsko-niemiecka wymiana handlowa w latach 2005–2015", *Studia Europejskie* 3: 79–105.

Strážay, Tomáš (2011). "Visegrad–arrival, survival, revival. Two decades of Visegrad cooperation". Bratislava: International Visegrad Fund.

Subasat, Turan & Bellos, Sotiros, (2013). "Governance and Foreign Direct Investment In Latin America: a Panel Gravity Model Approach", *Latin American Journal of Economics* 50(1): 107–131.

Tarasovič, Vladimír (2011). "The possibilities for cooperation of the Visegrad countries and their Eastern Neighbours in the development of security and defence policy in the EU and beyond: the Slovakian perspective", in Törö, Csaba (ed.), *Visegrad cooperation within NATO and CSDP*. Warsaw: The Polish Institute of International Affairs.

Ukielski, Paweł (2008). „Słowacja" *Rocznik ISP PAN Europa Środkowo-Wschodnia*, 2005(XV): 235-248.
Ukielski, Paweł (2009). „Słowacja", *Rocznik ISP PAN Europa Środkowo-Wschodnia* 2007(XVII): 297-308.
Ukielski, Paweł (2010a). „Słowacja" *Rocznik ISP PAN Europa Środkowo-Wschodnia*, 2008(XVIII): 345-358.
Ukielski, Paweł (2010b). „Polska pozycja w Unii Europejskiej a relacje Polski z Czechami, Słowacją i Węgrami", in Żukowski, Tomasz & Kloczkowski, Jacek (eds.) *Rzeczpospolita na arenie międzynarodowej. Idee i praktyczne dylematy polityki zagranicznej*. Ośrodek Myśli Politycznej: Kraków-Warszawa, available online at http://www.nowapolitologia.pl/sites/default/files/articles/polska-pozycja-w-unii-europejskiej-relacje-polski-z-czechami-slowacja-i-wegrami-295.pdf, (access: 20.09.2016).
Ušiak, Jaroslav (2013). *Security and Strategic Culture of the Visegrad Group Countries*. Banská Bystrica: Matej Bel University in Banská Bystrica.
Walsch, Christopher (2014). "Visegrad Four in the European Union. An efficient regional cooperation scheme?", *International Issues & Slovak Foreign Policy Affairs* 1(2): 25-41.
Wiszniowski, Robert & Glinka, Kamil (ed.) (2015). „New Public Governance in the Visegrád Group (V4)". Toruń: Wydawnictwo Adam Marszałek.
Więckowski, Marek & Michniak, Daniel & Bednarek-Szczepańska Maria et al. (2012). "Polish-Slovak Borderland: Transport Accessibility and Tourism", Warszawa: PAN IGiPZ.
Vlček, Dalibor & Kaščáková, Dominika (2012). "Foreign Policy of the Slovak Republic. Cornerstones, Aims and Implementation". Praha: Professional Publishing.
Zastempowski, Maciej & Przybylska, Natalia (2016), "Cooperation in Creating Innovation in Polish Small and Medium-Sized Enterprises in the Light of Empirical Studies", *Journal of Competitiveness* 8(2): 42-58.
Zenderowski Radosław (2013). „Twenty years of the independent Slovakia from Polish Perspective", *Politické vedy* 16(4): 134-144.
Zelenická Zuzana (2009). "The Visegrad Group and the EU—Balanced Relationship Between the Visegrad Group and the EU?", *Politické vedy* 4: 43-82.
Zhang, Kevin Honglin (2001). "What Attracts Foreign Multinational Corporations To China?", *Contemporary Economic Policy* 19(3): 336-346.
Zięba, Ryszard (2011). "Twenty Years of Poland's Euro-Atlantic Foreign Policy" *International Studies* 13(1): 11-21.

Other: newspaper articles, internet resources, miscellaneous sources.

Abend, Lisa (2014). "Why Nobody Wants to Host the 2022 Winter Olympics", *Time*, 03.10.2014, available at: http://time.com/3462070/olympics-winter-2022/, access (12.06.2016).

Agentúra FOCUS (2014). "Prieskum verejnej mienky pre Hospodárske noviny", September 2014, Internal documents available in the author's archive.

Aktuality.sk (2014). "Toto si myslíme o Poliakoch a Poliaci o nás", 12.09.2014, available online at https://www.aktuality.sk/clanok/261474/toto-si-myslime-o-poliakoch-a-poliaci-o-nas/, (access: 23.09.2016).

Bankier.pl (2014). „Tam mieszkam: Słowacja", wywiad Malwiny Wrotniak Chałady z Joanną Matloňová, 30.01.2014, available online at http://www ww.bankier.pl/wiadomosc/Tam-mieszkam-Slowacja-3047550.html, (access: 23.09.2016).

Bednár, Vladimír (2014). "Bezpečnostná spolupráca V4—nefungujúci concept", SME.BLOG, available online at http://vladimirbednar.blog.sme.sk/c/3 52829/bezpecnostna-spolupraca-v4-nefungujuci-koncept.html, (access: 08.05.2016).

Buras, Piotr (2014). "Has Germany sidelined Poland in Ukraine crisis negotiations?", Commentary, 27.08.2014, European Council on Foreign Relations, available online at http://www.ecfr.eu/article/commentary_has _germany_sidelined_poland_in_ukraine_crisis_negotiations301, (access: 11.05.2016).

Butler, Nick (2013). "Poland and Slovakia confirm joint bid for 2022 Winter Olympics and Paralympics", Inside the game, available online at http://www.insidethegames.biz/articles/1016844/poland-and-slova kia-confirm-joint-bid-for-2022-winter-olympics-and-paralympics, (access: 22.04.2016).

Český rozhlas (2015). „Od ledna bude obranu EU posilovat bojová skupina V4. Tvoří ji na 3700 vojáků", 29.12.2015, available online at http://www.r ozhlas.cz/zpravy/evropskaunie/_zprava/od-ledna-bude-obranu-eu-p osilovat-bojova-skupina-v4-tvori-ji-na-3700-vojaku--1568975, (access: 12.12.2016)

Danková, Janka (2016). "Univerzitná hokejová liga ako možnosť pokračovať v hokeji po mládežníckych súťažiach", EUHA—"Európska Univerzitná Hokejová Asociácia, available online at http://www.euhl.eu/sk/un iverzitna-hokejova-liga-ako-moznost-pokracovat-v-hokeji-po-mladez nickych-sutaziach/, (access 12.03.2016).

Dempsey, Judy (2014). "Poland's Foreign Policy Needs More, Not Less, Germany", Carnegie Europe, 10.11.2014, available online at http://carnegie europe.eu/strategiceurope/?fa=57176, (access: 1.05.2016).

Devlin, Kat (2015). "Anti-Russian views on the rise in Poland", Paw Research Centre, 19.05.2015, available online at http://www.pewresearch.org /fact-tank/2015/03/19/anti-russian-views-on-the-rise-in-poland/, (access: 11.05.2016).

Dušička, Martin (2015). "V Lešti vyvrcholilo najväčšie vojenské cvičenie v novodobej histórii Slovenska", TA3, 24.09.2015, available online at http://www.ta3.com/clanok/1069743/v-lesti-vyvrcholilo-najvacsie-v ojenske-cvicenie-v-novodobej-historii-slovenska.html, (access: 04.05 2016).

Dziennik Zachodni (2013). „Polski turysta na Słowacji: Głośny i cwany. Poszukuje wszędzie zniżek", 14.09.2013, available online at http://www.dziennikzachodni.pl/artykul/991692,polski-turysta-na-slowacji-glosny-i-cwany-poszukuje-wszedzie-znizek,id,t.html, (access: 23.09.2016).

EU Grants Map (2016). "Cyber Folklore", available online at http://www.mapadotacji.gov.pl/en/projekt/85, (access: 21.04.2016).

EurActive (2009). "EU agency vote revives Slovakia-Hungary language row", available online at https://www.euractiv.com/section/central-europe/news/eu-agency-vote-revives-slovakia-hungary-language-row/, (access: 08.12.2009).

Euroregión Beskydy (2016). "Všeobecné informácie o euroregióne", available online at http://www.regionbeskydy.sk/74/vseobecne-informacie-o-euroregione/, (access: 12.03.2016).

Euroregión Tatry (2016). "Publikácie", available at: http://www.euroregion-tatry.sk/w3/index.php/euroregiontatry-sk-o-nas/123-publikacie, (access: 12.03.2016).

EUSTREAM (2016). "Projekt spoločného záujmu (PCI)", available online at http://www.eustream.sk/sk_prepravna-siet/sk_prepojenie-pl-sk/sk_projekt-spolocneho-zaujmu-pci, (access: 08.05.2016).

Gazeta Krakowska (2014). „Polak, Słowak dwa bratanki. To je známe!", wywiad Marii Mazurek z Ivanem Škorupą konsulem generalnym Słowacji w Krakowie, available online at http://www.gazetakrakowska.pl/artykul/3486659,polak-slowak-dwa-bratanki-to-je-zname,id,t.html (access: 22.09.2016).

Gazeta Wyborcza (2008). „Słowacja: premier Fico przeciwny tarczy antyrakietowej", 21.01.2008, available online http://wiadomosci.gazeta.pl/wiadomosci/1,114873,4857521.html, (access: 22.09.2016).

Gazeta Wyborcza (2009). „Radosław Sikorski: Rosja w NATO? Czemu nie", 31.03.2009, available online http://wiadomosci.gazeta.pl/wiadomosci/1,114873,4857521.html, (access: 22.09.2016).

Gazeta Wyborcza (2010). „Prezydent Kaczyński: Zimowa olimpiada 2022 w Polsce!", 06.03.2010, available online at: http://wyborcza.pl/1,75248,7633740,Prezydent_Kaczynski__Zimowa_olimpiada_2022_w_Polsce_.html, (access:22.04.2016).

Global Firepower (2016a). "Active Military Manpower by Country", available online at http://www.globalfirepower.com/active-military-manpower.asp, (access: 10.05.2016).

Global Firepower (2016b). "Slovakia Military Strength", available online at http://www.globalfirepower.com/country-military-strength-detail.asp?country_id=slovakia, (access: 10.05.2016).

GlobalFirepower (2016c). "Poland Military Strength", available online at http://www.globalfirepower.com/country-military-strength-detail.asp?country_id=poland, (access 10.05.2016).

Gyárfášová, OI'ga (2014). "Rusko-ukrajinská kríza ako obraz slovenskej spoločnosti", *Zahraničná politika*, available online at http://zahranicnapolitika.dennikn.sk/rusko-ukrajinska-kriza-ako-obraz-slovenskej-spolocnosti/ (access: 10.05.2016).

HNonline (2016). "Slovenskí zbrojári ukázali svetu novinku, unikátne obrnené vozidlo", available online at http://style.hnonline.sk/hn-tech/660515-slovenski-zbrojari-ukazali-svetu-novinku-unikatne-obrnene-vozidlo, (access: 10.05.2016).
Katedra slovanských jazykov (2012). "Slávnostné otvorenie Centra poľského jazyka a kultúry na FF UMB", available online at: http://www.ff.umb.sk/katedry/katedra-slovanskych-jazykov/centrum-polskeho-jazyka-a-kultury/otvorenie-cpjak/otvorenie-cpjak.html, (access: 23.03.2016).
Kováč, Peter (2016a). "Armádny nákup obrnených vozidiel z Poľska padol", Denník SME, 19.06.2016, available online at http://domov.sme.sk/c/20216557/armadny-nakup-obrnenych-vozidiel-z-polska-padol.html, (access: 25.07.2016).
Kováč, Peter (2016b). „Oživenie zbrojárstva nevychádza, opravy húfnic pre Poľsko padli", Denník SME, 10.05.2016, available online at http://domov.sme.sk/c/20160234/ficovo-ozivenie-zbrojarstva-nevychadza-o pravy-hufnic-pre-polsko-padli.html, (access: 24.07.2016).
Koziej, Stanisław (2010). „Obronność Rzeczypospolitej Polskiej w latach 1989–2009", (skrypt internetowy),Warszawa/Ursynów, available online at http://koziej.pl/wp-content/uploads/2015/07/OBRONNOSC_III_RP.doc., (access 11.05.2016).
Lesná, Ľuba (2007). "Anti-missile shield on agenda for Moscow visit", The Slovak Spectator, 07.05.2007, available online at http://spectator.sme.sk/c/20005041/anti-missile-shield-on-agenda-for-moscow-visit.html, (access: 21.09.2016).
Law-Now (2016). "Slovak EUSTREAM and Polish GAZ-SYSTEM launch open season procedure for gas interconnector", 01.09.2016, avilable online at: http://www.cms-lawnow.com/ealerts/2016/09/slovak-eustream-and-polish-gazsystem-launch-open-season-procedure-for-gas-interco nnector, (access: 12.01.2017).
Łoginow, Jakub (2013). „Relacje z małą Słowacją pokazują, ile jest warta polska polityka zagraniczna", available online at http://www.porteuropa.eu/slowacja/polityka/5164-relacje-ze-slowacja-pokazuja-ile-jestwarta-polska-polityka-zagraniczna (access: 20.09.2016)
Matejko, Miroslav (2015). "Prelomové rokovanie v Bratislave pri crossborderových dohodách počas stretnutia krajín V4", Veliteľstvo vzdušných síl OS RS, 22.10.2015, available online at http://www.vvzs.mil.sk/57742/index.php?pg=7&day=2016-01-01&art_datum_od=&art_datum_do=, (access: 10.05.2016).
Naša univerzita (2006). "Ocenenie poľského profesora teoretickej chémie", 52(10), Bratislava: Comenius University, available at: https://uniba.sk/fileadmin/ruk/nasa_univerzita/NU2006-07/2006_10.pdf, (access: 05.03.2016).
North Atlantic Treaty Organization NATO (2015a). "NATO Welcomes its 24th Centre of Excellence", available online at http://www.act.nato.int/nato-welcomes-its-24th-centre-of-excellence, (access: 10.05.2016).

North Atlantic Treaty Organization NATO (2015b). "Response Force", available online at http://www.nato.int/cps/en/natolive/topics_49755.htm, (access: 05.05. 2016).
Organisation for Economic Cooperation and Development OECD (2016). "Further education reforms needed to improve performance and equity in Slovak Republic", 19.02.2016, available at: http://www.oecd.org/slovakia/further-education-reforms-needed-to-improve-performance-and-equity-in-slovak-republic.htm (access: 05.03.2016).
Organizacja Narodów Zjednoczonych (2016). "Rodzina Narodów Zjednoczonych w Polsce", available online at http://www.un.org.pl/agendy-onz-w-polsce/index.php, (access: 5.052016).
Permanent Mission of the Republic of Poland to the United Nations in New York (2016a). "Historical background", available online at http://www.nowyjorkonz.msz.gov.pl/en/poland_in_the_un/historical_background/, (access: 05.05.2016).
Permanent Mission of the Republic of Poland to the United Nations in New York (2016b). "Security Council should include one additional non-permanent seat for the Eastern European Group", available online at http://nowyjorkonz.msz.gov.pl/en/poland_in_the_un/speeches_and_documents/poland_on_un_security_council_reform_, (access: 05.05.2016).
Podhorská, Kvetoslava (2014). "Krakovskí umelci namaľovali Slovensko-poľskú úniu", 27.11.2014, available at: http://www.k13.sk/krakovski-umelci-namalovali-slovensko-polsku-uniu/, (access: 22.04. 2016).
Polska Agencja Prasowa PAP (2016a). „Duda: Polska i Słowacja mają podobne potrzeby i spojrzenia na przyszłość", 28.02.2016 available online at http://www.pap.pl/aktualnosci/news,477123,duda-polska-i-slowacja-maja-podobne-potrzeby-i-spojrzenia-na-przyszlosc.html (access: 21.09.2016).
Polska Agencja Prasowa PAP (2016b). "Slovak 'habilitation will not be automatically recognized by Polish universities", 08.06.2016, available online at http://scienceinpoland.pap.pl/en/news/news,410022,slovak-habilitation-will-not-be-automatically-recognized-by-polish-universities.html, (access 10.06.2016).
Polska The Times (2014). „Tajner: Korzyści z olimpiady? Nieobliczalne", 22.05.2014, available online at http://www.polskatimes.pl/artykul/3444861,tajner-korzysci-z-olimpiady-nieobliczalne,1,1,id,t,so,nk.html (access 10.06.2016).
PRAVDA.SK (2015a). "Plynovod z Maďarska na Slovensko by mohol začať fungovať v januári", 08.01.2015, available online at http://spravy.pravda.sk/ekonomika/clanok/341716-plynovod-z-madarska-na-slovensko-by-mohol-zacat-fungovat-v-januari/, (access 8.05.2016).
PRAVDA.SK (2015b). "Nová poľská vláda vymenila šéfa poľsko-slovenského centra NATO", available online at http://spravy.pravda.sk/svet/clanok/377511-nova-polska-vlada-vymenila-sefa-polsko-slovenskeho-centra-nato/, (access: 10.05.2016).

Rettman, Andrew (2012). "EU diplomats: Serbia to get candidate status", *EUobserver*, 20.02.2012, available online at https://euobserver.com/en largement/115407, (access: 23.09.2016).
RT (2015). "NATO to create new HQs in Hungary & Slovakia, boost response forces—Stoltenberg", 08.10.2015, available online at https://www.r t.com/news/317995-nato-boost-troops-bases/, (access: 05.05.2016).
Šebela, Miloslav (2014). "Krakov stiahol kandidatúru na olympiádu, s ním aj Jasná", *SME Sport*, 26.05.2014, available online at http://sport.sm e.sk/c/7215130/krakov-stiahol-kandidaturu-na-olympiadu-s-nim-aj-jasna.html, (access:20.02.2016).
Šefčovič, Maroš (2015). "My favorite Polish invention", BLOG POST, 12 October 2015 available online at https://www.wprost.pl/123952/Kaczynski-uznanie-niepodleglosci-Kosowa-niezwykle-skomplikowane, (access: 23.09.2016).
SIPRI (2016). „Military expenditure by country as percentage of gross domestic product 1988-2015", *Stockholm International Peace Research Institute*, available online at http://www.sipri.org/media/website-photos/sip ri-milex-data-1988-2015, (access: 01.05.2016).
Slovenský olympijský výbor (2013). "Slovenský olympijský výbor má 20 rokov", available online at: https://www.olympic.sk/userfiles/files/20-rokov-sov.pdf, (access:12.03.2016).
SME (1999)."Prípadné operácie NATO v Kosove sa dotknú aj troch nových členov", 24.03.1999, available online at http://www.sme.sk/c/21836 29/pripadne-operacie-nato-v-kosove-sa-dotknu-aj-troch-novych-clen ov.html, (access: 24.04 2016).
Šuša, Ivan (2012). "Ocenenie prof. P. Fobela a prof. D. Fobelovej v Poľsku", *Universitas Matthiae Belli* 19(2).
Světnička, Lubomír (2005). "Vojenská brigáda tří zemí skončí", *iDNES.CZ*, 30.04.2005, available online at http://zpravy.idnes.cz/vojenska-briga da-tri-zemi-skonci-do/zpr_nato.aspx?c=A050531_114318_zpr_nato_i nc, (access: 28.04.2016).
Vášáryová, Magda (2006). „Teraz znam Polaków lepiej", available online at http://www.polonia.sk/index.php?option=com_content&view=article &id=992:magda-vaaryova-teraz-znam-polakow-lepiej&catid=88:wywi ad-miesica&Itemid=99, (access: 21.09.2016).
The Economist (2011). "Radicova's lament. Another government is brought down by the euro crisis, 15.10.2011, available online at http://www. economist.com/node/21532304, (access: 21.09.2016).
The Warsaw Voice (2003). "The Polish View on the EU New Neighbors Initiative", 25.09.2003, available online at http://www.warsawvoice.pl /WVpage/pages/article.php/3566/article, (access: 23.09.2016).
Wilk, Remigiusz (2015). "Slovakia buys Scipio 8x8 IFVs", *IHS Jane's 360*, available online at http://www.janes.com/article/52821/slovakia-buys-sc ipio-8x8-ifvs, (access: 10.05.2016).

Wprost (2008). „Kaczyński: uznanie niepodległości Kosowa niezwykle skomplikowane", 18.02.2008, available online at https://www.wprost.pl/123952/Kaczynski-uznanie-niepodleglosci-Kosowa-niezwykle-skomplikowane, (access: 23.09.2016).

Index of names

A

Anyanwu, John C., 161
Ashton, Catherine, 67, 77

B

Bajda, Piotr, 52
Barroso, José Manuel, 216, 217, 231
Baška, Jaroslav, 125
Belka, Marek, 30, 36
Belousovová, Anna, 93
Busse, Matthias, 161
Buzek, Jerzy, 73

C

Carstensen, Kai, 161
Clausing, Kimberly, 162
Czaputowicz, Jacek, 13, 14, 15

D

Delors, Jacques, 73
Dienstbier, Jiří, 102
Dorobantu, Cosmina, 162
Dunning, John Harry, 161
Dzurinda, Mikuláš, 30, 34, 35, 88, 103, 104

E

Eising, Reiner, 19

F

Fico, Robert, 31, 32, 35, 36, 38, 52, 53, 54, 59, 82, 88, 93, 95, 97, 98, 107, 109, 110, 111, 112, 126, 145, 146, 149
Fobel, Pavel, 204
Fobelová, Daniela, 204
Fotyga, Anna, 79
Füle, Štefan, 67, 77

G

Gašparovič, Ivan, 30, 55, 57
Glváč, Martin, 126, 127
Gowin, Jarosław, 204
Guagliano, Claudia, 162

H

Havel, Vaclav, 102
Hofekcr, Carsten, 161
Hübner, Danuta, 230

J

Jagodziński, Andrzej, 206
Janicki, Hubert, 161
Juncker, Jean-Claude, 72, 231

K

Kaczyński, Jarosław, 31, 37, 92, 94, 107, 210
Kaczyński, Lech, 31, 37, 92, 93, 107, 210
Kašický, František, 124
Kiska, Andrej, 32, 55, 111

Index of names

Klich, Bogdan, 125
Kobieracki, Adam, 141
Komorowski, Bronisław, 31, 55, 110
Kopacz, Ewa, 32
Krištofík, Dušan, 204
Kubiš, Jan, 141
Kwaśniewski, Aleksander, 30, 65

L

Lajčák, Miroslav, 231

M

Maciejowski, Marcin, 207
Macierewicz, Antoni, 127
Marcinkiewicz, Kazimierz, 31
Matloňová, Joanna, 51
Mečiar, Vladimir, 34, 35, 103
Miková, Jana, 26
Miller, Leszek, 30, 36
Moravcsik, Andrew, 8, 9, 12, 13, 14, 15, 16, 18, 19, 22, 23, 28, 33, 42, 101, 158
Mottaleb, Khondoker A., 161

N

Najšlová, Lucia, 61
Niwelińska, Monika, 207

O

Obama, Barack, 90, 91
Oettinger, Günther, 81
Ondrejcsák, Róbert, 103, 106, 109, 126
Orban, Victor, 38
Owczarczuk, Magdalena, 162

P

Piksa, Agnieszka, 207
Poroshenko, Petro, 66
Putin, Vladimir, 92, 122

R

Rácz, András, 93, 94
Radičová, Iveta, 31, 35, 36, 38, 54, 109, 125
Riela, Stefano, 162

S

Saakashvili, Mikheil, 93
Sadlej, Andrzej Jerzy, 204
Sarkozy, Nicolas, 80
Sasnal, Wilhelm, 207
Schimmelfennig, Frank, 10, 16, 18, 22, 23
Šefčovič, Maroš, 72, 231
Siemoniak, Tomasz, 126
Sikorski, Radosław, 44, 67, 90
Škorupa, Ivan, 51
Suchodolski, Bogdan, 202
Szczygło, Aleksander, 124
Szigeti, Laszlo, 226
Szydło, Beata, 32, 38, 54
Szymczak-Gałkowski, Juliusz, 205

T

Tajner, Apoloniusz, 211
Toubal, Farid, 161
Tusk, Donald, 32, 38, 54, 72, 91, 92, 98, 107, 112, 125, 126, 148, 231
Tymoshenko, Julia, 65

V

Vášáryová, Magdaléna, 52, 53

W

Waszczykowski, Witold, 45
Westerwelle, Guido, 77
Włosowicz, Zbigniew, 126
Wojas, Joanna, 26, 165
Woynarowski, Jakub, 207
Wunnava, Phanindra, 161

Y

Yanukovych, Viktor, 66

Yatsenyuk, Arseniy, 66

Z

Zasępa, Tadeusz, 201
Zenderowski, Radosław, 50
Zhang, Kevin, Honglin, 162
Zubkov, Viktor, 93

ibidem*.eu*